MOTHER GOOSE
on the Loose
Updated!

ALA Editions purchases fund advocacy, awareness, and accreditation programs for library professionals worldwide.

MOTHER GOOSE on the Loose

Updated!

Betsy Diamant-Cohen

CHICAGO | 2019

A proven and trusted leader in the field of early literacy, **Dr. Betsy Diamant-Cohen** is a prolific author, inspiring mentor, charismatic presenter, and knowledgeable consultant, teacher, creator, and developer of the Mother Goose on the Loose program. She has revolutionized the way storytimes are presented to young children at libraries across the country and has empowered librarians to work confidently with this young population. For more information on Betsy or to check out the many Mother Goose–related products she has created (books, CDs, apps), visit her website (www.mgol.org).

© 2019 by the American Library Association

Extensive effort has gone into ensuring the reliability of the information in this book; however, the publisher makes no warranty, express or implied, with respect to the material contained herein.

ISBN: 978-0-8389-1646-9 (paper)

Library of Congress Cataloging-in-Publication Data

Names: Diamant-Cohen, Betsy, author.
Title: Mother Goose on the Loose : updated / Betsy Diamant-Cohen.
Description: First revised and updated edition. | Chicago, Illinois : ALA
  Editions, an imprint of the American Library Association, 2019. | Includes
  index.
Identifiers: LCCN 2018017957 | ISBN 9780838916469 (paper : alk. paper)
Subjects: LCSH: Language arts (Early childhood) | Early childhood
  education—Activity programs. | Children's libraries—Activity programs. |
  Nursery rhymes—Study and teaching (Early childhood)
Classification: LCC LB1139.5.L35 D5 2018 | DDC 372.6—dc23 LC record available at
https://lccn.loc.gov/2018017957

Book design by Kim Thornton in the Minion and Proxima Nova typefaces.

♾ This paper meets the requirements of ANSI/NISO Z39.48-1992 (Permanence of Paper).
Printed in the United States of America

23 22 21 20 19   5 4 3 2 1

For my parents, Shirley and Philip,
who lovingly sang nursery rhymes to me and my sister

For Regina,
who joyfully sang nursery rhymes with me during our travels together

For all the parents and children,
who are singing and will continue to sing nursery rhymes in the future

Contents

Preface: A Brief History of Mother Goose on the Loose / ix

Acknowledgments / xi

Introduction / xiii

Part I   **Learning All about Mother Goose on the Loose**

Chapter 1   Early Literacy, School Readiness, and Mother Goose on the Loose..........3

Chapter 2   Essential Components for an Early Literacy Program.......................15

Chapter 3   Mother Goose on the Loose Basics...19

Chapter 4   The Extra Element: Developmental Tips...31

Chapter 5   The Versatile Mother Goose on the Loose......................................37

Part II   **Planning Your Mother Goose on the Loose Programs**

Chapter 6   Planning Your Program...47

Chapter 7   Selecting Books, Rhymes, Songs, and Felt Pieces............................63

Chapter 8   Scheduling and Promoting Your Program.......................................71

Chapter 9   Before and after Your Program..75

Chapter 10   Evaluating Your Program..79

Part III   **Five Ready-to-Present Mother Goose on the Loose Programs**

     Program 1...92

     Program 2...108

     Program 3...118

     Program 4...128

     Program 5...138

Part IV	**Mother Goose on the Loose Resources**	
Resource A	The Mother Goose on the Loose Songbook and Rhyme Book	**149**
Resource B	Some Mother Goose on the Loose Felt Piece Patterns	**159**
Resource C	Suggested Supplies and Ordering Information	**195**
Resource D	About Barbara Cass-Beggs, by Michael Cass-Beggs	**199**

Subject Index / 201

Title Index / 207

Preface

A Brief History of Mother Goose on the Loose

AFTER BECOMING A CHILDREN'S LIBRARIAN, I observed programs where infants recited Mother Goose rhymes illustrated with colorful flannelboard characters. Finding library programs for babies fascinating, I recreated those enjoyable events in programs designed for parents and newborns from one to eighteen months. The first of these, "And Baby Makes Three," gathered infants and adults into a circle, included a Q and A between the parents and a professional as the babies crawled around, and made use of nursery rhymes and simple activities. A more intricate nursery rhyme program for children ages twelve to twenty-four months utilized nursery rhymes, flannelboard characters, songs, and fingerplays, as well as playtime with puzzles and other developmentally appropriate games.

In 1986, I moved to Israel, met and married my husband, and become the proud mother of a baby boy. I brought my son to a program called "Your Baby Needs Music," led by Barbara Cass-Beggs, a retired Canadian opera singer in her eighties. Barbara was a visionary who had developed her own unique system of teaching music to babies.

A typical Cass-Beggs program placed adults and babies in a circle and included a welcome song and numerous musical activities. While attending the sessions, I was amazed to watch my son become fully engaged with a complex but enjoyable mix of motion and music. Because of this positive experience, I later studied with Barbara and became a certified teacher of her "Listen, Like, Learn" method. Eventually, I designed a hybrid program of my own. Using the structure of Barbara's programs, I combined flannelboard characters, books, puppets, and library activities to create a book-based musical program for children called Mother Goose on the Loose (MGOL).

MGOL is an early learning program designed primarily for babies from birth to twenty-four months. It integrates elements of child development, storytime practices, and the "Listen, Like, Learn" teaching approach developed by Cass-Beggs. MGOL helps parents develop their children's early literacy skills in a fun and joyful environment using books, rhymes, songs, musical instruments, fingerplays, felt figures, puppets, stuffed animals, and other props. The activities help children build social and emotional skills in addition to early literacy skills by taking all parts of a child's development into consideration, intentionally focusing on the "whole child." MGOL activities build children's self-esteem and self-regulation, give them practice at being part of a group and working with others, provide opportunities for taking turns, exercise fine motor and gross motor skills, allow experimentation with objects to build STEM skills, ignite imagination, give information about the world around them, and increase parent-child bonding. MGOL incorporates unique activities designed to support children's strengths and minimize the challenges for optimal growth and development.

In 1998, I moved back to the United States and introduced MGOL at my new library. The program was a great success, partly because it coincided with an explosion in cognitive science showing that the "critical period" of neurological development takes place in the first years of life. Encouraged by the results, I began training MGOL facilitators first locally, then in-state, and eventually throughout the United States.

In 2002, the Godfrey Award for Excellence in Public Library Services for Families and Children recognized MGOL as "outstanding programming for young children and families." Because of MGOL, in 2004 I was named a "Mover and Shaker" by *Library Journal* and in 2013 was the proud recipient of the Association of Specialized and Cooperative Library Agencies' (ASCLA) Leadership and Professional Achievement Award for "revolutionizing the way librarians work with children from birth to age 3." MGOL was chosen as one of three National Early Literacy Best Practices by New York State in 2013 and highlighted as one of two brain-building, nationally replicated early literacy programs in a report coauthored by the Families and Work Institute, the Institute of Museum and Library Services (IMLS), and School Readiness Consulting in 2015. Recently, I was selected as the winner of the 2018 Alexandre Vattemare Award for Creativity in Libraries in recognition of the success and constant growth of Mother Goose on the Loose.

It has been more than twenty years since I first introduced MGOL to children's librarians in the United States. Due to the warm reception it still continues to receive and the praise that both librarians and parents have given, I feel there is something almost magical about it. How is it possible that an early literacy program engenders such enthusiasm from children, families, and facilitators? My theory is that MGOL remains successful because it celebrates the individuality of each person—presenter, parent, and child—while also creating a positive atmosphere in which everyone can thrive.

Although this book has scripts for five consecutive programs, MGOL provides a brain-based format that gives a structure for a well-constructed program while encouraging facilitators to use their own material to "fill in the blanks." Materials by the incomparable Barbara Cass-Beggs form the foundation of the program. Instead of focusing only on building language and literacy skills, the focus is on the *whole* child. Program facilitators are urged to use the "whole person" approach in their program planning and presentation by recognizing their own strengths and passions and then creating programs based on what is easy and fun for them. Because enthusiasm breeds enthusiasm, it is easy to see how positive personal connections and strong emotional attachments to the program form.

Children who regularly attend MGOL programs in the public library develop familiarity and comfort with libraries, books, words, music, rules, routine and structure, librarians, other children, and adult caregivers. MGOL turns young children's enjoyment of music and nursery rhymes into actual skills by interweaving them throughout the program with skill-building activities. Children are having so much fun that they are not aware that serious learning is taking place! MGOL as a whole exercises the brain, which increases total brain capacity by making all sorts of new connections.

MGOL is a perfect fit for the new emphasis public libraries are placing on family engagement. It can provide a springboard for programming that brings families together, strengthening relationships with their local librarians. MGOL is also meant to be a source of joy for the facilitating librarians, deepening their connections within the community and providing a time each week for musical fun, positivity, book play, and personal expression.

Acknowledgments

I WOULD LIKE TO THANK THE MANY PEOPLE WHO have helped me bring this book to reality.

Rahel, a top-class musician who brought Barbara Cass-Beggs to Israel and introduced me to "Your Baby Needs Music" classes, and Jim McClure, principal at Betsy's Folly Studios, have been invaluable partners for all the Mother Goose on the Loose (MGOL) recordings. My sister, Celia Yitzhak, supplied all the illustrations along with lots of love and laughter. She has illustrated, upon request, numerous expressive flannelboard characters for me over the years, and I am delighted to share her talents with the readers of this book. She has helped above and beyond the call of sisterly duty—responding to all my requests for illustrations even after hearing time and again, "This is the last one I will ask you to do."

I am grateful to visionary thinker and musician Barbara Cass-Beggs for her painstaking research, her love of music, her devotion to young children, and her work training me to become an instructor in her "Listen, Like, Learn" method. I thank her son, Michael Cass-Beggs, for granting me permission to reproduce some of Barbara's songs and music, helping me spread her wisdom and knowledge to a wider audience. (Please see resource D for Michael's tribute to his mother.)

Anne Lief Barlin's creative movement classes and books influenced the movement portion of MGOL. Nurit Shilo-Cohen, curator of the Israel Museum Ruth Youth Wing, supported weekly Wednesday-morning MGOL programs in the library over the course of many years and even brought her children when they were young. Miri Laufer and my first group of MGOL families inspired me by their enthusiasm and devotion. During our six years teaching nursery school together at Gan Horim Dovrei Anglit in Jerusalem, Bernice Brownstein taught me how to set limits lovingly for young children and about child development, circle times, and age-appropriate play-based learning activities.

Nancy Vorobey from the Maryland State Department of Education and Steve Rohde from the Maryland Family Network have been true advocates for addressing the whole child in both learning and childcare. They brought Betty Rintoul's Encouraging Connections training to Maryland, which supplied understandable and useful information about developments in brain research. Betty also provided valuable feedback on portions of this book and recommended relevant resources. Kim MacLean-Blevins provided additional background information and helpful feedback regarding the child development portions of this book.

I am grateful to have been employed by the Enoch Pratt Free Library, where professional development was supported and MGOL was adopted. Regina Wade taught me how to share brain research / child development information to make it accessible to everyone. She was a terrific partner in presenting numerous MGOL workshops. Ellen Riordan, former coordinator of children's services at the Enoch Pratt Free Library, shared her astute understanding of the importance of children's public library services and the role they can play in the future. I am thankful for our discussions on the implications that scientific research has on children's programming in public libraries. Selma Levi gave constant encouragement and support as a professional colleague and personal friend.

Former president of the American Library Association and current Librarian of Congress Carla Hayden, PhD, encouraged me to pursue a doctoral degree and served on my doctoral committee along with Nancy Kaplan, PhD, and Kathryn Summers, PhD. Thank you!

My original readers and cheerleaders: Brenda Bodenheimer-Zlatin, Fran Glushakow-Gould, Lisa Bloch-Rodwin, Naomi Hafter, Dina Sherman, Saroj Ghoting, and Lilach Horowitz are greatly appreciated. Carole Schlein created the first MGOL logo, and Celia Yitzhak and Paul Rothenberg updated it. Dorothy Valakos from the Baltimore Museum of Art spent hours discussing visual literacy in the context of MGOL. Crystal Lesher and Kate Moser created the first MGOL evaluation form on which the evaluations in this book are based.

Thanks go to the wonderful staff at ALA Editions for suggesting that I revise the original MGOL manual; to my editor, Jamie Santoro, for her encouragement and editorial excellence; to Jill Hillemeyer and Rob Christopher for their wonderful marketing; to Angela Gwizdala for copyediting, and to Rachel Chance for her enthusiasm. Heartfelt appreciation also goes to Jennifer Bergantz, my invaluable research assistant, administrative assistant, queen of Excel spreadsheets, and dear friend, for being a Jill of all trades when it comes to MGOL. Also, kudos to my son, Alon, who is mentioned in every training workshop, and to my daughters, Yoella and Maya, who helped with this revised edition.

I'd like to recognize Stuart, Alon, Maya, Yoella, and Gullumpy for providing constant love and support and my parents for bringing me up in an optimal learning environment with unconditional love, music, creativity, interaction, and lots of library visits. My love of books is due (at least in part) to my mother, Shirley Diamant, who sang nursery rhymes and read Nancy Drew stories aloud, and to my father, Philip Diamant, who read Thorton Burgess animal stories aloud at bedtime and quoted poets and philosophers at the dinner table.

Last but not least, I would like to acknowledge all the children throughout the years who have attended MGOL programs and rewarded me with their smiles and all the librarians who have reported back to me that MGOL has enriched their lives. Without you, none of this would have been possible.

Introduction

RESEARCH TELLS US THAT ENGAGING VERY YOUNG children with diverse forms of stimulation in a joyful environment with an adult that they love can significantly facilitate their developmental and educational success. *Mother Goose on the Loose: Updated* provides librarians, caregivers, and educators with the tools to encourage healthy child development while also providing an informal, inventive environment for parent education. This manual contains

- guidance on designing Mother Goose on the Loose (MGOL) programs;
- materials to create unique programs and organize a series of programs;
- tools to assess, evaluate, and promote your program;
- the latest compelling research on early literacy;
- complete scripts for five consecutive MGOL programs;
- a complete song and rhyme book;
- tips for communicating with parents, library administrators, and stakeholders;
- suggestions for incorporating digital media;
- and more!

Mother Goose on the Loose integrates the latest research in early literacy and infant brain development with traditional storytime elements. The easy-to-learn programs are fun to present, entertaining for children, and instructive to parents and caregivers. Activities are chosen intentionally in order to focus on the *whole* child. They also set in motion a lifelong love of learning, reading, and libraries for the young participants!

Each program offers the opportunity to share one or two developmental tips related to the activities with parents or other adult caregivers. MGOL differs from other programs for children because it is based on the work of a remarkable woman, Barbara Cass-Beggs, and her unique "Listen, Like, Learn" approach to teaching music. The program uses many of Cass-Beggs's wonderful songs—perfect for this age group—as a springboard to help create an optimal learning environment. Traditional folksongs, nursery rhymes, music, movement, language, drama, books, illustrations, and props have been seamlessly added to the mix to integrate many different artistic and educational elements. The end result is designed to provide children with an exciting opportunity to develop age-appropriate social skills and learning proficiencies. Rather than merely simplifying activities designed for older preschoolers, MGOL is specifically geared for babies and toddlers.

Presenting songs, rhymes, and activities in a framework of 80 percent repetition and 20 percent variety offers our youngest learners a perfect learning environment; it also helps busy librarians know the content of the program without having to reinvent the wheel for each presentation.

Organization

Part I, "Learning All about Mother Goose on the Loose," sets the scene for your program.

- Chapter 1, "Early Literacy, School Readiness, and Mother Goose on the Loose," discusses some of the fascinating research supporting the practices outlined in this book, including findings on early literacy, school readiness, emotional intelligence, and visual literacy.
- Chapter 2, "Essential Components for an Early Literacy Program," examines the developmental ideals furthered by the roles of repetition, ritual, fun, play, movement, music, and relaxation and by addressing multiple intelligences.
- Chapter 3, "Mother Goose on the Loose Basics," guides the reader through each segment of a successful presentation from the opening remarks to the closing songs.
- Chapter 4, "The Extra Element: Developmental Tips," explains what developmental tips are and how to deliver them while giving many sample tips.
- Chapter 5, "The Versatile Mother Goose on the Loose," deals with how to successfully expand the audience and dimensions of the program.

Part II, "Planning Your Mother Goose on the Loose Programs," features chapters that will help you make the program your own.

- Chapter 6, "Planning Your Program," offers the best tools to shape a unique program and series of sessions. It also provides information and planning sheets to help you create an ongoing MGOL series at your own institution.
- Chapter 7, "Selecting Books, Rhymes, Songs, and Felt Pieces," explains how to find rhymes and create, use, and store felt pieces, and it gives examples of ways books can be used in MGOL.
- Chapter 8, "Scheduling and Promoting Your Program," gives suggestions for scheduling sessions, publicizing the program, and recruiting participants.
- Chapter 9, "Before and After Your Program," covers information regarding room setup before the program and tips for running an informal playtime at the end.
- Chapter 10, "Evaluating Your Program," features informal and formal in-house evaluation tools specifically designed for MGOL.

Part III, "Five Ready-to-Present Mother Goose on the Loose Programs," contains complete scripts for five consecutive weekly programs with 80 percent repetition from week to week, including lyrics, developmental tips, and all script instructions.

Part IV, "Mother Goose on the Loose Resources," features key sources to keep your program up and running, including a Mother Goose on the Loose Songbook and Rhyme Book, patterns for creating felt pieces, and suggested supplies with ordering information. Also included is a brief memorial to the late Barbara Cass-Beggs by her son, Michael.

The Rewards of MGOL

You will quickly discover that babies and toddlers love MGOL sessions. Even if you were not trained in early childhood education, you will soon become familiar with the skills that can be taught to young children, feel comfortable running sessions, appreciate age-appropriate achievements, enjoy incorporating playful learning, and know how to model behavior for adults while engaging children.

I trust that you will gain a renewed or heightened sense of the value of our profession by becoming more actively involved in the important ways we contribute to the development of very young children. I also hope that you will find it great fun to offer innovative programs like MGOL and to encourage early literacy and a love of libraries in our youngest patrons.

Part 1

Learning All about Mother Goose on the Loose

Early Literacy, School Readiness, and Mother Goose on the Loose

EARLIEST CHILDHOOD IS A CRITICAL PERIOD FOR developing literacy skills. According to researchers in human development, literacy development begins at birth as children listen to sounds in their environment and respond with noises of their own. Early literacy refers to the knowledge and skills that children acquire before they enter school that will give them a strong foundation to help them learn how to read.

Markers of emergent literacy in babies include an "awareness" of the following:

- vocabulary: knowing names of things
- print motivation: learning basic rules of written language and showing an interest in and enjoyment of books
- writing: making a variety of marks that can range from circular, horizontal, separate scribble marks to letter-like forms or actual letters
- phonemics: being able to hear and manipulate the smaller sounds in words[1]

Children acquire these skills from experiences at home, in preschool centers, in libraries, and in kindergartens. The skills are a critical determinant of how well children will learn to read in elementary school.

In her book *Much More Than the ABCs,* Judith Schickedanz describes categories of early literacy that reflect book behaviors of very young children, illustrating the progression children can make toward literacy:

- Book-handling behaviors such as chewing and page turning are related to a child's physical manipulation or handling of books.
- When children pay attention and interact with pictures in books, they learn to look and recognize.
- By pointing to pictures of familiar objects, they show recognition, indicating a beginning understanding of pictures in books.
- When children imitate actions they see in a picture or talk about events in a story, they are showing that they comprehend the picture or story.

> MGOL was based on a body of research that is constantly being updated. When the foundational research has been corroborated, credit is given to the pioneering researchers upon whose backs we all travel. However, MGOL is always evolving; program techniques and tips are updated to incorporate new findings from recent research, and citations for this newer information are included.

- The final step in early literacy behavior is story-reading behavior. This is when a child verbally interacts with a book in ways that might include running fingers along printed words or babbling in imitation of reading.[2]

The number of vocabulary words that children know and can use when entering kindergarten affects their entire education; studies have shown that children growing up in impoverished households know fewer words.[3] Babies deprived of positive language encounters often have difficulty learning and may never reach their full intellectual capacity, while exposure to more words by age two results in larger vocabularies and faster language processing speeds;[4] this is why children find it easier to read when they have been read to as very young children.[5] Most of the children who are behind in reading at the end of first grade remain below level in sixth grade.[6] Studies have shown that children who start school with fewer literacy skills generally do not catch up with their peers.[7] Yet when children's brains have been nourished with words, they have faster language processing speeds, which makes language accrual easier.[8] In addition to building more vocabulary and conversational skills, this ability also provides a foundation for social-emotional and cognitive development.[9] Due in part to these findings, the Every Child Ready To Read @ Your Library curriculum was created.

> For the sake of brevity, this book will refer to the adults attending MGOL sessions as parents, even though in real life, the adults may be relatives or caregivers.

Every Child Ready to Read

Every Child Ready to Read (ECRR) is a research-based curriculum that was commissioned by the Public Library Association and the Association of Library Service for Children and gave children's librarians tools (such as PowerPoints, fliers, and more) to help them teach parents and caregivers how important it is for children to develop early literacy and to encourage them to take an active role in their children's literacy development. The first version of ECRR focused on six literacy skills: (1) vocabulary, (2) print motivation, (3) print awareness, (4) phonological awareness, (5) letter knowledge, and (6) narrative skills.[10]

The second edition of ECRR considered the critical dimensions of language and literacy to be (1) oral language, (2) phonological awareness, (3) print conventions, (4) letter knowledge, (5) vocabulary, and (6) background knowledge. This version focused on what adults could actually *do* with children to help them develop these skills and recommended five practices: talk, sing, read, write, and play.[11] ("Write" for babies means helping them develop the fine motor skills that will later enable them to write.) MGOL has always incorporated the five ECRR practices.

How MGOL Supports Early Literacy

As librarians, we want to instill a love of reading in all children. What better way to do this than to offer activities as playful opportunities to learn and develop early literacy skills? Listed below are some ways that MGOL supports the six literacy skills in ECRR.

Vocabulary

- Exposure to books, songs, and rhymes increases the variety of words children hear.
- Naming items in book illustrations and flannel-board characters adds to vocabulary.
- Loving verbal interactions with parents and caregivers leads to quality vocabulary acquisition.

Print Motivation

- Hearing fun stories teaches children how to enjoy listening to a book being read aloud and builds vocabulary. These positive associations with books encourage children to want to learn to read.

Print Awareness

- For young children, watching a librarian read a book aloud connects the written word to the spoken word. Understanding that print has meaning is *print awareness*.

Phonological Awareness

- Listening to rhyme patterns in words and songs helps children hear the sounds that, combined together, make up words. This ability helps beginning readers sound out new words.

Letter Knowledge

- Pointing out shapes and naming them, reading alphabet books aloud, and singing songs such as "BINGO" prepare children for learning about letters.

Narrative Skills / Comprehension

- Acting out rhymes helps connect words with motions.
- Repeating rhymes over and over helps children to learn word patterns through repetition.
- Listening and concentration skills, phonemic awareness, and imagination are fostered through rhymes about pigs flying in the air and pretending to be a teapot.
- Songs that have a beginning, a middle, and an end are telling a short story.
- Knowing when to go "uppity up" or "down-ditty down" requires listening to song lyrics and understanding what they mean.

What Is School Readiness?

School readiness refers to a number of different skills that, when combined together, mean a child is ready to start elementary school in every way. School readiness was first defined by a 1995 report written by the National Education Goals Panel as the following five domains:

1. social and emotional well-being
2. health and physical well-being
3. approaches to learning (meaning a positive attitude toward learning)
4. language development
5. general knowledge[12]

Since then, many US states have crafted their own definitions of school readiness based on these original five domains. In some states, science, math, social studies, and the arts are treated as separate domains rather than falling under the category of "general knowledge." Other states include creative thinking, learning through play, and partnerships for learning as new categories. No matter how the domains are defined, it is widely recognized that all children are born ready to learn, but a *school-ready child* is one who shows a healthy trajectory in terms of his or her physical, social, emotional, language, and cognitive development, along with an interest in learning and mastering new skills.[13]

How MGOL Supports School Readiness

When combined together, the school readiness domains form a well-rounded child, or "*a whole* child."[14] When it is time for these children to enter kindergarten, they already know how to get along in a classroom, to pay attention to the teacher, to follow directions, to believe in themselves and their capabilities, and to have a positive attitude toward learning.

During each MGOL session, children make connections among rhymes, illustrations, and activities that foster development of all domains of school readiness, as explained below.

What Is Social and Emotional Well-Being?

The social and emotional well-being domain of school readiness includes the ability to get along with others as well as a child's sense of self-worth.[15] Children who believe that they are capable human beings will be willing to try new things and risk failure. Their sense of self is not contingent on always succeeding and enables them to learn from their mistakes. Believing that they are capable of success gives them motivation to try to learn new things.[16] Often referred to as "executive function skills," social and emotional well-being includes being able to pay attention, to be flexible, and to have a good working memory that allows them to use what they already know to evaluate and plan. This ability to think before acting is called "self-regulation." Without adequate exposure to and experience with self-regulation or self-control, children can exhibit problem behaviors, such as being overly aggressive.[17] At the other end of the spectrum are children who exhibit so much control that they are socially withdrawn and unable to interact with others.[18]

An important skill for school readiness is being able to follow directions.[19] Infant programs clued into school readiness may include activities that encourage children to learn how to listen to directions or how to respond to directional cues from an adult.[20] Young children who have learned how to respond in a positive manner to directions will have an easier time responding to the requests of their first-grade teachers than those children who have not been in an adult-directed environment.[21] Plus, being able to think before they act will also keep them out of trouble as adults!

Emotional intelligence, or EQ, has been described as skills such as the ability to listen, to share, to verbally communicate feelings, to be enthusiastic and curious, to not be disruptive in class, and to be sensitive to others' feelings.[22] EQ is formed in the early years of a child's life. It involves touch, tone of voice, facial expressions, music, smell, and rocking and other rhythmic motions. Emotional literacy enables people to give names to emotions such as sadness and anger. The words children learn are then bridges between their emotions and their reasoning capacity.[23]

Although school readiness is undeniably tied up with knowledge, scientific studies show that social and emotional development are also vital components of school readiness.[24]

How MGOL Supports Social and Emotional Well-Being

MGOL helps children practice and develop many essential life skills. MGOL intentionally incorporates activities that help children build focus and practice self-control, which are different types of executive function skills. Each session has built-in opportunities for children to practice paying attention, listening to others, taking turns, and following a leader's instructions. They take on challenges and show appreciation to each other. Children who regularly attend MGOL sessions receive positive reinforcement for being patient, for taking turns, and for following directions. This builds self-esteem as well as self-regulation skills. Hearing praise builds children's sense of competence; interacting with a presenter who displays a positive attitude and uses encouraging vocabulary models how to show appreciation to others.

The activities interwoven throughout each session give children practice interacting with each other. Practicing positive social skills helps children learn how to get along with other children.

- Children become accustomed to accepting positive reinforcement for a job well done when they hear the applause of the group immediately after they follow directions in a doable activity.
- They also learn how to give positive reinforcement to others. Clapping for each other through an entire activity shows the children how to interact with others in a positive way, an important skill for school readiness.
- Hearing words such as *great*, *wonderful*, *fantastic*, *good job*, and *well done* after following directions for an activity gives an actual vocabulary of positive words to both the children and their caregivers.
- Young children are allowed to crawl around during the program except for entering the invisible circle around the flannelboard; this sets guidelines for behavior that even very young children can understand and comply with. In this friendly format, they have the opportunity to learn guidelines and stick to them.
- Freeze games teach the word *stop* without any negative connotations, giving children the opportunity to practice self-regulation skills.
- Tickle rhymes help children feel comfortable with their own bodies (self-esteem).

The benefits of these rhymes often fit into multiple categories. For instance, what is often considered a musical skill—learning to listen—is actually a very important social skill: being able to listen to others. Because MGOL has focused on building social and emotional skills along with early literacy skills from the very beginning, it was recognized in 2015 as "a brain-building powerhouse."[25]

What Are Health and Physical Well-Being, and How Does MGOL Support Them?

A child who is hungry has difficulty paying attention. A child with uncorrected vision problems will not be able to focus. While library programs cannot correct these issues, the librarian can use her position as an information professional to direct parents to resources such as food pantries or free health assessment clinics. Participation in positive prereading experiences like MGOL at the public library also brings many benefits. It can

- help children's eyes to focus,
- aid them in recognizing objects and developing sensory awareness,
- build fine motor skills with fingerplays (later used for holding writing implements), and
- give children time for physical closeness with their adult. This is crucial for healthy emotional and intellectual development.[26]

What Is a Positive Attitude toward Learning?

While there are many language and cognitive skills to acquire, before children enter first grade, they need to be motivated to learn to read and to learn in general. These attitudes develop very early and are based on what children experience more than on what they are told.[27] A positive association with reading and pleasure creates an enthusiasm for learning later on in life and translates into motivation to learn to read. Because children often adopt the attributes of their teachers and caregivers, it is important to promote this optimism and motivation for learning.[28] Early encouraging experiences at the library can produce positive lifelong effects.

How MGOL Supports a Positive Attitude toward Learning

By intentionally including fun activities that build emotional and social skills in the library environment, MGOL helps children develop positive attitudes toward learning. In the earliest years of children's lives, connections made between their feelings and their cognitive understanding teach them that there are things they can do with their feelings. For example, if children see librarians and other adults reading books, their brains absorb the fact that reading is a normal activity and everyone does it.[29] If, in addition to reading, the parent snuggles with a child while reading aloud, that child will connect books and reading with positive, loving experiences.

Positive Attitude toward Learning

- Attending a joyful program in the earliest years builds a positive attitude toward reading and books. This positive connection forms a solid foundation for years of literacy development.
- MGOL's physical setup, with the librarian in the front and children and their caregivers sitting around in a semicircle, is a forerunner to the classroom. Children with positive experiences in this format will enter the classroom setting with joyful recognition rather than trepidation.
- Children who have a warm connection with the MGOL facilitator will most likely begin their formal schooling expecting the teacher to be a combination leader/partner rather than an adversary.

What Is Language Development?

Infants are born with an "acute sense of hearing" as well as a "preprogrammed ability for language," but "this ability needs to be triggered and cultivated."[30] Exposure to a variety of sounds and speech is a major component of the entire learning process and can help trigger the baby's linguistic abilities. Part of this learning is baby talk, which is an intuitive baby language. However, baby talk is more like music in that it is nonsymbolic and nonverbal, and it "appeals directly to the emotions."[31]

Vocabulary is an important part of the language development leading to school readiness. A large vocabulary makes it easier for a child to read and to understand. Children with larger vocabularies have the language they need to express themselves and to explain things. One survey asking kindergarten teachers to rate the qualities essential for kindergarten readiness showed them putting the ability to verbally communicate needs, wants, and thoughts at the top of the scale and knowing the letters of the alphabet in the bottom 10 percent.[32] A child with developed language skills can use a variety of words correctly and interpret voice inflection. (Of course, this

EARLY LITERACY FAQS

Q: What are 21st Century Skills, and how do they relate to MGOL?
A: Twenty-first Century Skills are skills that the adults of the future will need in order to successfully deal with the challenges ahead of us. With the rapid rate of technological advancements and growing cultural diversity, it is impossible to predict what the world of the near future is going to be like. By teaching children to be creative thinkers, problems solvers, good communicators, and team players while still imbuing them with respect and honor of others, we can get them ready to handle whatever the future holds.[33]

Because the children of today are going to be the adults of the future, we need to prepare them with important life skills. In *Mind in the Making*, Ellen Galinsky reasons that in order to have a high-functioning technological world where kindness and community are still parts of the integral structure, we need to teach children how to figure out what others think and feel, to respect each other's differences, to determine what they want to communicate and to express themselves in ways others can understand, to work together, to be ready to tackle perplexing problems, to know what to focus on and what to ignore, to use creative thinking and problem-solving skills to make connections, to apply critical thinking, to recognize their interests and pursue them, to be willing to make mistakes and learn from them, and to have the persistence and determination to stick with a problem until it is solved. Described as the "Seven Essential Life Skills Every Child Needs," Galinsky places these 21st century skills into seven categories: (1) focus and self-control, (2) perspective taking, (3) communicating, (4) making connections, (5) critical thinking, (6) taking on challenges, and (7) self-directed and engaged learning.[34]

Q: What is VIEWS2, and how does it relate to MGOL?
A: VIEWS2 (Valuable Initiative in Early Learning) was a research study that measured the impact of early literacy storytimes in the public library, using early literacy domains that differ slightly from ECRR: communication, language use, phonological awareness, vocabulary, comprehension, print concepts, alphabetic knowledge, and writing skills.[35] This study found that storytimes do make a difference in children's early literacy behavior. The most effective or "supercharged" storytimes had three ingredients: (1) intentionality—purposely choosing activities to build skills and articulate early literacy connections to caregivers, (2) interactivity—presenting programs that are "shared enjoyable learning experiences" where children interact with the content of the storytime, and (3) community—relying on feedback and learning from peers to improve and hone one's practice.[36]

Programs that incorporate intentionality, interactivity, and community are now considered to be supercharged storytimes. MGOL has always been intentional with the "ulterior motive" of educating parents through modeling and giving developmental tips while also providing experiences that help children practice and develop social, emotional, and literacy skills. It is naturally interactive. MGOL librarians are facilitators; rather than striving to "perform" a program to passive audiences, they facilitate playful interactions between parents and their children. While MGOL has always strived to build community between participants, peer feedback has not yet been formally built into the program, although it has already resulted in fruitful adaptations and partnerships.

Q: What is the VIEWS2 Planning Tool (VPT), and how does it relate to MGOL?
A: VPT is the VIEWS2 Planning Tool that lists actions adults can take in order to address specific literacy skills, and it also describes what to look for to determine if children are exhibiting the desired behaviors.[37] It identifies specific skills such as communication (how to talk and share, language use, or how to use words) and places children in age-range groups of birth to eighteen months, eighteen to thirty-six months, and thirty-six to sixty months. Its format is similar to the Common Core Standards, Head Start Early Learning Outcomes Framework, and the Early Learning Benchmarks of many states. Because VPT provides details regarding observable early literacy behaviors, it helps MGOL facilitators articulate the changes they see in the children attending their programs.

in no way means that early letter recognition, word pronunciation, identification of patterns, and understanding syllables are not valuable.) Reading aloud to children in a sustained way has been shown to reduce aggression, hyperactivity, and difficulty with attention; the combination of reading and playing builds social and emotional skills as well as vocabulary.[38]

Simply talking "at" children or speaking aloud and expecting the children to listen are not recommended ways to build vocabulary. It is more important for parents to talk *with* their children rather than to bombard them with words. According to researchers Kathy Hirsh-Pasek and Roberta Michnick Golinkoff, the quality of language within caring relationships is more important than the quantity of words children hear.[39] The ideal learning situation is a "conversational duet."[40]

MGOL's philosophy and programming align perfectly with six evidence- and research-based principles for language development that were introduced in an article about providing support for ESL children:[41]

1. Children learn what they hear most.
2. Children learn words for things and events that interest them.
3. Interactive and responsive environments build language learning.
4. Children learn best in meaningful contexts.
5. Children need to hear diverse examples of words and language structures.
6. Vocabulary and grammatical development are reciprocal processes.[42]

Becoming familiar with book-reading behavior and developing a positive attitude toward books is also considered part of language development. When the librarian holds up a book with animal illustrations and sings a song about the sounds the animals make rather than reading the book aloud, parents who themselves have difficulty reading will be able to see a variety of ways in which to give their children early literacy experiences. You can tell them that book behavior for babies may involve chewing the book rather than turning the pages, which is absolutely fine (especially if the book is made of cardboard!).

Nursery rhymes are excellent vehicles for promoting linguistic awareness because they contain lots of words, use rhymes and rhythm patterns, and are easy to learn.[43]

In addition, when adults share songs that their parents and grandparents sang to them, they connect children with their heritage.[44]

Using Rhymes to Target Learning

Activities that accompany rhymes can be used to target specific skills, areas of learning, or multiple intelligences. The same rhyme presented in different ways may give children opportunities to practice building up skills in all the school readiness domains.

A Few Examples of Identifying the Learning Acquired through Rhymes

- Leaning from side to side at the appropriate time in "Mother and Father and Uncle John" helps children learn to listen and to respond physically to verbal cues (listening and following directions).
- Reciting "Peter Piper Picked a Peck of Pickled Peppers" aids in speech development by the constant repetition of the sound *p* makes (language development).
- "Two Little Dickey Birds," which contains the words *soft* spoken softly and *loud* spoken loudly, teaches new words and their meanings (vocabulary and narrative skills).
- Rhymes such as "Row, Row, Row Your Boat" that incorporate full-body movements are good for developing locomotion (gross motor, spatial awareness).
- Tapping sticks to rhymes like "Polly Put the Kettle On" or recorded music with a steady beat helps children to listen as well as to develop a sense of rhythm so they recognize the underlying beat in various musical works (learning to listen, sense of rhythm).
- Bouncing children on knees for "The Grand Old Duke of York" teaches "up" and "down" (vocabulary).
- "If You're Happy and You Know It" connects sounds with actions while also naming an emotion (emotional vocabulary).
- Singing a cleanup song such as "Toys Away" trains children to put away toys (or musical instruments, or anything else!) without seeing it as a chore. The cleanup song becomes part of the game, but the child learns how to pick up after him- or herself

(following directions).
- Partner rhymes such as "Pat-a-Cake" encourage feelings of friendship, love, and trust (building relationships).
- Tapping their names on a drum during the "Rum Pum Pum" drum sequence makes children aware of syllables (phonological awareness).
- "Where Is Thumbkin?" introduces children to conversation skills and manners (conversation and narrative skills).
- "Five Fat Sausages" familiarizes children with number names and counting sequences (math skills).
- When playing "Hickory Dickory Dare," children learn to wait their turn to throw a stuffed animal pig up in the air (self-regulation).

General Knowledge

General knowledge about the world helps develop learning readiness; general literacy knowledge "helps children understand books and stories once they begin to read."[45] Early literacy programs, such as MGOL, enhance general knowledge about the world. For example, simple songs such as "This Is the Way We Wash Our Face" teach how to use a washcloth. Songs about rain alert children to the pitter-patter sounds that rain can make against a window pane. Animal songs familiarize children with the names of animals as well as the sounds that they make. Rhymes can be used to teach manners, colors, and shapes. Rhymes can also build STEM skills; when children are given musical instruments to explore, they discover different properties (if I shake this rattle, it will make noise). They also learn cause and effect ("If I throw the pig up in the air, it will come back down"). Children expand their vocabularies as well as their understanding of the world when they are exposed to numerous words and concepts.

Music and Singing Stimulates Learning

Because the "Listen, Like, Learn" approach forms the foundation of MGOL, music is used as the conduit for building many early literacy skills.

The "Listen, Like, Learn" Approach in Action

- Singing songs that name specific body parts, how they move, and the sounds they can make expands children's body awareness and vocabulary (fine motor, gross motor, vocabulary, self-esteem).
- Singing songs to different tempos teaches the musical concept of fast and slow (music, vocabulary).
- Call-and-response rhymes that require the participants to sing back the word or phrase that the leader sings encourage accurate listening and singing while increasing vocabulary (vocabulary, paying attention, listening skills).
- Making connections between sounds of objects and animals familiarizes children with different sounds and helps them to recognize the world around them through their listening skills (phonemic awareness, general knowledge about the world).
- Physically ringing a bell high in the air while singing "ring them up high" in a high voice and then doing the same "down low" in a low voice teaches the musical concepts of high and low (musical concepts, vocabulary, spatial awareness).
- Shaking maracas up in the air while using the word *high* or down near the floor using the word

> **LET'S PLAY GAMES**
>
> Playing freeze games has had some surprising benefits. During the drum segment of MGOL, when the facilitator says, "And the drum says stop," all the children freeze. One of my colleagues was visiting a relative out of state. While entering a supermarket, she observed a little girl take a child-sized shopping cart and begin to race ahead of her father. As she was running, the father called out, "And the drum says stop." The daughter stopped immediately and waited while her father nonchalantly caught up with her. From this, my colleague knew they had attended MGOL programs at their local library and heard a developmental tip from their librarian about practicing freeze games at home!

low teaches the spatial concepts of high and low (spatial awareness, music, vocabulary).
- Shaking maracas and rattles vigorously helps provide an emotional outlet through music (expressing oneself, relieving tension in an acceptable way, physical exercise).
- Singing, listening, and rocking to lullabies helps children relax (self-regulation).
- High or very fast knee bounces can seem scary at first; by learning to enjoy them, children also learn what it feels like to overcome fears (building self-confidence).
- "The Eency Weency Spider" introduces beginning science concepts—the sun comes out and dries up all the rain (STEM, general knowledge about the world).

Visual Literacy

Exposure to book illustrations helps develop children's visual literacy. Although visual literacy is not officially considered part of school readiness, I agree with child psychologist Robert Coles, who said, "Visual literacy ought to be acknowledged as an important part of cultural literacy."[46] Visual literacy is "learning to look and construct meaning from objects and works of art."[47] It is considered a form of critical thinking because it requires interpretation of what is seen.[48]

Very young children enjoy their ability to visually recognize and name objects. There are always some toddlers in the supermarket joyously pointing out the objects they recognize: "Apples! Flowers! Cereal!" Children delight in this and are pleased with themselves. They often have had some sort of personal connection with the object; they have held apples, smelled flowers, or eaten cereal at some point. These personal connections enable them to decode visual representations of the experiences.

Children who see picture-book illustrations are also making personal connections. They recognize animals, objects, and patterns. By recognizing the same animal drawn by different illustrators and seeing different illustrations connected to the same rhyme, children start to understand that one thing can have several visual representations. They also may develop an aesthetic sense. I've seen children recognize new artwork by Eric Carle after being exposed to some of his illustrations at MGOL. Recognizing similarities in artwork can prepare the brain for recognizing letters and words later on.

Using flannelboard characters, puppets, and book illustrations to represent specific objects, rhymes, or actions helps children connect the sound of a word to a visual representation. This is a precursor to understanding that written letters represent words. Displaying illustrations of nursery rhymes encourages children to develop an interest in looking at artwork.

Community Development and Inclusivity

Offered as a free program at public libraries, MGOL brings together families from different ethnic, cultural, and economic backgrounds. In addition to celebrating diversity, parents and caregivers participate in activities that are designed to facilitate playful interactions with their children, thus increasing parent-child bonding, parent-child-librarian bonding, and group bonding. The informal atmosphere with the outward focus on children's development creates a powerful learning space for parents and caregivers.

- Parents watch the librarian and learn how to use familiar rhymes and storytime techniques to encourage their very young children to engage in literacy activities—even if the parents themselves are not quite comfortable with their own skills at reading aloud.
- Parents who observe the librarian read books aloud see examples of book-reading behavior. They hear how books can be read with expression; they see how to ask questions or say something about a particular illustration without actually reading the story. This exposure to age-appropriate books for use with infants and toddlers will help them when making book choices for their own young children.
- Often, informal parenting groups spring up after MGOL sessions; parents stay and schmooze together while the children play or nurse. The adults enjoy having a place to share information and socialize with other parents who have young children.

- Some parents do not realize what the realm of normal behavior for very young children is. By observing the "normal" behavior of a range of babies, they learn to have realistic expectations of their own children.
- By observing, parents can also learn effective ways for adults to interact with very young children in public spaces. Librarians can model methods for redirecting negative behavior in constructive ways and for showing positive reinforcement.
- MGOL gives parents myriad activities to use at home, in the car, while waiting in public places, and during toilet training. They learn different ways of sharing intimate time and making time useful with their child. The activities can be used to ease difficult transition times as well.

This manual includes a section on evaluation; facilitators are encouraged to write notes on their programming sheets at the end of each session and to take them into account when planning their next program. However, adding more self-reflection and a peer-review element could certainly make a great program even better!

Benefits for All

The benefits listed above are just some of the ways MGOL presents activities so children can develop their brains by learning a whole set of skills, parents and caregivers can practice skill-building and nurturing behavior, and everyone can have fun in a safe environment.

Notes

1. Eunice Kennedy Shriver National Institute of Child Health and Human Development, NIH, DHHS, *Put Reading First: Helping Your Child Learn to Read* (Washington, DC: US Government Printing Office, 2001).
2. Judith A. Schickedanz, *Much More Than ABCs: The Early Stages of Reading and Writing* (Washington, DC: National Association for the Education of Young Children, 1999).
3. Betty Hart and Todd Risley's groundbreaking research made the first scientific connection between early language exposure and intellectual development. It also documented disparities in ultimate educational achievement levels among children from different economic backgrounds. Hart and Risley, *Meaningful Differences in the Everyday Experience of Young American Children* (Baltimore: Paul H. Brookes, 1995). A more recent study showed similar results: Paul L. Morgan, George Farkas, Marianne M. Hillemeier, Carol Scheffner Hammer, and Steve Maczuga, "24-Month-Old Children with Larger Oral Vocabularies Display Greater Academic and Behavioral Functioning at Kindergarten Entry," *Child Development* 86, no. 5 (2015): 1351–70.
4. Dana Suskind, Beth Suskind, and Leslie Lewinter-Suskind, *Thirty Million Words: Building a Child's Brain* (New York: Dutton, 2015): 51, 48–49.
5. Catherine E. Snow, M. Susan Burns, and Peg Griffin, eds., *Preventing Reading Difficulties in Young Children* (Washington, DC: National Academy Press, 1998), 9–10.
6. Connie Juel, "Learning to Read and Write: A Longitudinal Study of 54 Children from First through Fourth Grades," *Journal of Educational Psychology* 80, no. 4 (1988): 437–47.
7. Donna Celano and Susan B. Neuman, *The Role of Public Libraries in Children's Literacy Development: An Evaluation Report* (Harrisburg: Pennsylvania Library Association, 2001), 9.
8. Suskind, Suskind, and Lewinter-Suskind, *Thirty Million Words*, 48–49.
9. Suskind, Suskind, and Lewinter-Suskind, 62.
10. Public Library Association (PLA) and Association for Library Service to Children (ALSC), *Every Child Ready to Read @ Your Library* (Chicago: American Library Association, 2004).
11. PLA and ALSC, *Every Child Ready to Read: Teaching Parents and Caregivers How to Support Early Literacy Development* (Chicago: ALA Editions, 2011).
12. Sharon L. Kagan, Evelyn Moore, and Sue Bredekamp, eds., *Reconsidering Children's Early Development and Learning: Toward Common Views and Vocabulary*, report of the National Education Goals Panel, Goal 1 Technical Planning Group (Washington, DC: Government Printing Office, 1995).
13. Adele Diamond, "The Evidence Base for Improving School Outcomes by Addressing the Whole Child and by Addressing Skills and Attitudes, Not Just Content," *Early Education and Development* 21, no. 2 (2010): 780–93.
14. Diamond, 780–93.
15. Office of Head Start, *Head Start Early Learning Outcomes Framework: Ages Birth to Five* (Washington, DC: US Department of Health and Human Services, 2015): 28–30, 32–33, https://eclkc.ohs.acf.hhs.gov/sites/default/files/pdf/elof-ohs-framework.pdf, accessed August 11, 2018.

16. Diamond, "Evidence Base," 2010.
17. Helena L. Rohlf, Anna K. Holl, Fabian Kirsch, Barbara Krahé, and Birgit Elsner, "Longitudinal Links between Executive Function, Anger, and Aggression in Middle Childhood," *Frontiers in Behavioral Neuroscience* 12, no. 27 (2018): 12.
18. Thomas R. Lynch, Roelie J. Hempel, and Christine Dunkley, "Radically Open—Dialectical Behavior Therapy for Disorders of Over-Control: Signaling Matters," *American Journal of Psychotherapy* 69, no. 2 (2015): 141–62.
19. *School Readiness Goals* (Camden, NJ: Center for Family Services, 2017), www.centerffs.org/headstart/school-readiness-goals, accessed August 11, 2018.
20. *Maryland Early Learning Standards: Birth–8 Years* (Baltimore: Maryland State Department of Education, Office of Early Childhood Development, 2016), 40, 135, 145, 150, 159, https://earlychildhood.maryland publicschools.org/system/files/filedepot/4/msde-pedagogy-report-_appendix_2016.pdf, accessed August 11, 2018.
21. Clancy Blair and Rachel Peters Razza, "Relating Effortful Control, Executive Function, and False Belief Understanding to Emerging Math and Literacy Ability in Kindergarten," *Child Development* 78, no. 2 (2007): 647–63.
22. Daniel Goleman, *Emotional Intelligence: Why It Can Matter More Than IQ* (New York: Bantam, 1995).
23. G. E. Joseph, P. S. Strain, and the Center on Social and Emotional Foundations for Early Learning, *Enhancing Emotional Vocabulary in Young Children* (Champaign: University of Illinois at Urbana-Champaign, 2003).
24. Amy Pace, Rebecca Alper, Margaret R. Burchinal, Roberta Michnick Golinkoff, and Kathy Hirsh-Pasek, "Measuring Success: Within and Cross-Domain Predictors of Academic and Social Trajectories in Elementary School," *Early Childhood Research Quarterly* (2018), https://doi.org/10.1016/j.ecresq.2018.04.001.
25. Families and Work Institute, IMLS, and School Readiness Consulting, *Brain-Building Powerhouses: How Museums and Libraries Can Strengthen Executive Function Life Skills* (Families and Work Institute, 2015), http://mindinthemaking.org/download/museums-and-libraries.pdf.
26. Jack Shonkoff, "The Timing and Quality of Early Experiences Combine to Shape Brain Architecture" (working paper 5, Center on the Developing Child at Harvard University, Cambridge, MA, 2007), https://developingchild.harvard.edu/resources/the-timing-and-quality-of-early-experiences-combine-to-shape-brain-architecture, accessed August 11, 2018.
27. Adriana G. Bus, Jay Belsky, Marinus H. van Ijzendoom, and Keith Crnic, "Attachment and Bookreading Patterns: A Study of Mothers, Fathers, and their Toddlers," *Early Childhood Research Quarterly* 12, no. 1 (1997): 81–98.
28. Allan M. Schore, "Effects of Secure Attachment on Right Brain Development, Affect Regulation, and Infant Mental Health," *Infant Medical Health* 22, no. 1–2 (2001): 7–66; Sarah Landy, *Pathways to Competence: Encouraging Healthy Social and Emotional Development in Young Children* (Baltimore: Brookes, 2009).
29. Jane Braunger and Jan P. Lewis, *Building a Knowledge Base in Reading*, 2nd ed. (Portland: Northwest Regional Laboratory, 1998).
30. Barbara Cass-Beggs, *Your Child Needs Music* (Mississauga, Ontario: Frederick Harris Music Co., 1986), 25.
31. Barbara Cass-Beggs, "How Music Is First Introduced," *Ostinato* 17 (January 1991): 122.
32. National Center for Educational Statistics, "Public School Kindergarten Teachers' Views on Children's Readiness for School," *Kindergarten Teacher Survey on School Readiness* (Washington, DC: NCES, 1993), http://nces.ed.gov/quicktables/displaytableimage.asp?ID=QTFImage1280, accessed July 27, 2017.
33. Partnership for 21st Century Learning, "Framework for 21st Century Learning," 2007, www.p21.org/our-work/p21-framework, accessed August 11, 2018.
34. Ellen Galinsky, *Mind in the Making: The Seven Essential Life Skills Every Child Needs* (New York: HarperStudio, 2010).
35. University of Washington ischool, "Valuable Initiative in Early Learning," *VIEWS2*, 2017, http://views2.ischool.uw.edu, accessed August 11, 2018. Dr. Eliza Dresang was the initiator and principal investigator of the VIEWS2 project.
36. These findings resulted in the 2016 publication of *Supercharged Storytimes* by Kathleen Campana, J. Elizabeth Mills, and Saroj Nadkarni Ghoting (Chicago: ALA Editions, 2016), 6.
37. VPT can be found online at University of Washington ischool, "Resources," n.d., http://views2.ischool.uw.edu/resources, accessed July 27, 2017.
38. Alan L. Mendelsohn, Carolyn Brockmeyer Cates, Adriana Weisleder, Samantha Berkule Johnson, Anne M. Seery, Caitlin F. Canfield, Harris S. Huberman, and Benard P. Dreyer, "Reading Aloud, Play, and Social-Emotional Development," *Pediatrics* 141, no. 5 (2018): e20173393.
39. Kathy Hirsh-Pasek, Lauren B. Adamson, Roger Bakeman, Margaret Tresch Owen, Roberta Mich-

nick Golinkoff, Amy Pace, Paula Yust, and Katharine Suma, "The Contribution of Early Communication to Low-Income Children's Language Success," *Psychological Science* 26, no. 7 (2015): 1071–83.

40. Roberta Michnick Golinkoff, Dilara Deniz Can, Melanie Soderstrom, and Kathy Hirsh-Pasek, "(Baby) Talk to Me: The Social Context of Infant-Directed Speech and Its Effects on Early Language Acquisition," *Current Directions in Psychological Science* 24, no. 5 (2015): 339–44.

41. Haruka Konishi, Junko Kanero, Max R. Freeman, Roberta Michnick Golinkoff, and Kathy Hirsh-Pasek, "Six Principles of Language Development: Implications for Second Language Learners," *Developmental Neuropsychology* 39, no. 5 (2014): 404–20.

42. Konishi et al., 406.

43. Peter Bryant, Morag MacLean, Lynette Bradley, and John Crossland, "Rhyme and Alliteration, Phoneme Detection, and Learning to Read," *Developmental Psychology* 26, no. 3 (1990): 429–38; Morag MacLean, Peter Bryant, and Lynette Bradley, "Rhymes, Nursery Rhymes, and Reading in Early Childhood," *Merrill-Palmer Quarterly* 33, no. 3 (1987): 255–81; Carl J. Dunst, Diana Meter, and Deborah W. Hamby, "Relationship between Young Children's Nursery Rhyme Experiences and Knowledge and Phonological and Print-Related Abilities," *Center for Early Literacy Learning (CELL)* 4, no. 1 (2011): 1–12; Susan Kenney, "Nursery Rhymes: Foundation for Learning," *General Music Today* 19, no. 1 (2005): 28–31.

44. Michael Sizer, "The Surprising Meaning and Benefits of Nursery Rhymes," PBS, www.pbs.org/parents/education/reading-language/reading-tips/the-surprising-meaning-and-benefits-of-nursery-rhymes, accessed July 23, 2015.

45. ALSC and PLA, *Every Child Ready to Read, 2nd Edition Kit* (Chicago: ALSC and PLA, 2011), section 1.5.

46. Robert Coles, "How to Look at a Mountain," interview by Milton Esterow, *ARTnews* 92, no. 3 (March 1993): 92–99.

47. Sharon Shaffer, *Preschoolers and Museums: An Educational Guide* (Washington, DC: Smithsonian Early Enrichment Center, n.d.), 14.

48. Kate Blake, "Learning to Look Across Disciplines: Visual Literacy for Museum Audiences," Visual Literacy Today, https://visualliteracytoday.org/learning-to-look-across-disciplines-visual-literacy-for-museum-audiences-by-kate-blake, accessed August 11, 2018.

Essential Components for an Early Literacy Program

AS LIBRARIANS, WE WANT TO LEAD PROGRAMS THAT will foster high EQ, early literacy, and well-being. By intentionally choosing activities that help young brains grow, we can assist in children's healthy development. When planning your sessions, use this list of important teaching elements, based on research regarding the way children learn.

- repetition
- ritual
- a fun, positive environment
- play
- being read to
- movement
- music
- time to relax
- appeal to multiple intelligences

Repetition

Repetition is soothing for young children. It helps them feel secure. Children are more likely to respond to activities and to participate if they already know the actions or the words to the songs. They know where they are in the program, and they are not worried about figuring out what will happen next. However, variation is important because it prevents boredom. It has been demonstrated that learning is enhanced when a known thing changes patterns or routines.[1] So not only do you *not have* to work up an entirely new program each session, *it is better if you don't.*

Without getting too technical, the right balance of repetition and surprise helps children's brains develop in a way that prepares them for reading and writing. The limbic system (the part of the brain that has to do with emotions) "LIKES repetition and predictability while the cerebral cortex [the 'thinking part of the brain'] CRAVES novelty and change."[2] So when you provide repetitive patterns that are pleasing to the ears but that also have some variation (nursery rhymes are an excellent example) or when you recite the same rhymes with different puppets, you are helping connect the part of the brain that has to do with emotions with parts that are later used for reading and writing.

Ritual

Ritual is a type of repetition. Rituals are specific activities that are repeated the same way at the same time during programs, and children love them. One programmatic ritual might be a song that starts and ends each session. Another could be an animal section in the middle of each session in which the same song is always sung to the same animal illustrations. Ritual helps many children feel grounded. If you don't already know how important this is, just try to leave out a "ritual" some time and listen to the clamor. For the children, the program seems incomplete without it. The ritual provides a shared experience that has meaning for the participants; it helps define the program.

Ritual not only gives structure to the program but gives structure to the mind. It creates a secure space for children because it is already familiar to them. Like repetition, a known ritual invites participants to join in. This participation activates memory, creates context, and eases transitions.[3] In other words, ritual creates another link between the emotions and the intellect.

A Fun, Positive Environment

Brain power is not just about what the brain can accomplish on its own—it is also about the type of environment in which the brain resides. Environment affects the mind, body, and spirit. Studies have shown that sensory-enriched environments have the power to improve stress management, immune systems, emotional stability, emotional adaptation, memory and learning, behavior, and life extension![4] In one scientific experiment, when laboratory animals were put in enriched environments, the *structures* of their brains changed, demonstrating concretely that environment can physically improve intelligence.[5]

The changes that take place in the brain of a child who feels consistently threatened also interfere with learning. If the environment is a fun one in which the child feels safe and secure, new information will be processed more quickly. Although children suffering from toxic stress are at risk of severe social, emotional, and cognitive impairment, studies indicate that making specific positive environmental changes early in their lives often results in the improvement of their lifelong mental and physical health.[6] Structural changes take place in the brain, allowing the new information to make connections on which other connections can be built. With repetition, these connections will become implanted.

Play

Noted child psychologist Jean Piaget argued that it is impossible to separate learning from play because there is a seamless and symbiotic relationship between the two.[7] He believed that children construct their knowledge of the environment by constantly interacting with objects and people through play. Oral language develops as children talk to each other. They learn to negotiate and settle disputes. Play involves imagination, which leads to creative thought. Play can expose children to print materials, and discourse with other children during play encourages them to practice narrative skills.[8]

As children play, connections in their brains are formed between what they are doing, what they think and feel about what they are doing, and what they are discovering as they are doing that particular thing.[9] Without the exploration of play, these connections would not be formed. Fred Rogers explained it this way: "Play gives children a chance to practice what they are learning,"[10] and scientist Alison Gopnik confirmed, "Play is the true work of childhood."[11]

Being Read To

Your reading habits, whether as a librarian or a parent, influence the reading habits of the children around you.[12] If you read, the children in your care will assume that they will be reading. If storytime is a warm cozy time, children will think of reading as a happy, secure activity. And like all happy, secure activities, children will want to repeat it.

However, not all parents have the literacy skills—or the confidence—to model positive reading behavior for their children. This is why public library programs are so important. Librarians can help educationally challenged parents by modeling creative ways to use books that do not involve sophisticated reading skills and by incorporating language development in their baby and toddler programs. They can also encourage well-educated parents to take the time to sit and read with their children by demonstrating that it can be a fun and valuable experience even if the child is very young.

Movement

The majority of children have to move; they can stop movement only with great self-restraint. However, incorporating movement into the program is more than just a method to keep children under control or to make the time go faster for everyone. Physical activity can actually create physiological changes in the brain.[13] Movement accelerates heart rates and can also correlate with increased attention levels. Greater attention often leads to greater memory performance. Movement activates the limbic system, which leads to the brain receiving increased sensory information and creating an emotional tone in which memory works more effectively. Studies have shown that exercise helps brain cells in the part of the brain that absorbs information to regenerate. By the same token, it is believed that lack of movement can lead to actual physiological deterioration of brain neurons.[14]

Clearly movement activities should always be included in children's programs. In addition to the physiological changes, there is the aesthetic experience, an awareness of the body and a sense of control (which can lead to self-control in other areas of life), and in short, a *total* experience that involves children's bodies, senses, emotions, intellects, and imaginations.

Music

Music is essential in programming for children. Music can be soothing or annoying. It can help someone relax or put a person on edge. It can encourage wild, large movements or tiny, calculated ones. Music with words helps children to learn vocabulary words painlessly, and it can incorporate patterns of speech and voice inflections. Through music, children learn rhyme, timbre, and tone. They learn concepts such as high and low, soft and loud, and fast and slow. They learn how to use their voices as musical instruments and connect with others through singing.

Music stimulates spontaneous motor movement; a five-day-old infant can turn its head to the left or right to discover the source of a sound, which is a key step in the infant's attaining sensory development and control and developing the part of the brain associated with each physical activity. As Barbara Cass-Beggs relates in her book *Your Baby Needs Music*, "Music not only gives children pleasure, but also improves their ability to concentrate, which enables them to make the most of their intelligence."[15] In addition, "songs encourage the enjoyment of sound, which leads to the understanding and enjoyment of speech."[16] Songs written or adapted by Cass-Beggs that use her "Listen, Like, Learn" approach encourage children first to *listen*, as music is a listening subject. Then they must *like* listening; otherwise they will not learn. From listening and liking, they will *learn*. The "Listen, Like, Learn" approach enables MGOL to reinforce developmentally appropriate concepts and offer age-appropriate learning opportunities in a musical format.

The movement stimulated by music is essential for a baby's physical and mental development. Singing to the baby triggers speech and encourages auditory discrimination. The "Listen, Like, Learn" approach involves listening, moving, singing, and participating in ways that encourage experimentation with sound, using a variety of percussive and melodic instruments. Music is a medium that supports the underlying aim of assisting in the development of the whole child so that he or she can gain a sense of self-confidence and security. The "Listen, Like, Learn" approach additionally helps parents learn many songs, rhymes, and musical exercises of babyhood.

Time to Relax

In today's busy world, it is important for everyone to find ways to relax, because stress can cause physical as well as emotional problems. Taking time to clear your mind, breathe deeply, and relax helps boost your brain[17] and also improves outcomes for young children.[18] Every MGOL program includes a lullaby where children are given time to relax and let their brains absorb everything they've learned. At the same time, parents learn words and melodies to lullabies while experiencing firsthand the calming effect singing lullabies can have on their children. Lullabies can be added to their "parenting toolbox" as a technique for helping their children relax.

Appeal to Multiple Intelligences

Howard Gardner says that people all learn differently and have certain skills that are stronger than others.[19] It is easier for people to learn using their strongest skills, or intelligences. Gardner identified eight different intelligences: (1) logical-mathematical (math and logic skills), (2) musical (keenly aware of rhythm, pitch, melody, tone, etc.; it may include musical talent to sing, play an instrument, or conduct), (3) spatial (being able to perceive, manipulate, and recreate aspects of the visual-spatial world; thinking in pictures), (4) bodily kinesthetic (athletic intelligence), (5) linguistic (the intelligence of language), (6) intrapersonal (self-intelligence), (7) interpersonal (social intelligence), and (8) naturalist (the intelligence of making distinctions in the world of nature).[20]

Because MGOL activities touch on multiple intelligences, children attending a session will be able to do something that is easy for them, using at least one of their intelligences. What a wonderfully validating feeling!

Notes

1. Jeb Schenck, "Movement and Decision-Making in Memory" (presentation, Learning and the Brain Conference VIII, Cambridge, MA, April 24–27, 2003); Stephen P. Rushton, J. Eitelgeorge, and R. Zickafoose, "Connecting Brian Cambourne's Conditions of Learning Theory to Brain/Mind Principles: Implications for Early Childhood Educators," *Early Childhood Education Journal* 31, no. 1 (2003): 11–21.
2. Betty Rintoul, "Encouraging Connections" (presentation, Learning by Heart: Emotional Intelligence and School Readiness Conference, Linthicum, MD, May 26, 2004).
3. Betsy Diamant-Cohen, Ellen Riordan, and Regina Wade, "Make Way for Dendrites: How Brain Research Can Impact Children's Programming," *Children and Libraries* 2, no. 1 (2004): 15.
4. B. L. Frederickson, "The Role of Positive Emotions in Positive Psychology," *American Psychologist* 56, no. 3 (2001): 218–26.
5. William T. Greenough, James E. Black, and Christopher S. Wallace, "Early Experience and Brain Development," *Child Development* 58 (1987): 539–59; Michael J. Meaney, "Maternal Care, Gene Expression, and the Transmission of Individual Differences in Stress Reactivity across Generations," *Annual Review of Neuroscience* 24, no. 1 (2001): 1161–92.
6. Sara B. Johnson, Anne W. Riley, Douglas A. Granger, and Jenna Riis, "The Science of Early Life Toxic Stress for Pediatric Practice and Advocacy," *Pediatrics* 131, no. 2 (2013): 319–27.
7. Jean Piaget, Play, Dreams and Imitation in Childhood (New York: W. W. Norton, 1962).
8. Kathleen A. Roskos, James F. Christie, and Donald J. Richgels, "The Essentials of Early Literacy Instruction," *Young Children* 58, no. 2 (March 2003): 52–60; Jennifer M. Zosh, Jessa Reed, Roberta Michnick Golinkoff, and Kathy Hirsh-Pasek, "Play and Its Role in Language Development," in *Encyclopedia of Language Development*, ed. Patricia J. Brooks and Verna Kempe (Thousand Oaks, CA: Sage, 2014), 467–71.
9. Stuart Brown with Christopher Vaughan, *Play: How It Shapes the Brain, Opens the Imagination, and Invigorates the Soul* (New York: Penguin, 2009).
10. Fred Rogers, *Mr. Rogers Talks with Parents* (Family Communications, 1983), 97.
11. Alison Gopnik, "How Much Do Toddlers Learn from Play?," *Wall Street Journal*, May 11, 2017.
12. Mary Renck Jalongo, *Young Children and Picture Books*, 2nd ed. (Washington, DC: National Association for the Education of Young Children, 2004).
13. Carla Hannaford, *Smart Moves: Why Learning Is Not All in Your Head* (Arlington, VA: Great Ocean, 1995); Jeb Schenck, "Building the Memory Bank," *Cable in the Classroom*, March 2003, 18–23.
14. John Ratey with Eric Hagerman, *Spark: The Revolutionary New Science of Exercise and the Brain* (New York: Little, Brown, 2013).
15. Barbara Cass-Beggs, *Your Baby Needs Music* (North Vancouver, British Columbia: Douglas and McIntyre, 1978), 4.
16. Cass-Beggs, 56.
17. Carol Gerwin, "Innovating in Early Head Start: Can Reducing Toxic Stress Improve Outcomes for Young Children?," Center on the Developing Child, Harvard University, August 14, 2013, https://developingchild.harvard.edu/science/key-concepts/toxic-stress/tackling-toxic-stress/innovating-in-early-head-start-can-reducing-toxic-stress-improve-outcomes-for-young-children.
18. Bethany Butzer, Denise Bury, Shirley Telles, and Sat Bir S. Khalsa, "Implementing Yoga within the School Curriculum: A Scientific Rationale for Improving Social-Emotional Learning and Positive Student Outcomes," *Journal of Children's Services* 11, no. 1 (2016): 3–24.
19. Howard Gardner, *Intelligence Reframed: Multiple Intelligences for the 21st Century* (New York: Basic Books, 2000).
20. MI Oasis, "MI Intelligences," http://multipleintelligencesoasis.org, accessed July 7, 2017.

Mother Goose on the Loose Basics

YOU MAY WONDER, "WHAT MAKES MOTHER GOOSE on the Loose (MGOL) different from other library programs for babies?" The difference is the structure. MGOL consists of ten sections patterned on the music basics of Cass-Beggs's "Your Baby Needs Music" classes and her "Listen, Like, Learn" approach. The program focuses on children's book illustrations and draws on my experience running library programs for young children. Each thirty-minute MGOL "session" builds on the previous session, and the ten sections within each session are presented in this order:

1. Welcoming comments
2. Rhymes and reads
3. Body rhymes
4. The drum sequence
5. Stand-up / sit-down activities
6. Animal activities
7. Musical instruments and scarves
8. Lullabies
9. Interactive rhymes
10. Closing ritual

Although individual content will vary from session to session, MGOL is based on this ten-section order. Each section takes no more than five minutes. An explanation of each of the ten sections follows; the next part of this book will tell you just what to do.

Section 1: Welcoming Comments

The welcoming comments provide a friendly introduction to the children and adults followed by a few brief explanations and instructions. The welcoming remarks are important because they put parents at ease with their children's natural behavior, and they let parents know what to do if their child does not follow certain guidelines. The welcoming comments consist of five parts: friendly introduction, a brief tidbit about the program, directions, child development facts, and guidelines. The introduction sets the tone for the program and is a part of creating an optimal learning environment, and the guidelines can address many situations before they become problematic.

Introduction

First, introduce yourself in a friendly way. Say your name and let everyone know that you are happy to see them: "Hi. My name is Betsy, and I am delighted that you are here with me for Mother Goose on the Loose today."

A Brief Tidbit about the Program

Let parents know that they are doing something valuable for their child by attending this session. You may want to say "Reciting nursery rhymes in a program like this helps your child build early literacy skills" or "Mother Goose on the Loose is a brain-based program consisting of thirty minutes of fun, skill-building activities." Alternately, you can describe some benefits of the program (aids speech development, improves motor coordination, develops attention span, encourages a love of books and book illustration, etc.).

Directions

Explain how each segment of the program works: "I will recite each rhyme first and then you should repeat it with me the second time. If you already know it, say it with me both times."

Ask everyone to sit in a semicircle with their children sitting in their laps, facing you. However, infants should be positioned to look at their parents' faces rather than yours.

Child Development Facts

Not all parents know what typical behavior is for a young child. Some think a child is supposed to sit still and listen to everything, even if their child is only nine or nineteen months old. So they get embarrassed if their child gets up and moves around, and they do not know how to respond. They may get angry at their child for "misbehaving" or feel that their child's inability to sit still reflects weak parenting on their part. They may feel embarrassed at their child's behavior and then choose not to return for another MGOL session. To avoid this from occurring, clearly state in your opening remarks, "Children this age do not sit perfectly still. In fact, they are often natural explorers. It is fine for your children to move around."

Guidelines

At the same time, offer guidelines starting with this specific occurrence. Say, "Pretend there is an invisible circle around the flannelboard. If your child enters this circle, please come up and physically bring him or her back to sit in your lap in the circle." You can explain that a child standing directly in front of the flannelboard blocks everyone else's view, and if a child comes up and takes a felt piece, a puppet, or musical instrument from behind the flannelboard, other children are likely to imitate by coming up and handling props also. Tell the adults that you'd like to keep all the props in a certain order for the program, which is why you need an immediate response if their child ventures into the invisible circle.

Now the adults know your two basic guidelines:

- It's fine (not disrespectful or unacceptable) for their children to walk or move around during the program.
- If the child comes within a certain distance of the flannelboard, the parent should come up and bring the child back.

Telling adults in advance that you would like them to physically get up, pick up the child, and bring the child back to the circle reinforces the fact that the child's behavior is not unusual and informs the adults what you expect them to do. Establishing these guidelines alleviates the embarrassment parents might feel in removing their children from the area. Verbalizing how you want parents or caregivers to handle those situations sets the scene for a relaxed program in a warm, nurturing environment where children are expected to act like children, where parents know how to respond to their children's actions, and where everyone can just relax and have a good time.

When everything is clearly spelled out, adults can pay attention to the program instead of worrying self-consciously about how to deal with their child's behavior. The children sense this ease in their parents and internalize it. You will not need to interrupt your session to give instructions to the adults or to worry about the props. It is a win-win situation for all.

Invitations (If Relevant for Your Session)

Invite everyone to stay for up to thirty minutes once the program is over. Explain that you will bring out some toys for the children to play with, and it is a great time for adults to chat with each other. Also, invite participants to check out books after the program. Finish up your directions by saying "Without further ado, Mother Goose on the Loose" and then begin your program.

Welcoming Comments FAQ

Q: Should I memorize the welcoming comments?
A: You don't need to memorize them; be as natural as possible and speak in your own voice. But remember to be concise, clear, and positive, like the example given here.

SAMPLE WELCOMING COMMENTS

Introduction

"Hello, everyone, and welcome. My name is_____, and I am a librarian here at [your library]. I'm delighted that you are here with me for Mother Goose on the Loose today.

"Mother Goose on the Loose is a brain-based program consisting of thirty minutes of fun skill-building activities. Reciting nursery rhymes in a program like this helps your child build important early literacy skills, and it's lots of fun for everyone."

Directions, Child Development Facts, and Guidelines

"Please sit in a semicircle facing the flannelboard, with your children on your laps, if possible. Children this age are not expected to sit perfectly still. In fact, they are often natural explorers. It is fine for your children to move around. However, please pretend there is an invisible circle around the flannelboard. If your child enters this circle, please come up and physically take him or her back to sit in your lap in the circle. A child standing in front of the flannelboard may block everyone else's view, and if a child comes up and takes a felt piece, a puppet, or musical instrument from behind the flannelboard, other children are likely to imitate by coming up and handling the props also. All the props are arranged in order for the program, and that is why a swift response is needed if your child ventures into the invisible circle. Otherwise, it's fine for them to wander around."

Extra Guidelines to Add When Needed: The Crying Child

"If your child starts to cry, feel free to go out of the room until he or she calms down and then come back in. I will not be at all offended if you walk out of the room in the middle of the program, and it is often easier for your child to calm down in a quieter atmosphere. Frankly, it's also easier for us to sing without trying to drown out a screaming child! But please, come back in when your child has settled down. You can go in and out as many times as necessary, but make sure to keep coming back."

Extra Guidelines to Add When Needed: Cell Phones Away

"Parents are a child's first and best teacher. Children learn the most by imitating the people they love. In order for your child to get the most out of this program, it's important for you to do all the rhymes and motions with the group in an enthusiastic manner. I made sure to have enough musical instruments and scarves to be able to give one to each adult as well as to each child because your participation is important. So for now, please put your cell phones away and participate fully in the program."

Directions and Invitations

"I will recite each rhyme twice. The first time, you can listen; the second time, recite the rhyme along with me. If you already know the rhyme, please feel free to say it both times.

"You are invited to stay afterward for up to thirty minutes for informal play and time to talk with other parents. Don't forget to check out some of the books on display after the program. And now, without further ado, Mother Goose on the Loose."

Benefits of the Welcoming Comments

- Leaders introducing themselves and welcoming everyone sets the tone for a comfortable place.
- Reminding adults that "children will be children," setting boundaries with an invisible circle, and asking parents to physically retrieve their children if they enter the invisible circle eliminates parents' feeling of distress and enables you to have a program that runs smoothly.
- (Optional) Mentioning benefits of attending MGOL helps parents understand the importance of participation in early literacy programs, lets them feel proud for bringing their children, and gives them a good reason for replicating the activities at home.

Section 2: Rhymes and Reads

Rhymes and reads begins with two opening rhymes, usually followed by reading a story from a book and then reciting a few other short rhymes or songs. Your opening should always be familiar. This means that section 1 (welcoming comments) and the first rhyme in section 2 (and sometimes the second rhyme as well) are basically the same from week to week, forming your opening ritual. If you are presenting a by-the-book MGOL program, always start with this rhyme:

**Old Mother Goose when she wanted to wander,
Would fly through the air on a very fine gander.**

Families traveling from state to state who attend MGOL programs at different libraries feel reassured by the familiarity of this starting rhyme; it signifies that the program is a MGOL program. Use hand motions while reciting the rhyme, or if you have a group of parents with babies, ask them to lightly tap the child's legs in rhythm to the rhyme for the first part and to lift up their babies and simulate flying them through the air for "would fly through the air." When the children are too heavy for lifting and flying overhead, it is easier to raise their hands up and move them in a semicircle over the head.

I often follow the first rhyme with "Goosey, Goosey Gander" and "Two Little Dickey Birds." I strongly recommend using Barbara Cass-Beggs's "Two Little Dickey Birds" regularly because her variation of "Two Little Blackbirds Sitting on a Hill" is a big hit with little children.

**Two little dickey birds sitting on a cloud.
One named Soft, the other named Loud.
Fly away, Soft; fly away, Loud.
Come back, Soft; come back, Loud.**

When reciting this, whisper the word *soft* and yell the word *loud*. Children enjoy the change of tone accompanied by the hand movements. At the same time, they are learning about soft and loud by actually acting out the meaning of the words as they say them.

Despite my recommendations, it is important for you to use the rhymes that you know and enjoy best. All rhymes can be matched with picture-book illustrations, felt pieces, props, puppets, or fingerplays. Hold open a collection of nursery rhymes as you recite a rhyme aloud, or prop open a book against the bottom of the flannelboard so that everyone can look at the illustration while doing the activity.

Choose a picture book to read aloud that is appropriate for your young audience, with colorful pictures and minimal text for this section. Pop-up books or books with flaps (like the Spot or Maisie books), books written in rhyme, large board books, and books with photographs of interest to babies (such as babies' faces) work well. If you want to choose a story that is a bit long, feel free to skip over pages so that the story remains short and interesting to the children. Be sure to check chapter 7 for a complete list of recommended books.

Because section 2 is the opening of the session, children are most attentive and can sit still most easily. This is a good time to expose them to book illustrations and to use books in an enthusiastic, happy way. It is the only time in the session when you will be reading a book from cover to cover.

Remember, you are modeling book-reading behavior to the adults by showing them that they do not need to be able to read proficiently in order to share books with their babies. Children who observe books being used in a joyous way will absorb the happy feeling related to books and carry it on later in life—one of the values that is now associated with school readiness!

The opening section should go on for no longer than five minutes. If the babies are getting restless, move directly into the body rhymes, because they are more interactive than the opening section.

Rhymes and Reads FAQ

Q: Why don't you start with a song about everyone's name?

A: Starting out slowly helps create a comfortable atmosphere, giving everyone time to adjust to you, your voice, the group, and the setting. Once the familiarity enables session attendees to relax, then welcoming each child by name becomes more meaningful.

Benefits of Rhymes and Reads

- It introduces your session with easy rhymes.
- It exposes children to book illustrations.
- It introduces felt characters.
- Reading one book from cover to cover models book-reading behavior.

Section 3: Body Rhymes

Section 3 matches rhymes with interactive body activities that name body parts and movements. Naming specific body parts as you interact with them teaches children the correct terms for parts of their anatomy as well as the words for what those parts do. For instance, fingers wiggle, but hands wave and clap.

Head Rhymes

Barbara Cass-Beggs suggested that body rhymes should start with the head and work their way down the body. Here is an example of a head rhyme:

> **Knock on the door.** *(Knock lightly on the top of baby's head.)*
> **Pull the bell.** *(Lift up a tuft of baby's hair.)*
> **Peek in.** *(Put a finger next to each of baby's eyes.)*
> **Lift up the latch.** *(Use your index finger to lift up the bottom of baby's nose.)*
> **Walk in.** *(Crawl your fingers toward babies open mouth.)*
> **Take a chair.** *(Gently pinch one cheek.)*
> **Sit down.** *(Gently pinch the other cheek.)*
> **"How do you do, Mrs. Brown?"** *(Hold the baby's chin in your hand and gently move it up and down.)*

Finger and Hand Rhymes

Next, move down to the fingers and hands. There are lots of choices for these.

- "Fingers Like to Wiggle Waggle" by Barbara Cass-Beggs is simple and fun.
- "Open Them, Shut Them" is a well-known fingerplay that children enjoy.
- Any song that uses clapping hands, rolling home, moving fingers, and waving can be considered a hand song.

In addition to hand songs, you can vary your program here with whole body songs:

- "We Hit the Floor Together"
- "The Wheels on the Bus"
- "If You're Happy and You Know It"

If you are singing "The Wheels on the Bus," a fun variation is to change the words so they are more relevant—instead of "all around the town," sing "on our way to the library!"

Tickle and Belly Rhymes

Move to the belly with one or two tickle rhymes, then go straight down to the legs or do knee bounces.

Knee Bounces

Before starting the knee bounces, give directions so the adults know exactly what to do. For example, "Sit up straight. Put your legs out straight in front of you. Place your child on your legs. Position your infants to face you, so they can have eye-to-eye contact with one of the people they love most. Place children who are a bit older on your outstretched knees facing me, so they can see the other children around the circle. Gently move your legs up and down one at time, as if you are riding a bicycle."

I often start with the knee bounce "Seesaw, Scaradown," singing it with the traditional words the first time ("This is the way to Londontown"). The second time around, I substitute the name of the city or neighborhood in which the program is taking place (e.g., "This is the way to Baltimoretown"). This personalizes the session for participants who enjoy singing the name of the area in which their library is located.

Children who have started wandering around often come back to sit on their parent's lap for this part. They love bouncing movements; there is often lots of giggling in this section. So don't do just one or two knee bounces. Do three or four or five! Children love variations of speed and height in bounces, such as in "The Grand Old Duke of York," when parents move their legs high up and then back down. They also delight in the leaning motions and the increase in tempo of "Mother and Father and Uncle John."

Body Rhymes FAQs

Q: I'm not familiar with foot-patting rhymes. Can you elaborate?

A: Foot-patting rhymes were very popular in the past but are rarely done nowadays because they require shoes off or bare feet. "Shoe a Little Horse" involves holding one of baby's bare feet in each of your hands and gently tapping the soles of the feet together. It's fun to invoke the imagination by pretending that you are a blacksmith helping put some horseshoes on your baby.

If you intend on using foot-patting rhymes in your session, ask parents to remove their children's shoes as part of your welcoming comments at the beginning of the program. With children who are either barefoot or just wearing socks, foot-patting rhymes are loads of fun.

Instead of foot patting, you can also try toe tickles such as "This Little Piggy." Leg rhymes involve moving the legs of your child in different directions—up and down, open and shut—and in different tempos. However, if you have used up the allotted five minutes on knee bounces and other body rhymes, don't worry about the foot patting or the leg rhymes, just go straight to the next section.

Q: What if my crowd is very quiet?
A: If your group seems passive during the knee bounces, they may not be ready to start the standing-up part. Try taking out the bells, and dive into some bell activities instead, switching the order of the sections. This technique can also be used when children are overactive and in need of distraction. Under normal circumstances, however, it is easy to go from here straight into the drum or standing-up sections.

Benefits of Body Rhymes
- They encourage positive physical contact between the adults and their children.
- They build vocabulary and increase positive body image by naming body parts and their specific actions.
- Bouncing builds a sense of balance. This later aids math skills![1]

Section 4: The Drum Sequence

The drum sequence is an easy phonological awareness exercise for young children. Centering on your drum and the verbal acknowledgment of each child's name, this activity strengthens the bonds between you and each child.

During the drum sequence, stand up and tap to the beat on your drum while reciting, "Rum pum pum, this is my drum. Rum pum pum, this is my drum." Continue in a singsong voice with "My name is _____. What's your name?"

Tap out the appropriate syllables on the drum while saying your name. Then invite your program participants to do the same using their names.

Because phonological awareness is one of the language skills leading to school readiness, recognition of syllables in this way is a valuable activity. Because parents may not understand what you mean when you say "Tap out the syllables" or they may not be able to hear the syllables you are tapping, demonstrate how to tap out some names using syllables. One example of this is "John" (one tap), "Cooper" (two taps), and then "Shaniqua" (three taps: Sha-ni-qua). Repeat these instructions with the examples *every time*. Ask "What's your name?" again, and walk around the circle of seated participants, holding out the drum to each child. If children are too young to tap the drum, tell the parents to hold their child's hand and help him or her tap. If the right number of syllables aren't tapped out, don't correct or explain; just keep moving around the circle. Eventually, parents and children who seem not to hear the syllables will begin to recognize them and then will be able to tap their own names in syllabic form.

As each name is tapped, give a personal greeting such as "Welcome," "Good morning," or "I'm glad you're here." If you have heard the name clearly, repeat the name along with the greeting. Try looking each person in the eye and smiling. This is a great way to build personal connections with your participants.

Drum Sequence FAQ

Q: What should I do if a parent never seems to tap out the right syllables?
A: Don't worry about it. Some cultures hear syllables differently. For instance, the name "Sylvia" in English is pronounced with three syllables, but in Spanish it is only pronounced with two syllables. Continue giving a warm greeting and smiling as each name is tapped.

Benefits of the Drum Sequence
- Tapping names on the drum teaches phonological awareness by encouraging children to hear syllables in words.
- Greeting children individually creates a bond between you and them.

Section 5: Stand-Up / Sit-Down Activities

The standing-up actions in section 5 involve activities that target gross motor skills, match vocabulary with movement, and last for about five minutes. This section of the program gives children the opportunity to stretch their muscles and expend some energy, which, in turn, gives them longer attention spans for the remainder of the program. Once everyone is standing, get them moving with a circle dance. Point while explaining that you would like them to move in this direction. I often start by singing Barbara Cass-Beggs's "We're Marching to the Drum" to the tune of "The Farmer in the Dell."

> "We're marching to the drum, we're marching to the drum, hi-ho-the derri-o, we're marching to the drum."

The second verse is

> "We're marching 'round the room…"

and the third verse goes back to

> "We're marching to the drum."

At the song's end, chant, "And the drum says *stop*," while giving a big bang on the drum for stop. Encourage everyone to freeze when they hear "*stop*." Walk around the circle and ask each child, "Can you hit *stop*?" If they are too young to do it themselves, encourage their parents to gently use the child's hand to hit *stop* on the drum. As they hit *stop*, say something encouraging: "good," "great," "wonderful," "fantastic," "terrific," or other positive terms. You will see smiles spreading over children's faces as they are complimented for doing what they were asked. You are modeling ways to give positive reinforcement for the parents and familiarizing them with a vocabulary of positive words to use. This is a great time to insert a developmental tip. Tell parents that by playing games such as this, they are teaching their children concepts such as "stop" in a positive way, without negative connotations, like the story of the little girl in the grocery store in chapter 1.

While everyone is standing up, add some circle games or stretching rhymes. Old favorites such as "London Bridge" and "The Hokey Pokey" work well. If your group consists of babies, parents can carry the babies around the circle with them. Toddlers who have started walking will delight in doing all the actions on their own.

When it is time for everyone to sit back down again, use a rhyme to turn sitting down into a game. My favorite is "Handy Spandy." Together, everyone jumps into the circle, out of the circle, up, and then down. Without giving instructions, this fun activity gets everyone to sit down.

> **Handy Spandy, sugar and candy, we all jump in.**
> **Handy Spandy, sugar and candy, we all jump out.**
> **Handy Spandy, sugar and candy, we all jump up.**
> **Handy Spandy, sugar and candy, we all sit down.**

Stand-Up / Sit-Down Activities FAQ

Q: My crowd is so large, there is no room to move around while standing up. Should I skip this portion?
A: No. Use rhymes for standing without moving around in a circle. "I'm a Little Teapot" and "Jack-in-the-Box" are especially good for large crowds or in small spaces where large movements are not practical.

Benefits of Stand-Up / Sit-Down Activities

- By the middle of the program, exercise is needed.
- Using freeze games teaches the word *stop*.
- They provide more opportunities to use your vocabulary of positive words.
- After the energy is expended, children are able to sit for a while longer.

Section 6: Animal Activities

The animal activities in section 6 feature book illustrations, animal puppets, toy animals, or stuffed animals and connect them to the appropriate animal sounds. Once everyone is seated after the stand-up / sit-down activities, they are tired out and ready to listen. This is the optimal time to use book illustrations that require responses from the children.

Matching sounds to visual representations is an early literacy skill. For example, show children illustrations of animals and have them sing about the noises that animals make. The best songs are short and simple, such as "I Went to Visit the Farm One Day" by Barbara Cass-Beggs. You can use the same book every week for one or two years, and children will still enjoy seeing their animal friends and imitating the sounds they make. Children never tire of seeing farm animal illustrations from Eric Carle's *The Very Busy Spider* because they are large and colorful. This activity presents a wonderful opportunity to model how to use books without actually reading them. Parents and caregivers learn how to "read" the pictures with children who are too young to read. They can sing animal songs, name the animal, describe the animal, talk about where they might have seen the animal, make up stories about the animal, and so on. Even a parent who does not know how to read or who does not speak English can use books with their children in this way.

Every once in a while, it is good to add some variation. If you use the Eric Carle book, sing a verse about the owl in the moonlight (rather than the other animals, who are out during the day: "I went to visit the farm one night, I saw an owl by the moonlight…") or alternate the order of the animals. Now and then, use a book with different illustrations for the same animals. You can also vary the gender, sometimes using "he" and sometimes using "she" to refer to the animals.

While sitting in front of the semicircle, singing the song and showing the illustrations, you will notice that even very young babies seem to look at the illustrations intently. Older children enjoy calling out the names of the animals and joining in with the sounds that they make. When children first make a connection between the animal picture and its sound, sometimes they are unable to restrain their enthusiasm. A quick glimpse of the cow just as you have turned the page may bring mooing even before the verse about the cow begins. What a joyful introduction to books! It reminds me of the connection between school readiness, children's enthusiasm for books, and knowledge about the world around them.

Some librarians use iPads here to show photographs of the same farm animals. By touching the icon, the actual animal noise is heard. Because a cow doesn't really say "moo," children can have fun trying to imitate the real sounds. This is just one more connection for the neural pathways.

Children may begin to get restless, so change gears with puppets and stuffed animals! Bring out your duffle bag or canvas bag filled with the animals and play another guessing game with animal sounds. Display an ear or tail peeking out of the bag's top, and ask, "Who does this belong to?" Then pull out the stuffed animal or puppet and say, "Look, it's a cow!" and launch into a song about that particular animal. I often use another song by Barbara Cass-Beggs, "When the [Cow] Gets Up in the Morning," but there are many other animal songs that can be used. "Old MacDonald" can be too long, so if you plan to use that, only sing a few verses. Other fun ones are "I Had a Little Rooster by the Old Barn Gate" or "We're on the Way to Grandpa's Farm." Plastic farm animals can also be used as props.

You may want to substitute or include other animal activities, such as "The Eency Weency Spider" or "I Had a Little Turtle."

Smaller crowds always enjoy doing "Hickory Dickory Dare." Any animal can be substituted for "pig."

Hickory dickory dare.
The pig flew up in the air.
Farmer Brown soon brought her down.
Hickory dickory dare.

Recite the rhyme, throw the puppet up into the air at the appropriate place, and catch it as it comes down. Then explain that you are going around the circle to give each child a chance to throw the animal up in the air. Remind parents with children who are too little to do it on their own to help by taking the children's hands in their own and tossing the pig up in the air together. Without this reminder, parents tend to throw the animal in the air without including their children at all, which is of little to no value to the children! Tell everyone to applaud after each effort to show appreciation for a job well done. Then walk around the circle, giving the puppet to each child. Every time a child throws it up in the air say "Yay!" or applaud. The parents will follow your lead. In just a few weeks, you will see how even the very youngest children try to throw the puppet up in the air in order to receive the positive feedback.

Even older children enjoy this activity. They usually like to throw the pig up quite high and appreciate your noticing their skill. A compliment such as "Wow, what great pig-throwing skills" is usually rewarded with a big smile from the older child.

Upon returning to your seat, repeat the rhyme one more time. Throw the pig in the air, catch it, put the pig in the tub, and then begin your next activity.

Animal Activities FAQs

Q: *What if a child won't let go of the pig puppet (or any puppet)?*
A: If a child is having difficulty parting with the pig, count to three and then help by gently lifting the pig out of their arms and throwing it up in the air. You will not

be doing anyone a favor by letting a child cling to the pig and stopping the activity. But don't force the pig away either—a soft count to three followed by a gentle tug and clapping with verbal encouragement usually diverts a tantrum. Children who see other children throwing the pig up in the air are more likely to understand that the pig is for throwing and not for keeping. If a child finds it difficult to part with the pig each week, you might recommend that the parent bring in a stuffed animal from home to keep the child company at this time. Also, start your pig-throwing rhyme with a child who is already familiar with the activity and will willingly participate. Work your way around the circle, and by the time you reach the reluctant child, his or her attitude might have changed.

Q: What if the children are coming up to the front and taking the stuffed animals?
A: To avoid havoc, drop each animal into the storage tub as soon as you are done singing about it. The container should either be behind you or inside of the flannelboard/easel where little hands cannot reach it. This is when the instructions given at the beginning of the program really come in handy!

Benefits of Animal Activities

- Using a book joyfully without actually reading is a valuable early literacy experience.
- Learning animal sounds is easy for young children.
- Correctly recalling and reciting the animal sounds builds self-confidence.
- Puppets grab the attention of most children.

Section 7: Musical Instruments and Scarves

Musical instruments and scarf activities directly follow the animal section. Children usually are squirmy by this point and being given a musical instrument or colored scarf easily captures their attention.

Before you begin this segment:

- Be aware of the safety issues of each instrument. Consider that children often put things in their mouths; do not use anything with little pieces that a child could choke on or with sharp edges that can cut tongues. (Large Easter eggs with small beans inside need to be sealed tightly enough that they cannot open; bells need to be checked for any areas in which little tongues can get caught.) Heavy pieces that can bruise or things that can poke (such as mallets or sticks) need to be used under close supervision.
- You may want to give some general cautions. Although children are not supposed to run with their instruments, it sometimes happens, and so a cautionary word to parents at the beginning of the musical instrument session is a good idea.
- Remind the adults that for very young children, instruments should be used for free activity, experimentation, exploration, and the creation of a variety of sounds.

Lift the canvas bag with one type of instrument (bells, for instance) from behind the easel. Walk around the circle and hand one bell from the bag to each child and adult. Handing the bell directly to the child rather than giving it to the adult to hand to the child increases your direct interaction with each child. If using cluster bells, present the handle to the child rather than the ringing part. Because very young children are able to grab, presenting the stem of the bell first makes it much easier for them to take the bell from you.

Once everyone has an instrument, go back to your seat and use a variation of Cass-Beggs's "We Hit the Floor Together" by singing out the name of the instrument and the way it is played. For instance, sing, "We *ring* our *bells* together," "We *tap* our *sticks* together," or "We *shake* our *rattles* together." Follow this introductory song immediately by singing these directions: "Ring them *up high*, ring them *down low*, ring them *in the middle*." *Up high* should be sung in a high voice, *down low* in a very low tone, and *in the middle* in your regular tone of voice. The words *high, low,* and *middle* will be easy for the children to learn because they are using movements that correlate to the meaning of the words they are verbalizing. Varying the tone of voice increases the learning to include another meaning of the words *high* and *low*; *high* is experienced as a tone as well as a physical space, and the same for *low* and *middle*. And experience is what strengthens brain connections!

Follow this with one or two songs related to what the instrument or prop can do. Ringing and singing "Jingle

Bells" (or a similar Barbara Cass-Beggs song "Ring Your Bells") might be next if you are using bells, sticks can be tapped in varying tempos to "Grandfather's Clock Goes Tick Tock," and shaking maracas may help keep the beat when listening to recorded music. Try playing to the beat using a variety of music from week to week including classical music, folk songs in languages other than English, rock and roll, gospel, zydeco, bluegrass, and children's songs. A list of recommended recordings can be found in chapter 7.

Fun instruments for young children include drums, tambourines, all kinds of bells, Chick-ita shakers, rattles, maracas, woodblocks, a xylophone, triangles, rhythm sticks, cymbals, chimes, and even everyday kitchen items such as wooden spoons and pot lids. Exposing children to a large variety of instruments gives them varied experiences. Finally, recite the "Up high, down low, in the middle" ditty, and walk around the circle with an open canvas bag singing the put-away song geared for the specific item; if you have just used bells, the song would be "Bells Away."

If there is time, follow the first musical instrument with another prop. Bells can be followed by colored scarves, rhythm sticks can be followed by bells, or bells can be followed by maracas. Because colored scarves are wonderful for igniting the imagination, I almost always use them as the second prop. Distribute your second set of props following the same method. A scarf can be a flyswatter ("Shoo Fly, Don't Bother Me") or a washcloth ("This Is the Way We Wash Our Face"). Ask everyone to put the colored scarves over their heads and play peek-a-boo while singing a peek-a-boo song. Try waving scarves to recorded music or act out animal movements using the scarves (e.g., snakes slither, frogs jump, birds fly).

Musical Instruments and Scarves FAQs

Q: What else can you do with musical instruments?
A: For an occasional variation, place a tub of musical instruments in the middle of the circle and invite all the adults and children to choose an instrument to play. Sing "We play our instruments together because it's fun to do." Ask everyone to stand up, put on a lively recording (something by John Philip Sousa works well), and parade around the room. At the end of the session, sing the cleanup song again, walk around the circle with your open canvas bag, and collect the items. "Instruments Away" is a generic song that works when using multiple instruments.

Q: How do you deal with collecting instruments and scarves that you see have been "mouthed"?
A: Ask parents to hand you any wet items (children put things in their mouths) rather than depositing them in the bag. Once the session is over, sterilize the wet instruments by washing or disinfecting them.

Benefits of Musical Instruments and Scarves

- Children explore sounds and textures while using instruments and scarves.
- Playing to the beat gives children practice using their listening skills.
- Play and imagination are encouraged when colored scarves are used.
- Using music from different sources exposes children to a variety of cultures.

Section 8: Lullabies

The hustle and bustle of using musical instruments and props makes some children tired but revs up the energy level of others. At this point, a lullaby helps children to relax while sharing physical closeness with their adults. Not all children will be prepared to sit quietly, rocking with their caregivers, but it is a valuable part of the session.

This section shows parents how lullabies work. Explain to parents that lullabies are best when children are snuggled close while singing and rocking. Hearing the adult's heartbeat and experiencing the rocking motions reminds children of the uncomplicated time when they were still in the womb. Incorporating lullabies into your program teaches them to parents who may not know any lullabies.

Learning lullabies gives adults new techniques for calming down their children. Parents who experience the way soft singing combined with rocking and hugging calms a child can tuck it away in their parenting tool kit for further use when needed. All children have meltdowns once in a while. At those trying times, we hope that parents will be able to pull a lullaby from their toolbox and use it.

The lullaby also sets the tone for the next activity. The bit of quiet gives children extra fortitude and patience to wait their turn for the interactive rhymes segment.

Lullabies FAQ

Q: What if I don't know any lullabies?
A: Any song can be a lullaby, as long as you sing it softly and slowly. This is great information to share with parents. You can model what you mean by turning "Twinkle, Twinkle" into a gently sung lullaby.

Benefits of Lullabies

- Lullabies give parents relaxation techniques to use with their children.
- Lullabies give children a rest before the grand finale because they will have to be patient while waiting for everyone to pull Humpty Dumpty off of his wall.

Section 9: Interactive Rhymes

Interactive rhymes give each child a chance to shine individually via successful interaction with a rhyme activity. In addition to learning how to follow directions, by performing an easily achievable task that is recognized and acknowledged by their peers, children build self-esteem and practice self-regulation skills.

After children have had a quick lullaby rest, they are ready for more action or to finish the program. Because the program is not quite over, give them some action. Choose an interactive activity that involves large motor skills. You can place a candlestick on the floor and recite "Jack Be Nimble" while inviting children to take turns jumping over the candlestick. Remind parents to clap as each child completes the task. Rather than going around the circle in order, let the children decide for themselves if they want to come up and jump over the candlestick. The most enthusiastic ones will come up first, and the more reticent ones will have time to watch and decide if they would also like to join in the activity.

Don't recite the rhyme as each child jumps; you could get hoarse reciting it every time. Just count to three and say "Jump!" if needed. When children need help, invite the parents to help them jump over. Or if the child feels connected to you, gently help him or her over the candlestick. Don't forget to clap as each child makes the jump.

In a group with nonwalking infants, bring the candlestick to each parent and let them lift their baby over it while reciting the rhyme, using their child's name.

Or put three pieces on the flannelboard: Little Bo Peep on the top, a cluster of sheep or some sheep faces in the middle of the board, and some big green bushes on top of the sheep with just a bit of sheep peeking out. Recite "Little Bo Peep" and invite children to find the hiding sheep by taking turns coming up to the flannelboard and pointing them out. Show how to pull the bush off to show the sheep. Give positive feedback by applauding when children achieve their goal. Don't worry if different children point out the same sheep; the objective here is to get them moving and looking carefully at a picture.

My favorite interactive activity is Humpty Dumpty, and my Humpty felt piece is fluorescent green. Recite the rhyme as Humpty sits on his wall and pull him off as he has "a great fall." Invite all the children to come up one by one and pull Humpty off of the wall, mentioning that each child has just one turn. Tell the adults that if children do not go back to their seat after taking a turn, traffic jams form at the front. Encourage the adults to physically bring their children back to their laps if this should occur. Also, invite the adults to bring up their babies and help manipulate their babies' hands to pull Humpty off of the wall, if needed. Be sure to ask everyone to clap each time Humpty is pulled off his wall so the children will feel appreciated for a job well done.

When sitting in the chair next to the flannelboard/easel, you can see the faces of the children as they come up to the front. Very young children, sometimes as young as three months, will lift up their fingers to push Humpty off and smile with the triumph of accomplishment when they know they have successfully completed the task at hand. This is why the interactive section is my favorite part of MGOL.

Once you have established this routine, it is not unusual for a number of children to come running up to the flannelboard as soon as they see Humpty appear. It is valuable to reiterate that everyone has *one* turn and to compliment the children who wait patiently.

Because this activity is so rich in skill-building, it is a great place for developmental tips regarding self-regulation, following directions, building patience, taking turns, strengthening feelings of competency, showing appreciation for others, being self-confident, and so on.

Interactive Rhymes FAQ

Q: What do I do if a child keeps returning to the easel even after she has had a turn, and I see the parent is getting tired of continually retrieving the child?
A: Ask the child if she would like to join you in clapping for the other children. Invite her to stand next to you or to sit on your lap and clap even more enthusiastically as each child pulls Humpty off of the wall. In addition to enjoying the clapping, the child with you is learning how to enjoy showing appreciation to others.

Benefits of Interactive Rhymes

- Performing an easily achievable task that is recognized and applauded by all builds a child's self-esteem.
- Social development is enhanced by taking turns and learning to appreciate the achievements of others.
- Children learn self-regulation by coming up to the flannelboard when they are ready and going back to their place when their turn is over.

Section 10: Closing Ritual

Always closing with the same sequence of activities creates a powerful ritual. In "Can You Kick with Two Feet?," everyone sits in place and has a chance to exercise various parts of their body. "It's Time to Say Good-Bye" and "We're So Happy" signify the end of the program by ending on a positive note and encouraging everyone to come back again next week. This song by Cass-Beggs lets everyone know the program is over while also reminding them that we are glad they attended. Another phrase, a singsong "Good-bye, everybody! See you next week" reminds program participants that the program is ongoing and we hope they will return. Always starting and ending the program in the same way familiarizes babies with the ritual and adds to their sense of security. Knowing what to expect at the beginning and end of the program also eases transitions for toddlers.

Closing Ritual FAQs

Q: Because the closing ritual is always the same, can you suggest some good rhymes?
A: "Can You Kick with Two Feet?" by Barbara Cass-Beggs gives everyone an opportunity to sit in place and exercise various body parts. Following this with "It's Time to Say Good-Bye" indicates that the program is over.

Q: Should I ask everyone to leave the room as soon as the program ends?
A: Informal playtime after the session has officially ended is a great time to chat with participants and answer any questions they might have. It is also a good time to recommend books for checking out. But before anything else, be sure to put the lid back securely on your storage tub. Then place some age-appropriate toys for the children on the floor, and start a conversation going among the adults by asking a generic question such as "What new thing is your child doing this week?" At this age, children are doing new things all the time. So one parent might answer and then another will comment, and another will comment, and eventually you will have a group conversation. So far, this has worked every time for me!

Q: How do I get people to eventually leave the room?
A: After twenty or thirty minutes of informal play, sing "Toys Away" and collect all the toys around the room. Parents understand that this is the signal for them and their children to leave.

Benefits of the Closing Ritual

- Singing the same closing songs weekly prepares children for the ending transition.
- The program ends on a positive note.
- This closing ritual reminds everyone to come back next time.

Note

1. Andrea Frick and Wenke Möhring, "A Matter of Balance: Motor Control Is Related to Children's Spatial and Proportional Reasoning Skills," *Frontiers in Psychology* 6, 2049 (2016), 10.3389/fpsyg.2015.02049.

The Extra Element: Developmental Tips

PARENTS ARE THIRSTY FOR KNOWLEDGE ABOUT THEIR children and will often appreciate bite-size tips about their children's development.

Using Developmental Tips during Your Program

Developmental tips are (very) short informational blurbs for the adults. They are not part of the ten segments and can be used anywhere or anytime during each session.

Because we don't want to turn MGOL into a parenting class and we certainly don't want to be didactic, try to loosely follow a limit of one or two developmental tips per program. Parents really seem to appreciate these tips; by returning week after week, they learn quite a bit. This is helpful to parents of young children who want to know about their child's development but are too busy or too tired to do much research. It also reinforces the value of MGOL and helps encourage parents to keep attending with their children. Once a quick tip has been mentioned during one session, it is not unusual for a parent to return the next week and say, "I thought about that tip all week. Where can I get more information about that?"

Types of Tips

Different types of tips cover varying topics.

- Explain why an activity is beneficial to children and perhaps include a reference to a scientific study. For example, "Learning rhymes are great because they help a child develop a sense of balance, and according to research, a good sense of balance can strengthen mathematical abilities."
- Give a parenting tip related to the activities being done with the children: "Freeze games are great because they teach your child to react instantaneously to the word *stop*. This can be useful when it is urgent that your child stop something immediately."
- Offer a tip endorsing library programs: "Participating in library programs week after week helps children socialize with others and increase their attention spans."
- Suggest activities to do at home that will make life easier for parents. For instance, after the group sings "This Is the Way We Wash Our Face" using scarves as pretend washcloths, you might say, "Try singing songs about activities that children might find difficult, such as taking baths or having their diapers changed. You'll see how using a song can turn the dreaded activity into a fun game."

Below are some developmental tips for you to use in your sessions. These include tips for well-known nursery rhymes that are not included in this book. The lyrics are readily available online or in nursery rhyme collections. Choose a developmental tip that fits your activity and mention it during your MGOL program. Remember to use only one or two tips per session! Try to use different tips each week so that parents are constantly hearing new things about their babies. Feel free to insert your own tips, like things that you have learned from your own reading and attendance at conferences.

Familiarity and Comfort

Tell parents that attending MGOL programs at the library regularly aids children's development. Complete the following phrase with one of the words below.

MGOL helps children develop familiarity and comfort with _____.

- books
- words
- music
- different styles of art
- rules
- routine and structure
- themselves and their bodies
- other children
- caregivers who regularly attend the program with them
- program participants from a variety of backgrounds
- librarians
- public libraries

Development of Motor Skills

Recite these tips before or after specific rhymes and activities. These are ways in which MGOL helps children develop motor skills. The program

- aids in speech development ("Peter Piper Picked a Peck of Pickled Peppers")
- develops a sense of rhythm ("Grandfather's Clock Goes Tick Tock")
- improves hand-eye coordination ("I Had a Little Turtle")
- teaches children to respond physically to verbal cues ("Mother and Father and Uncle John")
- helps them feel comfortable with their own bodies ("Here Are Baby's Fingers")
- helps muscles with development and coordination through movement ("Open Them, Shut Them")
- is a fun way to get some physical exercise ("London Bridge")
- promotes the use of the voice ("When the Cats Get Up in the Morning")
- develops locomotion ("I'm Driving in My Car")
- shows children how parts of the body can develop movement ("Can You Kick with Two Feet?")
- helps with understanding up and down ("Ring Them Up High")
- demonstrates blowing the scarves as a way of moving them ("Wind, Oh Wind")

Development of Musical Skills

MGOL helps children develop a range of musical skills. They learn to

- recognize fast and slow (tempo; "Row, Row, Row Your Boat")
- recognize loud and soft (volume; "Two Little Dickey Birds")
- recognize sounds ("I Hear Thunder")
- connect sounds with actions ("We Ring Our Bells Together")
- develop a sense of rhythm ("Hot Cross Buns")
- listen and sing accurately ("I Went to Visit the Farm One Day")
- listen to sounds and patterns as a precursor to word awareness (hearing nursery rhymes being read)
- use music as an emotional outlet ("The More We Get Together the Happier We'll Be")
- relax with lullabies ("Hush-a-Bye")
- recognize the underlying beat in various musical works (shaking maracas or tapping sticks to recorded music)
- become familiar with different types of music (using recorded classical, folk, rock and roll, jazz, blues, gospel, children's songs, klezmer, and other musical selections)
- become proficient in singing and moving simultaneously by using songs with actions ("This Is the Way We Wash Our Face")
- listen, like, and learn ("The Wheels on the Bus")
- enjoy musical skills through participation and total involvement ("Peek-a-Boo")

Emotional Development

MGOL aims to give children an emotional outlet by

- relaxing with lullabies ("Twinkle, Twinkle")
- learning the vocabulary for different emotions ("If You're Happy and You Know It")
- expressing emotions through words (reading a story involving emotions)
- expressing emotions through sound (crying at the end of "1, 2, 3, 4, 5, Once I Caught a Fish Alive")
- expressing emotions through music ("Tapping Sticks in a Happy Way, in a Sad Way")
- expressing emotions through movement (acting out various emotions)

Development of Social Skills

MGOL activities help children develop their social skills, such as

- taking turns (throwing pigs up in the air to "Hickory Dickory Dare")
- waiting patiently (pulling Humpty Dumpty off of his wall)
- putting toys away when asked ("Instruments Away")
- learning the rules and sticking to them (invisible semicircle around the flannelboard)
- interacting with others in a positive way (clapping for others when they successfully perform a task)
- receiving positive reinforcement for a job well done (hearing the applause)
- giving positive reinforcement to others (using many encouraging words)
- feeling friendship, love, and trust through partner rhymes ("Row, Row, Row Your Boat")
- developing social responsiveness ("Where Is Thumbkin?")
- gaining self-confidence by recognizing sounds and mimicking them ("Baa Baa Black Sheep")
- overcoming fears (bouncing up and down during "The Grand Old Duke of York")
- bonding with others ("We're So Happy")
- experiencing the enjoyment and awareness of everyday activities ("Knock on the Door")
- learning how to stop ("Drum Freeze Game")
- learning how to redirect negative behavior in a constructive way (instructions given during the welcoming remarks)
- learning the phrase "Thank you" (after a child comes up to the flannelboard to find Little Bo Peep's hidden sheep)
- learning how to act in a group setting (the whole atmosphere of MGOL)
- learning how to play with other children (spending informal playtime together after the program has finished)
- reciting rhymes about body parts (improves self-awareness and positive body image; "My Face Is Round")

Development of Preliteracy Skills

MGOL encourages children to develop preliteracy skills like

- connecting the sound of a word to an object ("I'm a Little Teapot")
- connecting the written word to the spoken word (reading a book aloud)
- enjoying listening to a book being read (listening to a story)
- developing an interest in illustration (using illustrations when reciting rhymes)
- learning syllables ("Rum Pum Pum")
- learning word patterns through repetition ("Old Mother Goose")
- acquiring vocabulary (exposure to at least thirty minutes of rhymes each week)
- connecting words with motions ("And We Creep, and We Creep, and We Creep, and We Stop!")
- introducing phonemic awareness (clapping and tapping to "Pizza, Pizza, Hot")
- exercising the brain, which increases brain capacity (exposure to a variety of rhymes, songs, and activities regularly in a nurturing atmosphere)
- building a positive attitude toward reading and books (interacting with books in a joyful way)
- learning how to read books through following the pictures (using book illustrations to tell a story)
- developing listening and concentration skills (each rhyme is repeated twice)
- encouraging imagination (pretending you are

"Mary, Mary Quite Contrary" planting your garden)
- becoming familiar with science concepts ("Little Arabella Miller")
- seeing how to turn the pages of a book (observing book-reading behavior)

Development of School Readiness Skills

MGOL helps children develop school readiness skills in different categories:

- listening to directions ("Open Them, Shut Them")
- developing positive feelings about the "authority figure" in the front of the room (responding to positive reinforcement)
- enjoying interaction with books (recognizing characters like the Duke of York related to fun rhymes)
- developing self-regulation skills (stopping during freeze games, putting instruments away)
- becoming exposed to numerous vocabulary words (hearing and reciting an assortment of rhymes and songs)
- hearing sounds made by consonants and vowels (hearing rhymes and songs)
- bouncing rhymes improve balance (knee bounces)
- better balance strengthens mathematical ability (knee bounces)
- developing familiarity with structure and routine, such as in a school schedule or in a MGOL program (the ten sections)
- expanding memory of words, meanings, and social cues (responding to a visual or verbal cue with specific motions)

Development of Visual Skills

MGOL encourages children to develop visual skills when they look at book illustrations:

- helps children recognize works by different illustrators (naming illustrators while using their illustrations; e.g., Eric Carle)
- helps children learn that different illustrations can be used to represent the same song or animal (using different illustrations for the same song or rhyme)
- shows children that we all come in a variety of sizes, shapes, colors, and abilities (promoting diversity by using illustrations that depict children of all varieties)
- helps children enjoy visual stimulation (such as when the colored scarves are being waved)
- helps children look closely at pictures for clues (decoding a picture on a felt piece to figure out what it represents)
- encourages children to look closely at pictures to find the answers to questions (calling out answers; e.g., "What's under the flap?")
- helps children learn that there are visual representations for real objects (showing an illustration of an umbrella one week and using a real umbrella another week)

Development of General Knowledge of the World around Them

MGOL helps develop general knowledge by facilitating

- families to come together in a welcoming community space (the program itself)
- exposure to others from different ethnic, cultural, and economic backgrounds (everyone is welcome in the public library)
- singing songs about everyday events ("This Is the Way We Wash Our Face")
- singing songs about common objects ("I'm a Little Teapot")
- singing songs about animals and nature ("Twinkle, Twinkle, Little Star")
- singing songs about science ("Zoom, Zoom, Zoom")
- singing songs about numbers ("Five Fat Sausages")

Texting Tips

A relatively new way to get tips to parents is through texting. After signing up for a service, parents can get an app that sends tips or receive one text a day with a developmental tip. Sites that provide this service include READY4K!, developed by researchers at Stanford University (https://ready4k.parentpowered.com/sign-up.html)[1]; "Text4baby," sponsored by Zero to Three (www.zeroto

three.org/resources/services/text4baby); "Positive Parenting Tips" by the Children's Trust Fund (http://ctf4kids.org/text-msgs); "Ready, Set, Kindergarten" by the Brooklyn Public Library (www.bklynlibrary.org/ready-set-kindergarten-txt); and "Vroom" from the Bezos Family Foundation (www.joinvroom.org/parents). You can use some of your developmental tips to alert parents about these wonderful resources!

Getting Tips from Websites

Many websites offer parenting tips written in such clear language that they work well as developmental tips. Tandem Partners in Early Learning has tips, links to library websites, and an application for a San Francisco library card on its website (www.tandembayarea.org/resources/for-parents-families). Mind in the Making has partnered with First Book to create tips based on the "The Seven Essential Life Skills Every Child Needs," discussed in chapter 1. Each tip is partnered with a picture book and comes with a downloadable handout (often available in Spanish too) that can be distributed to parents (http://mindinthemaking.org/firstbook). Earlier is Easier provides tips related to the five ECRR practices—talk, sing, read, write, and play (www.earlieriseasier.org). Too Small to Fail has a "Talking Is Teaching" website that gives early literacy tips and also has videos that reflect a range of culturally diverse families (http://talkingisteaching.org/resources/talk-read-sing-together-every-day-tips-families). ¡Colorín Colorado! offers downloadable tips in English and Spanish (www.colorincolorado.org/reading-tip-sheets-parents). Reading Rockets has translated their downloadable tip sheets into Spanish, Arabic, Tagalog, and other languages (www.readingrockets.org/article/reading-tips-parents-babies).

Many public libraries have created their own materials to supplement Every Child Ready to Read with tips. One of my favorites is the Colorado Libraries for Early Literacy site (www.clel.org/early literacy-reminders).

Other Resources

If you are looking for tips that cover all the domains of school readiness, check out the "Early Literacy Handbook and Tip Cards" available via ALA Editions. I developed these with Saroj Nadkarni Ghoting specifically for MGOL and storytime programs in response to requests from children's librarians. If you want to see some great examples of ways to deliver early literacy tips, check out Libby Krabbenhoft's "Early Literacy Messages in Action" on the Jbrary blog (https://jbrary.com/early-literacy-messages-in-action).

Note

1. Research has shown that the READY4K! program developed by Stanford University doctoral students costs less than $1 per parent and resulted in parents spending more time doing literacy-related activities with their children.

The Versatile Mother Goose on the Loose

AFTER TWENTY-FIVE YEARS, I'VE RUN A LOT OF MGOL programs and trained many MGOL facilitators around the world. I often receive feedback from facilitators, and this chapter is dedicated to the versatility needed when working with young children and a frequently changing audience. Adaptations are often needed for different ages and abilities, varying program spaces and group sizes, a wide range of cultures and languages, addressing social justice concerns, and for incorporating different types of media.

Adapting MGOL for Different Ages and Abilities

Babies

Q: When should a mother start bringing her baby to MGOL?
A: Mothers have brought babies as young as three weeks old. There is no one time when they "should" come. In addition to being age appropriate for babies, with minor adaptations, MGOL can work for children up to age seven! I once ran MGOL as an afterschool program for kindergarten children, and they had a great time.

Q: Do very young infants benefit from MGOL?
A: Yes! Children benefit from being with their parents in a joyful, close atmosphere, and that's what MGOL is. The parent can do things with the baby, like helping the baby grasp a bell and ring it, and the baby smiles. The youngest babies show they are involved by smiling or focusing on the leader. They really pay attention to things.

Q: What should I tell a parent whose baby falls asleep and sleeps through the entire program?
A: Children need their sleep! It's fine to let a child sleep, but encourage parents to continue to sing and join in with the activities. There will be plenty of time for them to share the songs and rhymes with their babies at home, and this is a great opportunity for parents to learn them.

Q: When do babies start actually paying attention to book illustrations and making the connection between "that thing" and the words you are reading?
A: By three or four months, children can follow the pictures in Eric Carle's *The Very Busy Spider* while we sing a song about sounds made by the animals. The babies may not make the connection, but there is definitely *something* going on. By three months, babies already react to the activities. They smile when they pull Humpty off of the flannelboard and everyone claps. Babies can indicate that they want to go up to the flannelboard when Humpty is brought out because they know that the pulling off and applause will follow.

Q: What should I do if a parent has twins?
A: Generally, parents of twins have figured out a way to sit with both children on their lap. However, doing knee

bounces with more than one baby can be hard on the knees! So if one of the babies seems willing, ask the parent if you can use their baby to demonstrate the knee bounces with you.

Q: Is there a way to deal with an older child who seems bored while accompanying a baby sibling and parent?
A: Show the child a stuffed animal or puppet and explain that it feels sad because its parents didn't come. Ask if the child could pretend to be the animal's parent for the session. This often totally engages the older sibling and provides extra visual treats for everyone watching the animal tap its name on the drum and participate in the program.

Differing Abilities (Special Needs)

Q: How do I accommodate children with special needs and differing abilities in this program? Do I have to change the program or buy new props?
A: MGOL can accommodate children of all abilities. Here are some examples of how you might adapt the activities to match what the children can do:

- When children can't use their legs, don't sing the song inviting them to kick with two feet. But playing peek-a-boo with the scarves and singing the sounds animals make while displaying animal puppets still work well.
- A child who cannot move most body limbs often has a caregiver who can assist with scarves and musical instruments, so the child is still able to participate in the experience. You may want to give them more time with the props if you sense it is a unique experience for them.
- If a deaf parent comes with a hearing child, arrange for a sign language interpreter to be present. Babies love this. Research shows that young children can actually learn to sign before they can communicate verbally.[1] Watching the signing fascinates them.
- Give visually impaired babies things to hold, like a stuffed animal bird for "Two Little Dickey Birds." This tactile connection helps increase understanding of the rhymes.
- If you speak quickly, try slowing down your speech.
- Offer noise-canceling headphones when a child is sensitive to loud sounds.
- To adapt MGOL sessions to meet different needs, special props are usually not needed. Just consider who your audience is and then tailor the program with what you already have to emphasize what the children can already do—and, of course, provide lots of positive reinforcement.

Adapting MGOL for Different-Sized Groups

Differing Attendance

Q: What is the ideal number of participants for a MGOL session?
A: While the ideal number of people attending a MGOL program is twelve adults and twelve children, sometimes the group can grow much larger than this. Although the quality will be compromised, attendees are still getting a valuable experience. Modifications will need to be made regarding seating, types of activities offered, how props are handed out and collected, and number of activities presented.

Large Crowds

Q: What if so many people are attending my sessions that asking them to sit in a circle is impractical?
A: Ask them to sit in concentric circles facing the easel. Make sure there is at least an aisle-width space between each circle so you can comfortably walk between the circles to hand out and collect the musical instruments and scarves. Try to find a helper (perhaps a Friend of the Library who likes children, a volunteer, or an older sibling of one of the participants). Invite your helper to sit on the other side of the easel and divide all your props into two bags. Place an extra tambourine and puppet on your helper's side of the shelf. When it is time to walk around the circle, you can start at one end, and your helper can start at the other end and begin handing out props, giving puppet kisses, or asking children to tap their names on the drum. After you meet in the middle, you can both go back to the front of the room.

Stand-up / sit-down activities are important to include even if the room is too crowded for large movements.

Stick to standing-up rhymes that can be done in one place, such as "I'm a Little Teapot" or "Jack-in-the-Box."

You may want to limit the one-to-one activities. Try to keep the drum sequence. You may not have enough time for each child to throw a puppet in the air and get applause, to play peek-a-boo with you, and to have a turn pulling Humpty Dumpty off of his wall. That's fine! Decide what to keep in and what to leave out according to what is most comfortable to you. You might choose to use different activities on alternate weeks. Because it will take longer to hand out and collect the props, you may need to trim down the number of activities presented in your program.

Small Crowds

Q: What if only one parent comes to a session with one child?

A: I believe that this is the most challenging session to present. You don't want to seem too intense, but there is no one else to look at! Even if the child starts off paying attention, at some point, he or she may get up and wander around. Then what do you do? The parent may continue singing along with you, but if the parent gets up and follows the child, you are left sitting by yourself, singing songs and putting felt pieces on the flannelboard for a nonexistent audience.

This has happened to everyone at least once, and there is no one-size-fits-all solution.

- If you are comfortable continuing, do so. The child may get tired of exploring and return to finish the session with you.
- If you have not yet brought out the musical instruments, skip to that section. Walk up to the parent and child and ask if they'd like to play some musical instruments with you. Depending on your comfort level, you can stand with them and do the activities together, or you can go back to your seat and hope that they follow.
- Another technique is to ring the bells loudly enough for them to hear, pretend the parent and child are still sitting in the circle, and place two musical instruments down where they were sitting. Begin singing the songs and ringing; they may return to join you.

- You may want to shorten your program and just finish up with one or two songs.
- Even if you have a very abbreviated session with no participants at the end, be sure to tell the adult how happy you are that he or she came. Give reassurance that children are not expected to sit perfectly still and explain that with more participants, it is easier for children to remain engaged. Use this as an opportunity to ask the adult if he or she has other friends who might like to join in the next session.

Adapting MGOL for Different Spaces

High-Traffic Program Space

Q: Is there an ideal space for presenting MGOL sessions?

A: The ideal place for presenting sessions is in a program room with a door that closes. Not everyone has that luxury, however. When your program takes place in the middle of the children's room or in a space that has lots of people walking in and out, there are a few things you can do to make the program run smoother.

- Consider investing in a portable speaker that can be clipped to your belt. It will project your voice so it can be heard over the hubbub of people moving around.
- Using carpet squares, a rug, or even masking tape on the floor helps define the programming space. Attendees know where to sit, and defined borders can keep other people from walking directly through the program area.

Presenting MGOL outside of the Library

Q: If you are doing MGOL as an outreach program, what is the most important thing to keep in mind?

A: According to Dora Garraton, who leads a roving MGOL program in Indiana, it is most important to be portable, keeping everything accessible and organized. Use a folding flannelboard and bring a small portable speaker that syncs to your MP3 device so you don't have to plug anything in (because there may not be outlets nearby). Prepare by placing the felt pieces on the flannelboard one on top of the other in opposite order, so when you take one piece off, the next one is already there. Use a bag that zips to keep items away from wandering hands. Also, bring fuzzy socks because some daycares request that shoes be removed.

Adapting for Childcare Situations

Q: What should I do for the welcoming comments if I am presenting the program in a childcare setting where parents are not present, and there is not a one-to-one ratio of adults to children?
A: Bring some masking tape and make a circle on the floor around the easel. After welcoming everyone cheerfully, ask the children to pretend it is a magic circle around the easel that should not be crossed until they are invited to do so. Then continue with the directions and begin.

Q: Aren't some of the activities (the knee bounces) meant for a child to be bouncing on a parent's lap? What if the program is in a daycare where parents aren't present?
A: Children can do their own knee bounces without parents. They simply stretch their straightened legs out in front and bounce them up and down. Depending on the rhyme, they may also lean from side to side or kick their legs faster and slower. Children also enjoy tickling themselves during tickle rhymes. Although these actions were originally meant for parents and children together, if you present it as a fun activity to do on their own, the children are thrilled with the movements and don't mind at all.

Q: A local childcare facility has asked if I can run MGOL sessions there, but our library is very busy, and it would be hard for me to leave the building during my work hours.
A: Find a convenient time for them to come to the library, and schedule once-a-month sessions just for them. The group dynamics don't always work when combining a group of children and teachers with child-adult family units; the childcare children sometimes get restless when they do not each have a lap to sit on. Limit their visits to once a month rather than weekly, but be sure to make their visits special. Name tags are helpful when there is not a one-to-one adult-child ratio. From the start, let the daycare center know that teachers are expected to participate rather than using the time to go on the computer or choose books. At the end of each session, remind the group that they are all welcome to come and visit with their families anytime.

Adapting MGOL for Different Cultures and Languages

Q: How can I help non-English speakers feel comfortable during the program if I don't speak their language?
A: You can address diversity in your welcoming message by saying "hello" in the different languages spoken by participants or add "hello" in new languages regularly. Find a translator app (such as "SayHi Translate") to help with correct pronunciation and communication with non-English speakers.

Q: How can I get the non-English speakers more involved?
A: Ask the adults if they would like to share a simple song or fingerplay with the group. Perhaps they can teach it to you, and you can add it to your regular sessions. Ask if they can bring in a children's song recording in their language and have everyone shake their maracas along to the beat for the first verse or two. If books in their language are available, look for an illustration to match one of the well-known rhymes that you regularly use.

Q: There is a large Spanish-speaking population that uses the library, and I don't speak Spanish. How can I accommodate them?
A: *Early Literacy Programming en Español*, a book published by ALA Neal-Schuman in 2010, is based on my experiences developing a version of MGOL called "Buena Brasa, Buena Casa" with Dr. Annie Calderón.[2] In case you do not speak Spanish, the book explains how to find a Spanish-speaking partner to run the program with you. Lots of information, including a complete script for a program, song lyrics, rhymes, activities, and developmental tips, are presented in both Spanish and English. A CD of the recorded script comes along with the book. In addition, the "Escucha y Disfruta con Mama Gansa"

CD, available through Amazon or CDbaby.com, contains good songs for MGOL programs in both English and Spanish.³ The Spanish songs are sung by my favorite opera singer, Evelio Mendez. His version of "The Great Spider" uses his opera voice, and it is magnificent!

Q: How else can I make non-English-speaking families feel welcome?
A: Get their input! Ask if there is something you can do to help them feel more comfortable. Allow them to film your sessions so they can watch and practice the rhymes at home.

Adapting MGOL to Address Social Justice Concerns

Q: I want to make sure that everyone in my community feels included. Songs about "ladies" and "lords" seem old-fashioned and caste-sensitive; songs that include descriptive words like fat *or* small *can be seen as derogative.⁴ What should I do?*
A: Change the rhymes! Feel free to substitute your own words for any of the rhymes. Massage the lyrics until they create the image that you want. Also, pay attention to gender when singing songs about animals. Don't always use "he"; many animals are female!

Q: How can I include families with same-sex partners or who don't conform to gender binaries?
A: A discussion on the Storytime Underground website about countering ethnocentrism in storytime included some great ideas, such as using nongendered caregiver terms that don't make assumptions about relationships. For instance, say "grown-up" instead of "parent," use "friend" instead of "he" or "her," write names without pronouns such as "Sue" rather than "Mrs. Brown" on name tags, and ask people what pronouns they use.⁵

Q: Are there any rhymes that I should avoid?
A: Some rhymes have sexist, racist, or violent undertones that we do not want to pass on to our children. If you like something about the rhyme, feel free to change the words and continue using the rhyme. I had a great mouse puppet, so I changed "Three Blind Mice" to "Three Gray Mice." In my version, they all ran after the farmer's wife

ADAPTING NURSERY RHYMES

Some traditional rhymes that you may choose to omit or revise because of violent themes, sexist stereotypes, or problematic depictions include the following:

In "Georgie Porgy," he "kissed the girls and made them cry" but ran away when the boys came out to play.

In "This Is the Way the Ladies Ride," the females ride gently and the males ride roughly.

In "The Farmer in the Dell," he "takes" a wife.

The second verse of "Goosey, Goosey Gander" describes throwing an old man down the stairs; this verse can be omitted.

Some sources speculate that "Peter, Peter Pumpkin Eater" may have murdered his wife, chopped her up, and kept the pieces inside a scooped-out pumpkin. I prefer the revised *Positively Mother Goose* version where Peter "had a wife who was a leader / In a pumpkin they did dwell and loved each other very well."⁶

because she fed them cheese by the slice. It creates a great visual image and works perfectly with the mouse puppet.

The original "Old Woman Who Lived in a Shoe" whipped her children soundly. My version has her kissing them all soundly.

My friend Felecia, who is black, did not like singing "Baa Baa Black Sheep"; she felt the reference to "my master" connected it to slavery. So we changed to the words to

Baa baa black sheep, have you any wool?
Yes, I have some—four bags full.
One for my mommy, and one for my dad,
One for the little girl and one for the lad.

We made the rhyme even more fun by adding verses with sheep of different colors and creating red, blue, green, pink, orange, and yellow felt sheep to use. Everyone enjoyed singing the song and substituting a new color each time a different sheep appeared on the flannelboard.

Don't throw away nursery rhymes because they were created as unpleasant political commentary and are outdated. The original version of "Two Little Monkeys" is offensive and derogatory. Yet because of word changes and the warm, welcoming, and diverse atmosphere in which the rhyme is used, the original meaning has been transcended, and it has become a beloved rhyme for children from all backgrounds. Using monkey puppets makes it clear that this rhyme is now clearly about monkeys and nothing else. We are not yet living in a perfect world. Being able to reword racist, sexist, and violent rhymes to make them into fun, loving, and relevant rhymes is an ode to our ability to rise above injustice and to make the world a better place.

That being said, if a program attendee expresses discomfort with a rhyme, I would not use it.

Q: What should I do if a participant expresses discomfort over some content, such as the word *fat in "Five Fat Sausages"?*
A: Everyone has their sensitivities, and our goal is to make everyone feel welcome and wanted. If you are strongly attached to a rhyme, try to find a creative adaptation that works for both of you. Alternately, choose to use a different rhyme. Because there are many songs and rhymes, it is easy to add new ones to your repertoire.

Adapting MGOL to Include Digital Media

Using Digital Media

Q: Is there a place for digital media in MGOL?
A: Absolutely! Digital media in a MGOL program should be handled with careful consideration and in moderation, but it can definitely be used in ways that fit with a program's intent. Don't overwhelm your audience and do encourage parent-child interaction. Digital media should be used to enhance your program rather than replace it.

Our goal is to encourage parents to interact with their children physically, mentally, and emotionally. Time and again, studies have shown that human interaction and the emotional tone conveyed during those connections influence children more than interactions with electronic media. One study found that when reading e-books together, more attention was focused on the behavior ("Point here. Swipe that.") than on the actual content.[7] Another study showed that children learned less when conversations with their parents were interrupted by a phone call.[8] According to Lisa Guernsey, director of the Learning Technologies project at the New America think tank, "Learning language (not just learning words) is dependent on social interactions between people."[9] We need to empower parents to feel confident about themselves. We also need to remind them that no matter what their literacy level, they can provide the most valuable learning experiences for their children.

Q: Why add a digital activity then?
A: Because swiping and tapping are part of the modern experience, brief exposure to tablet use is a beginning step for bridging the digital divide. It also creates an opportunity to give developmental tips regarding digital media use to parents and caregivers. A tip might be "Electronic devices surround us, and many apps advertise themselves as being educational, even for our youngest children. But studies show that young children benefit most from these games when they are played together with an adult, involving human connection and conversation. So remember, your personal interaction with your baby is the most beneficial contact of all."

Another tip might alert parents that "educational" labels on apps can be misleading. Tell them about reliable review resources such as digital-storytime.com or commonsensemedia.org, and give them guidelines: "When looking for a good app, ask if it promotes engaged and not distracted learning, if the material is meaningful, if it's age appropriate, if children need to think rather than just use it mindlessly, and if it encourages social interaction."[10]

It is awkward to make a comment about using digital media out of context. But during or immediately following a digital activity is a perfect time for commenting about the importance of joint media engagement. We can give parents information so they can make informed decisions regarding the quality of the apps they use with their children, the amount of time children spend on electronic devices, and the importance of human interaction. We want parents to understand that using an app together with their child is much more valuable than using electronic media as a babysitter. Young children learn best through active play with objects, with other children, and with the significant adults in their lives.

Remind parents of the fun fingerplays, freeze games, and other activities that took place during MGOL, and encourage them to repeat these with their children at home too.

To encourage the use of digital media in a way that fits with the MGOL program, the "Felt-Board Mother Goose on the Loose" app can be downloaded from iTunes.

A few examples of other ways to appropriately use digital media in MGOL sessions are the following:

- If your program takes place in a room with a smart board, try making the board red for the activity when you sing, "If you're wearing red today, stand up and shout 'Hooray!'"
- After singing "I Went to Visit the Farm One Day" and making animal sounds while looking at illustrations of farm animals, use a farm animal app on a tablet. Display photos of a few different animals and listen to the animal noises when you touch each photo. Actual animal sounds differ from the English words we use for animal sounds (e.g., pigs don't actually say "oink"), so the addition of photographs and recorded animal sounds enriches this activity.
- Find recordings of familiar songs in different languages and share them with your group.

Q: There are some great nursery rhyme apps that could be adapted for MGOL. Can some of the traditional nursery rhyme activities be replaced with digital activities?
A: If you want to use an app in this way, choose a high-quality app that presents the rhyme in an active, engaging way, allowing children's hands-on participation. Limit your replacement to *one rhyme per session*.

Q: Is there a downside to using digital media with children?
A: Children need physical play experiences. They need to move their bodies, to experiment with objects, and to learn social skills while playing with others. The danger of digital media is that it can take time away from the important activities of childhood. It also distracts adults from spending valuable time with their children. Parents and caregivers must be reminded of the valuable role they play in their child's development.

MEDIA MENTORS

In 2015, the Association for Library Service to Children (ALSC) officially recognized children's librarians as "media mentors";[11] in 2016, ALA Editions published an ALSC-sponsored book explaining how to become a media mentor,[12] and the American Academy of Pediatrics (AAP) switched from telling parents to keep young children away from digital media to "teach them to use it as a tool to create, connect, and learn."[13] Yet there are still conflicting views regarding the use of digital media for children under the age of two.

Q: What else is beneficial about using digital media in programs?
A: Librarians help parents by showing them how to talk, sing, read, write, and play with their children. We demonstrate loving ways to read books, how to have fun with words, and how to talk about the world and what's going on around us. MGOL is about strengthening connections between children and the adults in their lives, giving parents different tools to help them assist in their child's development, and presenting age-appropriate activities that build social, emotional, and cognitive skills through the framework of early literacy programming. Isn't it great that we now have more items to add to our toolbox to encourage conversation and imagination, grow vocabulary, and give parents a wider variety of ways to play with their children?

MGOL Fits Every Situation

Once you have become familiar with the "plain vanilla" version of MGOL, feel free to make it your own in order to fit your setting. Because it gives a structure that works without telling you what you must do within that structure, MGOL is an easy program to adapt. It has been used with children in hospitals, with incarcerated parents who have children visiting them in prisons, with preschoolers, with home daycares, in kindergartens, in parks, in children's museums, in toy stores, and in a variety of other places. (To learn about other MGOL adaptations and using MGOL outside of the library, read my new book *Mother Goose on the Loose: Here, There, and Everywhere*, also published by ALA Editions.)[14]

Onward

You are now ready to put together your own MGOL program. You may want to go directly to the ready-to-present programs in part III, or you may want to use the planning materials in part II to get started.

Notes

1. Rachel H. Thompson, Nicole M. Cotnoir-Bichelman, Paige M. McKerchar, Trista L. Tate, and Kelly A. Dancho, "Enhancing Early Communication through Infant Sign Training," *Journal of Applied Behavior Analysis* 40, no. 1 (2007): 15–23.
2. Betsy Diamant-Cohen, *Early Literacy Programming en Español* (Chicago: Neal-Schuman / ALA, 2010), www.alastore.ala.org/content/early-literacy -programming-en-espa%C3%B1ol-mother -goose-loose%C2%AE-programs-bilingual-learners.
3. The CD is available on CD Baby or Amazon, and individual songs can be downloaded.
4. Brytani, "Storytime for Social Justice: Ethnocentrism," Storytime Underground, May 15, 2017, http:// storytimeunderground.org/2017/05/15/storytime -underground-ethnocentrism/, accessed August 11, 2018. Due to some scientific inaccuracies but also as a response to the "current effort against fat-shaming," Hap Palmer changed the word fat to heavy in his iconic "The Elephant" song. Palmer, response to "Your wonderful song, 'The Elephant,'" e-mail from author, 2018.
5. These ideas were taken from a Google document accessed via a link on Brytani's Storytime Underground post titled "GuerillaStoryTime Idea—J Meeting 01/01/17," https://docs.google.com/document/d/1Umh2DubG-L83wnQqix_JF0FvA2qFdAOeenxIdjAC9fQ/edit, accessed August 11, 2018.
6. Diana Loomans, Julia Loomans, and Karen Kolberg, *Positively Mother Goose* (Tiburon, CA: HJ Kramer, 2001).
7. Julia Parish-Morris, Neha Mahajan, Kathy Hirsh-Pasek, Roberta Michnick Golinkoff, and Molly Fuller Collins, "Once upon a Time: Parent-Child Dialogue and Storybook Reading in the Electronic Era," *Mind, Brain, and Education* 7, no. 3 (2013): 200–211, doi:10.1111/mbe.12028.
8. Jessica Reed, Kathy Hirsh-Pasek, and Roberta Michnick Golinkoff, "Learning on Hold: Cell Phones Sidetrack Parent-Child Interactions," *Developmental Psychology* 53, no. 8 (2017): 1428–36.
9. Lisa Guernsey, "How True Are Our Assumptions about Screen Time?," NAEYC for Families, http://families.naeyc.org/learning-and-development/music -math-more/how-true-are-our-assumptions-about -screen-time, accessed July 8, 2017.
10. Jennifer M. Zosh, Sarah Roseberry Lytle, Roberta Michnick Golinkoff, and Kathy Hirsh-Pasek, "Putting the Education Back in Educational Apps: How Content and Context Interact to Promote Learning," in *Media Exposure During Infancy and Early Childhood*, ed. Rachel Barr and Deborah Nichols Linebarger (New York: Springer International, 2017), 259–82.
11. Cen Campbell, Claudia Haines, Amy Koester, and Dorothy Stoltz, "Media Mentorship in Libraries Serving Youth," Association for Library Service to Children, adopted March 11, 2015, www.ala.org/alsc/sites/ala.org.alsc/files/content/2015%20ALSC%20White%20Paper_FINAL.pdf.
12. Claudia Haines and Cen Campbell, *Becoming a Media Mentor: A Guide for Working with Children and Families* (Chicago: ALA Editions, 2016).
13. AAP Council on Communications and Media, "Media and Young Minds," *Pediatrics* 138, no. 5 (2016).
14. Betsy Diamant-Cohen, *Mother Goose on the Loose: Here, There, and Everywhere* (Chicago: ALA Editions, 2019).

Part II

Planning Your Mother Goose on the Loose Programs

Planning Your Program

PART III OF THIS BOOK FEATURES FIVE COMPLETE, ready-to-present programs that you can use over and over. You may want to start with the premade scripts to get familiar with facilitating the program, but once you are comfortable, create your own! You will find that it is more fun to customize your own plan and create your own series using a personalized combination of elements.

The "Secret Formula"

The rule of thumb for repetition in MGOL programming is to keep about 80 percent the same from week to week. Repeating rhymes gives children the opportunity to learn to recognize the words, the word patterns, the timbre, and beat of the rhyme. About 20 percent of the material used during each session should be new. This 80-to-20 percent ratio will hold everyone's attention while children concentrate and learn better. (Your 80 percent repetition should not include the developmental tips, which should vary from week to week, or the book being read aloud after the opening rhymes, which should also change from session to session.)

Activities

Each activity has an action, prop, or song associated with it. I recommend keeping some activities the same during specific segments, such as the beginning and ending rituals. But other than that, you are encouraged to use the songs and rhymes that you know and love, as long as they are combined with a skill-building activity. Tailor your activities to involve more movement for toddlers and more sedentary activities for babies.

Use the session planning sheet provided in this chapter to guide you with planning your very first program. Fill in the blanks with the titles of the rhymes you want to use. Later on, you will fill the "prop" or visual representation to go along with each rhyme. Once you have practiced your "plain vanilla version" and are comfortable presenting it, add some variety to the segments. You might pair a new action with a familiar rhyme, you might want to teach a new rhyme using familiar props, or you might want to vary the visual representation and keep the rhyme and accompanying activity unchanged. For example, using rhythm sticks instead of scarves, displaying a book illustration to accompany a rhyme rather than using the familiar felt character, and playing the bells after the knee bounces rather than after the animals are all forms of variation. Customize your plan by filling in the blanks with the songs, rhymes, and books that you would like to use. **Consider using the suggested materials but know you are free to decide. Remember, the suggested materials have been recommended for good reasons!**

Note: You can choose to fill in the blanks from resources in this book.

1. A list of sixty-six songs and rhymes with lyrics and directions exists in resource A, "The Mother Goose on the Loose Songbook and Rhyme Book," arranged alphabetically.
2. There is a list of book titles in chapter 7 for reading aloud and using as illustrations for activities.
3. A recommended list of recorded music to use while playing musical instruments or waving colored scarves can also be found in chapter 7.
4. You may also want to add your own favorites.

Once your session plan is ready, add one or two developmental tips on the bottom of the planning sheet and write DT1 and DT2 to signify where in the script you expect to deliver the tips. A wide range of developmental tips can be found in chapter 4.

Mother Goose on the Loose Session Planning Sheet

Date of program: _____ Session number: _____

Section 1: Welcoming comments
Introduce yourself and welcome everyone.   State expectations ("Children this age don't sit perfectly still").   Set guidelines ("If they come within this invisible circle, please come and get them").   Explain how it works ("I'm going to say things twice").

Section 2: Rhymes and reads		
Section	**Rhyme/read**	**Prop**
Opening		
Opening rhyme	"Old Mother Goose"	
General rhyme		
General rhyme		
Puppet kisses		
Book to read aloud		
Tickle rhyme		
General rhyme		

Section 3: Body rhymes		
Head		
Head		
Fingers		
Tickle		
Hands		
Knee bounces		
Knee bounces		
Knee bounces		

Section 4: The drum sequence		
Children tap out names with syllables.		
Drum sequence	"Rum Pum Pum"	

Section 5: Stand-up / sit-down activities		
Stand-up action 1		
Stand-up action 2		
Stand-up action 3	"Handy Spandy"	
Section 6: Animal activities		
Book	"I Went to Visit the Farm One Day"	
Puppets		
Puppets		
Section 7: Musical instruments and scarves		
Musical instrument	"We Ring Our Bells Together"	
Musical instrument		
Musical instrument		
Musical instrument		
Musical instrument	"Bells Away"	
Colored scarves		
Colored scarves		
Colored scarves		
Colored scarves		
Colored scarves	"Wind, Oh Wind" / "Scarves Away"	
Section 8: Lullabies		
Lullaby		
Section 9: Interactive rhymes		
Interactive rhyme		
Section 10: Closing ritual		
Closing rhyme	"Can You Kick with Two Feet?"	
Closing rhyme	"We're So Happy"	

Developmental tip #1: _____

Developmental tip #2: _____

Observations: _____

Betsy Diamant-Cohen, Mother Goose on the Loose: Updated (Chicago: ALA Editions, 2019).

Once you have filled out the worksheet above, download the Word document at https://mgol.net/resources/program-planning-sheet, fill in the blanks with your choices, and save it with the date of your first session as its title. Print it and use it as an outline for both planning and presenting.[1] Then save it again with a new date, and it will be ready to modify for your next session.

Preparing for Your Program

Once you've decided what to do for your first MGOL session, it is time to figure out how to do it. Look over your list of rhymes and decide how you would like to present each one. Choose which rhymes to represent with a book illustration. Ask yourself, "Does the rhyme need a felt piece for the flannelboard, a puppet, or something else to go along with it?" Programs run smoothest when you have a visual representation for everything except the standing-up rhymes. But realistically, if this is your very first session, you may not yet have all the felt pieces you need. So instead of a felt figure or book illustration, you may choose to use another prop or a written reminder.

Setup Outline and Order

Add a brief description of the props you have chosen to go with each rhyme on your master list of rhymes and activities to remind yourself which rhyme to present next. The next page contains an example of the completed planning sheet for session 1 in this book.

Mother Goose on the Loose Session Planning Sheet

Date of program: _____   Session number: _____

Section 1: Welcoming comments
Introduce yourself and welcome everyone.
State expectations ("Children this age don't sit perfectly still").
Set guidelines ("If they come within this invisible circle, please come and get them").
Explain how it works ("I'm going to say things twice").

Section 2: Rhymes and reads		
Section	**Rhyme/read**	**Prop**
Opening	"Old Mother Goose"	Mother Goose felt figure
Opening rhyme	"Goosey, Goosey Gander"	Goose on Stairs felt figure
General rhyme (DT1)	"Two Little Dickey Birds"	Two Little Dickey Birds felt figure
Puppet kisses	"Two Little Monkeys"	Monkey puppets or Monkeys Jumping on Bed felt figures
Book to read aloud	*Freight Train*	*Freight Train*
Tickle rhyme	"The Little Train Went up the Track"	*Freight Train* or Train felt figure
General rhyme	"We Hit the Floor Together"	Alien felt figure

Section 3: Body rhymes		
Head	"Knock on the Door"	Door felt figure
Head	"Eye Winker"	Baby Faces
Fingers	"Fingers Like to Wiggle Waggle"	Boy Wiggling Fingers felt figure
Tickle	"'Round and 'Round the Garden"	*Corduroy* or Teddy Bear felt figures
Hands	"Pat-a-Cake"	Chef's Hat felt figure
Knee bounces	"Seesaw, Scaradown"	What's next card #1 (See explanation of these cards below.)
Knee bounces	"To Market, To Market"	*My Very First Mother Goose* (Use a sticky note to mark pages 24–25.)
Knee bounces	"Mother and Father and Uncle John"	*My Very First Mother Goose*

Section 4: The drum sequence		
Children tap out names with syllables.		
Drum sequence	"Rum Pum Pum"	What's next card #2

Section 5: Stand-up / sit-down activities		
Stand-up action 1	Freeze game: "We're Marching to the Drum"	What's next card #2
Stand-up action 2	Stretch: "Stretch Up High"	What's next card #2
Stand-up action 3	Circle dance: "London Bridge"	What's next card #2
Stand-up action 4	"Handy Spandy"	What's next card #2
Section 6: Animal activities		
Book	"I Went to Visit the Farm One Day"	The Very Busy Spider
Puppets	"When the [Cow] Gets Up in the Morning"	Farm animal puppets
Puppets	"Hickory Dickory Dare"	Pig puppet or Pig felt figure and what's next card #3
Section 7: Musical instruments and scarves		
Bells	"We Ring Our Bells Together"	What's next card #3
Bells	"Ring Your Bells"	What's next card #3
Bells	"Ring Them Up High"	What's next card #3
Bells	"Grandfather's Clock Goes Tick Tock"	Grandfather's Clock felt figure
Bells	"Bells Away"	What's next card #4
Colored scarves	"Wind, Oh Wind"	What's next card #4
Colored scarves	"Peek-a-Boo"	What's next card #4
Colored scarves	"This Is the Way We Wash Our Face"	Hands Washing felt figure
Colored scarves	"Scrunch Your Scarf into a Ball"	What's next card #5
Colored scarves	"Wind, Oh Wind" / "Scarves Away"	What's next card #5
Section 8: Lullabies		
Lullaby (DT2)	"Twinkle, Twinkle"	Draw Me a Star
Section 9: Interactive rhymes		
Interactive rhyme	"Humpty Dumpty"	Humpty Dumpty and Wall felt figure
Section 10: Closing ritual		
Closing rhyme	"Can You Kick with Two Feet?"	What's next card #6
Closing rhyme	"We're So Happy"	What's next card #6

Developmental tip #1: _____

Developmental tip #2: _____

Observations: _____

Betsy Diamant-Cohen, Mother Goose on the Loose: Updated (Chicago: ALA Editions, 2019).

Sorting, Listing, and Gathering

Now that your program has been planned, list the items you will need, using these four categories: felt figures, books, props, and written reminders.

Felt Figures and Books
Your program plan should mention multiple books, including one for reading aloud and several with illustrations to go along with rhymes.

Props
Props are tangible objects that are not felt pieces or books. Props can include puppets, musical instruments, colored scarves, electronic devices, and toys.

Puppets and Stuffed Animals
Puppets are used for giving kisses to the children, to "act out" rhymes such as "The Eency Weency Spider," and for farm animal songs about the sounds different animals make.

Always be prepared to make substitutions when necessary. A pig puppet seems right for "Hickory Dickory Dare." However, if you don't have a pig puppet, change the rhyme to "a duck flew up in the air," and use your duck puppet instead!

Musical Instruments, Colored Scarves, and Tote Bags
You will most likely need musical instruments and colored scarves. These can be kept in tote bags that are easily stored by hanging on a coat hook. Although only one tambourine or drum is needed, make sure that you have enough instruments and scarves to give one to each person—children and their adults.

Equipment
Flannelboard easel with a shelf and a plastic storage tub. (See page 195 for more information.)

Recorded Music, If Any
If you plan on using recorded music in your program, you may need a CD player, CDs, and a list that includes the track numbers and names of the songs. If using a tablet, phone, or MP3 player, be sure to bring your device and check to see that the song or songs you want are already on an easily accessible playlist.

Other Props
Other props might include a jack-in-the-box if you are doing the "Jack-in-the-Box" rhyme, an umbrella if you are singing "Rain, Rain, Go Away," or other rhyme-related objects. Unusual musical instruments for a kitchen band may include wooden spoons, clean and empty cottage cheese containers for tapping with the spoons, and empty water bottles filled with lentils and hot-glued shut.

FELT FIGURES, BOOKS, AND PROPS FOR PROGRAM 1

Felt Figures
- Old Mother Goose
- Goosey, Goosey Gander
- Two Little Dickey Birds
- We Hit the Floor Together
- Knock on the Door
- Fingers Like to Wiggle Waggle
- Pat-a-Cake
- Grandfather's Clock Goes Tick Tock
- This Is the Way We Wash Our Face
- Humpty Dumpty (and wall)

Books
- Anne Schreiber's *Monkeys*
- Donald Crews's *Freight Train*
- Margaret Miller's *Baby Faces*
- Don Freeman's *Corduroy*
- Iona Opie's *My Very First Mother Goose*
- Eric Carle's *The Very Busy Spider*
- Eric Carle's *Draw Me a Star*

Props: Puppets and Stuffed Animals
- two monkey puppets
- four farm animals in a tote bag
- one pig puppet or stuffed animal

Props: Musical Instruments, Colored Scarves, and Tote Bags
- one tambourine or small hand drum
- one tote bag with bells
- one tote bag with colored scarves

Written Reminders

When just getting started with MGOL, it can be challenging to remember the full program script, the order of rhymes and songs, and the developmental tips to share with your audience. That is why guides are built into the program for you! Placing all your props in the tub by their order of use and using written reminders when you don't have a flannel piece or book corresponding to the rhyme give you a quick and easy visual representation of your script. You won't need to read from a script during your session, and it looks to participants as if you have everything memorized.

There are four types of written reminders that may be useful to you during your MGOL program: a welcome card, developmental tip cards, what's next cards, and sticky notes.

Welcome Card

Because the main welcoming points are always repeated, creating a laminated welcome card ensures that it can be reused for all your MGOL sessions.

Developmental Tip Cards

Here is an example of the two developmental tip cards for session 1.

Welcome Card

> Welcome: *Introduce yourself.*
>
> If possible, please sit in the circle with your child on your lap.
>
> Children don't naturally sit still, and that is fine.
>
> But please pretend that there is an invisible line around the flannelboard.
>
> If your child comes within that line, please physically walk up and bring him or her back.
>
> I'm going to say everything twice—you can listen and repeat or recite the rhyme both times with me.
>
> Please stick around afterward to look at books and chat.
>
> (Optional: Talk about the value of MGOL.)

Developmental Tip Cards for Session 1

> **DEVELOPMENTAL TIP #1**
>
> **Demonstrate the meanings of the words *soft* and *loud*.**
>
> This next rhyme introduces the concepts of *soft* and *loud*. Notice how we whisper the word *soft* and shout the word *loud*. What a fun way to demonstrate the meaning of words!

> **DEVELOPMENTAL TIP #2**
>
> **Lullabies are important.**
>
> Holding your children closely enables them to hear your heartbeat. They associate the sound with being a fetus safely enclosed in the womb, and it helps them relax. It's good to learn lullabies to keep in your "parenting toolbox." Use them with your children the next time they have a meltdown by holding, rocking, and singing to them softly.

What's Next Cards

When you have no visual prompt reminding you what comes next in your program, a glance at what's next cards during your session will remind you.

Each what's next card can be written on a piece of paper or a note card. In the examples below, titles of rhymes to be recited are in regular font, actions are in capital letters, and spoken comments have a dash before them. Here's an example of the what's next cards for session 1 in this book.

What's next #1

"Seesaw, Scaradown"

What's next #2

USE tambourine on shelf.

"Rum Pum Pum"

"We're Marching to the Drum"

"Stretch Up High"

"London Bridge"

"Handy Spandy"

What's next #3

USE puppets in tote bag.

"When the [Cow] Gets Up in the Morning"

THROW a puppet up.

"Hickory Dickory Dare"

PASS OUT bells from bag.

"We Ring Our Bells Together"

"Ring Your Bells", "Ring Them Up High"

What's next #4

COLLECT bells—"Bells Away."

PASS OUT scarves from bag.

"Wind, Oh Wind"

"Peek-a-Boo"

What's next #5

"Scrunch Your Scarf into a Ball"

"Wind, Oh Wind"

COLLECT scarves—"Scarves Away."

What's next #6

"Can You Kick with Two Feet?"

"It's Time to Say Good-Bye"

"We're So Happy"

—Bye, everyone! See you next week. Please choose some books to check out and take home!

Sticky Notes

Sticky notes with written reminders can serve as bookmarks to flag the illustrations you want to display when placed within the book. Placed on a book's back cover, they remind you what to do next and are easy to see when holding up the book to face your audience.

Sticky Notes for Session 1

Note #1 on back of Anne Schreiber's *Monkeys*

Show front cover.

Recite "Two Little Monkeys."

Use puppets.

Give puppet kisses.

Note #2 on back of Donald Crews's *Freight Train*

Read book aloud.

Show front cover.

Recite "The Little Train Went up the Track."

Note #3 on back of Margaret Miller's *Baby Faces*

Show front cover.

Recite "Eye Winker."

Note #4 on back of Don Freeman's *Corduroy*

Show front cover.

Recite "Round and Round the Garden."

Note #5 posted inside Iona Opie's *My Very First Mother Goose*

Recite "To Market, To Market."

Recite "Mother and Father and Uncle John."

Note #6 on back of Eric Carle's *The Very Busy Spider*

Recite "I Went to Visit the Farm One Day" using different animal illustrations.

Note #7 on back of Eric Carle's *Draw Me a Star*

Display a star illustration.

Recite "Twinkle, Twinkle."

Gather and Make

Once your lists have been created, collect everything you will need for the program.

1. Gather together all the books that you plan to use. If this is your first session, many of them are probably still on the library shelves.
   - Retrieve all the books that will be used in your program.
   - Write all the sticky notes and reminder cards you will need.
   - Find the illustrations you want to show and flag them by using sticky notes or paperclips to mark the specific pages.
   - If you plan to read the book aloud or to display the book's cover rather than an inside illustration, put your sticky note on the back of the book.
2. Bring the puppets you will be using over to your planning area.
3. If you plan on using felt pieces but haven't made them yet, now is the time to do so. Use the list of rhymes that you have chosen to be represented by a felt piece. If you already have the pieces, that's great. If not, use in the information in chapter 7 to learn how to make your own. Feel free to use the patterns in resource B. Now is the time to make any pieces that you don't already have!
4. Go through your lists one last time to make sure you have everything you need for your program. If something is missing, find it, make it, borrow it, or buy it.

Organizing Your Materials

Organize your materials in the order in which they will be used. Books, felt pieces, and cards should all be interspersed. The piece for the first rhyme should be on the top of the pile, facing you. Keeping your pile in order, place it in a plastic storage tub with a securely fastened cover. Add in the canvas bags with instruments, puppets, and other props you intend to use. Close the lid and put the tub away until it is time to set up for your program. This organization will help you find, use, and discard props easily throughout the program. Your goal is to sit in the front of the room next to the easel without needing a script in your hand. You should be able to reach for the necessary prop (lined up in order of use) on the easel shelf when needed and then drop it in the tub when you are finished.

Preparing for Your Program

1. Practice running through your session a few times while looking at your printed plan.
2. Listen to recordings of the songs you want to use, and practice rhyme lyrics if you don't already know them.
3. Do a dress rehearsal: Set up the flannelboard/easel. Take out the storage tub and set up everything that is going to be used in your first session. Practice each rhyme, using the visual representations when possible. Then drop the items you used in the tub when the rhyme has finished.
4. Invite a colleague or two to watch a practice run-through, point out the things that work best, and offer suggestions for improvement.
5. Time yourself. Each person speaks at a different pace. If your practice session lasts more than thirty minutes, reduce the number of items in a section while keeping to all ten sections in their designated order. If you have a very large group, you may also have to reduce the number of rhymes used per session.
6. As soon as your practice program has finished, put everything back in the storage tub in the correct order for the program.
7. Review your written session plan and have one more practice session with another colleague. When you feel ready, schedule your very first MGOL session and begin presenting your program!

Planning Your Second, Third, Fourth Sessions, and More

When you are ready to plan for your second session, review the previous week's planning document.

- For each session, change a developmental tip or two. Change your read-aloud book too. Substitute your new rhymes, illustrations, or felt pieces. Then resave the document with your new presentation date.

- Look at your list for new illustrations and felt pieces that will be needed. Then fetch the books, use sticky notes to mark the illustrations, and make one or two new felt pieces.
- Find other props you plan to use, put everything in order, and store it all in the plastic tub until it's time for your program.
- After a few sessions, you can recycle in items you have taken out from earlier sessions. That's all there is to it!

Here is a table to show what the five consecutive programs included in this book look like.

FIGURE 6.1

Five Consecutive Programs

	+Program 1	*Program 2	$Program 3	^Program 4	§Program 5
Rhymes and reads	"Old Mother Goose"	"Old Mother Goose"	"Old Mother Goose"	"Old Mother Goose"	"Old Mother Goose"
	"Goosey, Goosey Gander"	"Goosey, Goosey Gander"	"Goosey, Goosey Gander"	"Two Little Dickey Birds"	*"Good Morning, Mrs. Perky Bird"
	"Two Little Dickey Birds" (DT1)	"Two Little Dickey Birds"	"Two Little Dickey Birds"	^"Zoom, Zoom, Zoom"	"Two Little Monkeys"
	"Two Little Monkeys"	*"Good Morning, Mrs. Perky Bird"	*"Good Morning, Mrs. Perky Bird"		^"Five Fat Sausages"
		"We Hit the Floor Together"			
	Freight Train—Donald Crews	*Busy Fingers*—C. W. Bowie	*Stripes of All Types*—Susan Stockdale	*Opposite Surprise*—Agnese Baruzzi	*Zoom, Zoom, Baby*—Karen Katz
	Tickle: "The Little Train Went up the Track"	*"Pizza, Pizza, Hot"	$"If You're Happy and You Know It"	"I Hear Thunder"	"I Hear Thunder"
	"We Hit the Floor Together"	*"I Hear Thunder"	$"The Eency Weency Spider"	^"Five Fat Sausages"	"We Hit the Floor Together"
Head	Head: "Knock on the Door"	Head: "Knock on the Door"	$Head: "My Face Is Round"	$Head: "My Face Is Round"	$Head: "My Face Is Round"
Fingers	Head: "Eye Winker"	Head: "Eye Winker"	Head: "Eye Winker"	Head: "Knock on the Door"	§Fingers: "This Little Piggy"
Hands	Fingers: "Fingers Like to Wiggle Waggle"	Fingers: "Fingers Like to Wiggle Waggle"	Fingers: "Fingers Like to Wiggle Waggle"	^Tickle: "The Garden Snail"	Hands: "If You're Happy and You Know It"

Tickle rhymes	Tickle: "'Round and 'Round the Garden"	Tickle: "'Round and 'Round the Garden"	$Hands: "Open Them, Shut Them"	^Hands: "Open Them, Shut Them"	^Hands: "Zoom, Zoom, Zoom"
	Hands: "Pat-a-Cake"	*Hands: "Open Them, Shut Them"	Tickle: "The Little Train Went up the Track"	$Hands: "If You're Happy and You Know It"	
Knee bounces	Knee bounce: "Seesaw, Scaradown"	Knee bounce: "Seesaw, Scaradown"	Knee bounce: "Seesaw, Scaradown"	$^Knee bounce: "See the Ponies Galloping"	§Knee bounce: "Row, Row, Row Your Boat"
	Knee bounce: "To Market, To Market"	Knee bounce: "To Market, To Market"	$Knee bounce: "See the Ponies Galloping"	Knee bounce: "Mother and Father and Uncle John" (DT1)	Knee bounce: "Humpty Dumpty" (new with leaning)
Knees and/or Legs	Knee bounce: "Mother and Father and Uncle John"	Knee bounce: "Mother and Father and Uncle John"	Knee bounce: "Mother and Father and Uncle John"	*Knee bounce: "The Grand Old Duke of York"	*Knee bounce: "The Grand Old Duke of York"
Feet/toes		*Knee bounce: "The Grand Old Duke of York"	*Knee bounce: "The Grand Old Duke of York"		§Foot patting: "Shoe the Little Horse"
The drum sequence	"Rum Pum Pum"	"Rum Pum Pum" (DT1)	"Rum Pum Pum"	"Rum Pum Pum"	"Rum Pum Pum"
Stand-up / sit-down activities	"We're Marching to the Drum"	"We're Marching to the Drum"	*"And We Walk" (DT1)	$"The Hokey Pokey"	"We're Marching to the Drum"
	"Stretch Up High"	*"And We Walk"	$"The Hokey Pokey"	*"And We Walk"	^"I'm a Little Teapot"
	"London Bridge"	"Handy Spandy"	$"Jack-in-the-Box"	^"I'm a Little Teapot"	$"Jack-in-the-Box"
	"Handy Spandy"		"Handy Spandy"	"Handy Spandy"	"Handy Spandy"
Animal activities	"I Went to Visit the Farm One Day"	"I Went to Visit the Farm One Day"	"I Went to Visit the Farm One Day" (DT2)	"I Went to Visit the Farm One Day"	"I Went to Visit the Farm One Day"
	"When the [Cow] Gets Up in the Morning"	"When the [Cow] Gets Up in the Morning"	"When the [Cow] Gets Up in the Morning"	"When the [Cow] Gets Up in the Morning"	"When the [Cow] Gets Up in the Morning"
	"Hickory Dickory Dare"	"Hickory Dickory Dare"		$"The Eency Weency Spider"	"Hickory Dickory Dare" (DT1)

(continued)

FIGURE 6.1 (cont'd)

Musical instruments	"We Ring Our Bells Together"	"We Ring Our Bells Together"	"We Shake Our Shakers Together"	"We Shake Our Shakers Together"	"We Ring Our Bells Together"
	"Ring Your Bells"	"Ring Your Bells"	"Grandfather's Clock Goes Tick Tock"	^"Hickory Dickory Dock"	^"Hickory Dickory Dock"
	"Ring Them Up High"	*"Are You Sleeping Brother John / Frère Jacques"	$"Shake Your Rattles like the Leaves"	^"I'm Driving in My Car"	§"Ring Them Up High" (DT2)
	"Grandfather's Clock Goes Tick Tock"	"Bells Away" (DT2)	"Shakers Away"	"Grandfather's Clock Goes Tick Tock"	$"Jack-in-the-Box"
	"Bells Away"			"Shakers Away"	"Bells Away"
Colored scarves	"Wind, Oh Wind"	"Wind, Oh Wind"	"Wind, Oh Wind"	"Wind, Oh Wind"	"Wind, Oh Wind"
	"Peek-a-Boo"	"Peek-a-Boo"	"Peek-a-Boo"	*"Oh Where, Oh Where Has My Little Head Gone?"	"Peek-a-Boo"
	"This Is the Way We Wash Our Face"	"This Is the Way We Wash Our Face"	*"Oh Where, Oh Where Has My Little Head Gone?"	§Creative movement activity	§"The Wheels on the Bus"
	"Scrunch Your Scarf into a Ball"	*"Oh Where, Oh Where Has My Little Head Gone?"	"This Is the Way We Wash Our Face"	^Wave scarves to recorded music	
	"Wind, Oh Wind" (leading into)	"Wind, Oh Wind" (leading into)	"Scrunch Your Scarf into a Ball"	"Wind, Oh Wind" (leading into)	"Scrunch Your Scarf into a Ball"
	"Scarves Away"	"Scarves Away"	"Scarves Away"	"Scarves Away"	"Scarves Away"
Lullabies	"Twinkle, Twinkle" (DT2)	"Twinkle, Twinkle"	$"ABC Song"	$"ABC Song"	§"You Are My Sunshine"
Interactive rhymes	"Humpty Dumpty"	"Humpty Dumpty" (DT3)	"Humpty Dumpty"	^"Jack Be Nimble"	"Humpty Dumpty"
Closing ritual	"Can You Kick with Two Feet?"	"Can You Kick with Two Feet?"	"Can You Kick with Two Feet?"	"Can You Kick with Two Feet?" (DT2)	"Can You Kick with Two Feet?"
	"We're So Happy"	"We're So Happy"	"We're So Happy"	"We're So Happy"	"We're So Happy"
		8 changes	8 changes	9 changes	7 changes

Note: New additions are indicated with an asterisk in program 2, a dollar sign in program 3, a caret symbol in program 4, and a sectional symbol in program 5, so you can see how the program changes over time. The secret sauce is to keep 80 percent of the program the same and to change just 20 percent of the program each week.

Go for It!

Using the formula mentioned above, you can create your own MGOL program. Keep your sessions consistent with a mix of repetition and variety by making a copy of the planning worksheet, filling it out each week, and changing only a few things from the week before. By following this method, you will always be introducing new material while keeping a substantial amount of the familiar material from week to week. You have just created your own customized MGOL program.

Note

1. For my doctoral project, I created an "online planning center" for easily constructing MGOL sessions. The mathematical formats are embedded into the program. When a change is desired, the facilitator can choose from a list of suggested choices or write in his or her own songs or rhymes. The versatility of this online planning center can streamline planning time and ensure high-quality programming. It is my hope that sometime in the near future that this tool will become available to children's librarians.

Chapter 7

Selecting Books, Rhymes, Songs, and Felt Pieces

YOUR INGREDIENTS ARE NECESSARY FOR COOKING up a MGOL program: books, rhymes, songs, and felt pieces. One book is read aloud in each MGOL session, and books are chosen for their content as well as for their illustrations. Rhymes and songs with activities form the basis of every program. Rhymes build vocabulary and assist with language development. Each rhyme or song (except for standing-up rhymes) has an accompanying visual representation, which often is an illustration from a picture book or a felt piece. These build visual literacy and enhance the oral language of the rhyme.

Choosing Books

The only time a book is read aloud cover to cover in a MGOL session is during the rhymes and reads section. While some children have a hard time keeping focused, others love this part.

Here are a few suggestions concerning book selection:

- Choose books with a simple story line, minimal text, and large, bold illustrations.
- Don't limit yourself to new books only; there are some wonderful older books to choose from.
- Don't worry about a worn cover; it's what's inside that matters.
- Make sure *you* like the book.

Here are my suggestions for using books as read-alouds:

- Books without a story line can be used by naming large, colorful pictures of objects; animals; or facial expressions.
- If a book has fabulous illustrations but is too long for babies and toddlers, it's fine to read from only a few pages. Use paper clips to fasten pages together ahead of time to ensure you don't read more than intended.
- Reading a short poem from a poetry anthology can substitute for a book being read aloud.
- Using vocabulary that is new to children is fine as long as it is a *very short* book.

Recommended Books to Read Aloud

Although the basic criteria for selecting read-alouds are minimal text and large, colorful pictures, some categories lend themselves well to MGOL. These include individual rhyme books, "call out what you see" books, board books, pop-ups and pop-outs, and older books.

Individual Rhyme Books

Some books have words to classic lullabies that may be hard to remember or provide words and illustrations to one rhyme, such as Keith Baker's *Big Fat Hen*. It is not unusual to find parents reciting the words along with you when the rhyme or song is familiar.

"Call Out What You See" Books

Lift the flap and fold-out books such as Agnese Baruzzi's *Opposite Surprise* are often favorites with very young children. They love the surprise and discovery of what is hiding beneath the flap. Toddlers enjoy calling out what they see when it is revealed. Concept books with shapes and colors give the same opportunity for MGOL participants to say aloud what they see.

Board Books

Board books are meant for babies, so the pictures and content are often perfect for reading aloud. If you have enough copies of the same board book, keep them in a canvas bag and hand out one book to each parent. Before you begin reading aloud, invite the parents to join in by reading aloud quietly to their child. They may or may not take you up on this offer. Then collect the books, singing "Books Away" as you come around with the opened canvas bag.

Pop-Ups and Pop-Outs

Children are fascinated by the unusual illustrations created by books with complicated pop-ups and pop-outs, known as paper engineering. One example is Philippe Ug's *In the Butterfly Garden*. Infants and toddlers are not ready to handle these fragile books on their own, but they love seeing the imaginative structures that instantaneously appear and disappear.

Eric Carle's *Papa, Please Get the Moon for Me* has a page that folds out to become double its size, showing a gigantic moon. Singing "Oh Mr. Moon" as a lullaby while showing this illustration leaves a big impression on little children.

Older Books

Don't be afraid to use older books. Some older picture books are gems and perfectly appropriate for a very young audience. Unless they are well-known classics, these books will not be readily available at the local bookstore, so you will be doing a service to both the children and their parents by introducing them to lovely illustrators and authors from the past.

Choosing Books for Illustrations

Some books have wonderful illustrations. Showing these illustrations is a versatile way to visually represent rhymes. The easiest way to display an illustration is to show the cover or use a sticky note to mark the page, but you can also turn the illustration into a felt piece using a color photocopier.

Nursery Rhyme Books

Some nursery rhymes are privileged and have an entire book devoted to them, such as Keith Baker's beautifully illustrated *Big Fat Hen*. Each illustration in his book is a two-page spread. In a case like this, it is best to choose one illustration that you particularly like and use a sticky note to mark the page. Or you can simply show the cover of the book as the visual representation for the rhyme.

Picture Books

Even though a picture book may have nothing whatsoever to do with nursery rhymes or songs, if you see an appealing illustration, use it! *One Two, That's My Shoe!* by Alison Murray has a lovely illustration of a dog with a wagging tail. It could become a great flannel piece for "How Much Is That Doggy in the Window." *What's Your Sound, Hound the Hound?* by Mo Willems has engaging illustrations of a cat, a dog, a chicken, and a cow. These could be used as felt pieces for a song about the sounds that animals make.

Song Books

Compilations of songs and fingerplays often have illustrations along with the lyrics and music. Feel free to photocopy the title of the rhyme or the lyrics too, if they fit in with the illustration. By combining the printed words along with the illustration for a fun activity, you are building print awareness and print motivation.

Books Not to Forget

Here are some newer books and old favorites that work wonderfully in MGOL sessions.

Baker, Keith. *A Big Fat Hen*. San Diego: Harcourt, 1997.

Bowie, C. W. *Busy Toes*. Dallas: Whispering Coyote Press, 1998. (This book is also available in Spanish as *Laboriosos Deditos de los Pies*. Watertown: Charlesbridge, 2004).

Campbell, Rod. *Dear Zoo*. Berkeley: Four Winds Press, 2017.

Cimarusti, Marie Torres. *Peek-a-Moo!* New York: Dutton Children's Books, 1998. (There are also more in this series.)

Cocoretto, ill. *Construction (Wheels at Work)*. Swindon, UK: Child's Play, 2018. (This is a wonderful new board book series.)

Crews, Donald. *Freight Train*. New York: Greenwillow Books, 2017. (There are other great books by Crews too.)

Fleming, Denise. *Barnyard Banter*. New York: Henry Holt, 2008.

Katz, Karen. *Where Is Baby's Belly Button?* New York: Little Simon, 2000.

Laden, Nina. *Peek-A Who?* San Francisco: Chronicle Books, 2000.

Martin, Bill Jr. *Brown Bear, Brown Bear, What Do You See?* New York: Henry Holt, 1992.

Miller, Margaret. *What's on My Head?* New York: Little Simon, 1998. (Miller has lots of good books.)

VanVoorst, Jenny Fretland. *Who Lives in the Forest (Who Lives Here?)*. Minneapolis, MN: Jump!, 2017. (There are lovely full-color animal photographs in this easy-to-read nonfiction book.)

Zelinsky, Paul. *The Wheels on the Bus*. New York: Dutton Children's Books, 1990.

Books to Use with Lullabies

Bleck, Linda. *A Children's Treasury of Lullabies*. New York: Sterling Children's Books, 2014.

Cooper, Floyd. *Cumbayah*. New York: Morrow Junior Books, 1998. (I suggest singing only one or two verses.)

Crews, Nina. *I'll Catch the Moon*. New York: Greenwillow: 1996. (Open this one to the last page with the picture of the girl lying in bed looking out at the moon.)

Fox, Mem. *Baby Bedtime*. San Diego, CA: Beach Lane, 2014.

Grosléziat, Chantal, et al. *Songs from the Baobab: African Lullabies and Nursery Rhymes*. Montréal: Secret Mountain, 2011.

Grosléziat, Chantal, et al. *Songs in the Shade of the Flamboyant Tree: French Creole Lullabies and Nursery Rhymes*. Montréal: Secret Mountain, 2012.

Pinkney, Brian. *Hush Little Baby*. New York: Greenwillow/Amistad, 2006.

Thomas, Joyce Carol, with Brenda Joysmith (ill.). *Hush Songs: African American Lullabies*. New York: Hyperion Books for Children, 2000.

Finding Rhymes

There are many places to find rhymes and songs for use in your MGOL programs in addition to the materials in this book. Nursery rhyme collections, song books, and poetry books can spark great ideas. Many online sites have videos of librarians doing fingerplays and other early literacy activities.

- At Jbrary (http://youtube.com/user/Jbrary/playlists), you can access playlists containing videos of two wonderful librarians (and sometimes some friends) doing fingerplays and tickles, lap bounces, baby time rhymes and songs, egg shaker songs, body parts songs, diaper changing songs, lullabies and soothing songs, scarf rhymes, and more!
- The official MGOL YouTube channel contains many videos of nursery rhyme presentations by fellow librarians. These are not professional videos but viewing them along with other clips gives great examples of our colleagues sharing rhymes and related useful activities (https://bit.ly/2P42ImV).
- The MGOL YouTube Channel also features selected "Rhyme of the Month" videos from each of MGOL's monthly newsletters (https://bit.ly/2P2icYq).
- Searching on YouTube for "babytime songs library," "lapsit," "baby rhyme time" will also take you to similar videos from libraries around the world.

- Some public libraries have their own channels for nursery rhyme videos. For instance, the Mooresville Public Library in Indiana has "Nursery Rhyme Time with Miss Michelle"; the Aurora Public Library in Ontario, Canada, has "Online Rhymes: Fingerplays, Songs, Rhymes and More"; and the Johnson County Library in Kansas has "6 by 6 Finger Play and Wordless Books."

Choosing Music

Using recorded music during the instrument or prop sessions can be a vehicle for exposing children to new sounds. There are plenty of wonderful tapes and CDs with children's songs, and these are fine to use. However, this is also an opportunity for you to expose children and their parents to other types of music. Classical music often has a steady tempo. Music from other countries can increase cultural awareness. Rock and roll, jazz, blues, and country songs add a bit of variety to the mix. I like to use some of my personal favorites while shaking maracas, waving scarves, or tapping sticks to the music.

Music That Works Unexpectedly Well with MGOL

The Beatles, "All My Loving"
Beethoven, Ludwig van, *Moonlight Sonata*, first movement
Chopin, Frederick, "Minute Waltz"
Crosby, Stills, Nash, and Young, "Our House" (on *Déjà Vu*)
Debussy, Claude, "Clair de Lune"
Denver, John, "Country Road"
Elgar, Sir Edward, "Pomp and Circumstance"
Handel, George Frederick, *The Water Music*
Haydn, Franz Josef, *Surprise* Symphony, second movement
Kingsley, Gershon, "Pop Corn" (played by Hot Butter)
Libana, "Oi Dai" (on *Borderland*; a song from Karelia, Russia)
Mallett, Dave, "The Garden Song"
Mozart, Wolfgang Amadeus, *Quintet in E Flat Major* and *Eine Kleine Nachtmusik*
Pachelbel, Johann, "Pachelbel's Canon" (also known as Canon in D Major)
Peter, Paul, and Mary, "If I Had a Hammer"
Rameau, Jean-Philippe, "Gavotte" (from *Pieces de Clavecin*)
Staines, Bill, "A Place in the Choir" (on *Whistle of the Jay*) and "The Happy Yodel" (on *Miles*)
Stewart, Georgiana, "Let's Go Fly a Kite" (on *Musical Scarves and Activities*)
Strauss, Johann, "The Blue Danube"
Talking Hands, Talking Feet, "Water, Water" (on *Heartbeat of the Future*)
Taylor, James, "You've Got a Friend" (on *Sweet Baby James*)
Vivaldi, Antonio, *The Four Seasons*

If you are looking for more MGOL-suitable songs to add to your repertoire, there are five MGOL CDs that are available via Amazon.com or CD Baby, and most songs can also be downloaded individually from iTunes.[1] In additional to an instructional CD that has an entire MGOL session with directions and developmental tips, "Listen, Like, Learn with Mother Goose on the Loose" has 121 songs and rhymes, "Escucha y Disfruta con Mama Gansa" has songs and rhymes in both English and Spanish, and another CD contains material in both English and Hebrew.

Creating Felt Pieces

Felt pieces stick easily onto the felt covering a flannelboard. They also come off with ease without leaving any marks. Seeing felt pieces being placed on a flannelboard, staying there, and then being removed has a magical quality for children. In addition, because felt is fuzzy, it helps create a warm, cozy feeling.

Felt pieces for the flannelboard play many important roles. They serve as

- a visual representation of the rhyme,
- a cue for the participants regarding the upcoming activity and a prereading developer,
- an introduction to the world of art,
- a foray into the world of abstract concepts,
- a placeholder for the facilitator, and
- a promoter of diversity.

Visual Representation of the Rhyme

If you were going to tell a story, you would want multiple felt pieces. For "One, Two, Buckle My Shoe," perhaps you would place a shoe, a door, a pile of sticks, and so forth on the flannelboard whenever they appeared in the story. Although storytelling requires several pieces to represent characters and objects, visually representing a rhyme requires *just one illustration*.

Each rhyme is not simply recited; there should always be some type of action that goes with it. For "One, Two, Buckle My Shoe," you can act out buckling your shoe, shutting the door, and picking up sticks. Or you can clap hands or ring bells to the beat as you recite the rhyme. Doing these actions would be impossible if you had to continually put new pieces on the flannelboard! "One, Two, Buckle My Shoe" has so many parts that trying to add a felt piece for each new object mentioned in the rhyme would result in frenetic activity, drawing attention away from the rhyme's intended actions. Participants would watch and look for each new piece rather than concentrating on acting, clapping, or ringing along. That's why using just one felt piece (a shoe or a door or a pile of sticks) to represent the rhyme is fine.

A Placeholder That Gives Practice for Recognizing Words

While you are presenting your program, the top felt piece on the pile on your easel's shelf represents a rhyme or activity to remind you which rhyme comes next. It will also replace your need to announce what rhyme comes next to the audience.

Using felt pieces makes your job much easier by helping children focus their attention, providing concrete images for spoken concepts or objects, and developing children's visual learning skills. For instance, the piece for "The Wheels on the Bus" can be a bus, a wheel, or anything else mentioned in the song. After using this piece a few times, children make a connection between the felt piece and "The Wheels on the Bus." When reading, once children's eyes and brains grow accustomed to the way certain words look (like the word *the*), children no longer have to sound it out. They recognize the pattern of those three letters put together (t-h-e) and know what word it represents. Flannel pieces serve the same function, building prereading skills.

An Introduction to the World of Art

Using actual illustrations, photographs cut from magazines, felt patterns from this book or online sites, and your own felt creations introduces the world of art while building prereading skills. Illustrations cut from discarded library books and glued onto felt familiarize children with actual artwork. They introduce children and their parents to the beauty accessible in books. I once found a discarded book with nursery rhyme illustrations by Randolph Caldecott (the Caldecott best illustrated book award is named for him). The artwork made great flannelboard pieces, and I used them along with other illustrations from discarded books by artists Dick Bruno, Eric Carle, and Nancy Tafuri.

Color photocopies make this possible too. Look through your nursery rhyme collections and find new illustrations to go along with a rhyme you have already been reciting. Make photocopies of the illustrations, glue each one to a piece of felt, and use them in rotation when you recite the rhymes.

Don't limit yourself to one piece per rhyme, however. Once participants have grown used to a felt piece, try using a different one for the same rhyme. Eventually, program participants will associate all the new felt pieces with the rhyme. Then you may want to reintroduce your original piece or create a new one to represent the same rhyme.

A Foray into the World of Abstract Concepts

Exposing participants to a number of different visual representations for the same rhyme introduces them to the concept that the same object can be described or shown in different ways. By experiencing one idea being expressed visually in different ways through multiple illustrations for the same rhyme, children become exposed to abstract concepts.

Rotating a variety of characters for some rhymes is like a guessing game. Children wonder "Which character will represent the rhyme this time?" and will delight in the occasional changes.

Promoting Diversity

Make felt pieces that include children from different races and ethnic backgrounds; try using illustrations from foreign language books to add flavor to your offerings. Diversity is important because children come in a variety of sizes and shapes. They have different skin tones and facial features. Some use assistive devices. Most children love to see themselves represented in programs, and there is no one size fits all.

How to Make Felt Pieces for Use in MGOL Programs

Felt sticks to felt, so anything can become a flannelboard character as long as it has a felt backing. There are many different ways to create felt pieces. You can use book illustrations, design your own pieces, use the illustrations in this book, ask other people to make them, highlight local resources, recycle pages from discarded books by cutting out pictures, use online templates, find graphics from the surrounding environment, or buy them.

Browse through Nursery Rhyme Collections

The obvious place to look for nursery rhyme illustrations is in nursery rhyme collections. Some of them are perfect for photocopying just as they are, such as many of Rosemary Wells's illustrations in collections by Iona Opie or illustrations from Clare Beaton books. However, often the illustrations are too small, or sometimes they are too big. So before making your color copy, remember that the ideal size for a flannel piece is bigger than your fist and smaller than 7½ × 10½ inches. You may have to play with the enlarging or shrinking settings on your copy machine until you get the ideal size. When you have to change the settings, it is useful to make more than one photocopy. Keep the spares in a folder for a year or so later. When it is time to replace your flannel piece, you will be glad you already have the right-size illustration ready and waiting.

Design Your Own

Try designing your own flannelboard pieces or ask a talented artist on the library staff or in the community to use a black permanent marker to draw the outline of a character on some felt. Cut around the edges and you'll have a new felt piece.

Use the Illustrations in This Book

If you are looking for templates to use as felt characters or to add as illustrations for advertising your MGOL sessions, see resource B in this book. My favorite artist is my sister, Celia. She has drawn whimsical illustrations to represent many MGOL rhymes. Feel free to photocopy them, scaling them to size, then cut them out along the thick black line, and glue them onto a piece of felt. Color them in or leave them as is. My favorite is the alien who illustrates "We Hit the Floor Together" by hitting the floor with all three of his hands!

Ask Other People to Make Them

Another way to incorporate visual literacy into your program is to find an artist to design flannelboard pieces for you. Try partnering with art teachers at local high schools or colleges with an art department. Offer to supply felt and Tacky Glue and ask if the students can each design and donate one flannelboard piece for the library. You may receive some very creative and imaginative ones! Or ask a local quilting club to contribute a few pieces. Carole Schlein, a student from the Maryland Institute College of Art, became a MGOL intern for me at the Enoch Pratt Free Library. During her year's internship, she designed an Impressionist sheep, shoe, and plate of cherries; a cubist London Bridge, turtle, and goose; and a pop art pease porridge and tea kettle. Although each of these pieces was for the flannelboard, she used a variety of techniques, including embroidery and silk screening. Her contributions to MGOL provided a visual treat for adults and children alike. By creating a town-wide project out of making felt props for MGOL, Laurie Collins of Ipswich, Massachusetts, brought the community together while receiving high-quality pieces that are used in programs and on display at the library.

Highlight Local Resources

Try approaching a local art museum and ask if they will work with you. Photographs of objects or pictures in the museum's collection can be cut to size, glued to felt, and used as props in your MGOL programs. For instance, a reproduction of a teapot might work well for the song "I'm a Little Teapot." After using this for a few weeks, you can mention that the actual teapot is on exhibit at the museum. If there is a reciprocal agreement between the museum and the library, tell library visitors that they can check out museum passes so they do not need to pay admission fees in order to visit the museum (if your library offers this service).

Recycle!

Instead of discarding pictures books with torn pages, ripped bindings, or scribbles, look to see if any of the illustrations would make good flannelboard pieces. Cut them out and attach them to felt using Tacky Glue. You may want to mention the illustrator's name when using those particular flannelboard pieces. After seeing one particular turtle illustration as a flannelboard character in the library program for a few weeks in a row, young children will squeal with delight when they recognize that same turtle illustration in a nursery rhyme book that their family has borrowed from the library.

Felt pieces can also be made out of stray puzzle pieces as long as they are big enough for your audience to see and not so heavy that they will slide down the flannelboard.

Go Online

Downloadable patterns for felt characters are available for free on many online sites, such as DLKteach (http://dltk-teach.com/rhymes/index-feltboard.htm) or MakingLearningFun (http://makinglearningfun.com/themepages/FeltBoardPrintables.htm). Online searches using terms such as "nursery rhyme characters clipart," "coloring pages," and "felt board templates" will provide many usable images. To experiment with the look of your felt characters, try printing images on clear T-shirt transfer paper and then using it on your felt.

Use Other Sources

Felt pieces can be made out of photographs cut from magazines, posters, fliers, discarded library books, or anything interesting that you see! Use Tacky Glue to attach them to felt, flannel, sandpaper, or Scotch-Brite pads. Don't use Velcro; although it will stick to a flannelboard, it pills the felt and leaves it looking unkempt.

Buy Them

Commercial flannel pieces are readily available, but often they do not have the same "warm" feeling to them. One exception is the charming felt finger puppets made by Artfelt, which work well with nursery rhymes and come with lyrics and suggestions in both Spanish and English (http://artfelt.net).

To Laminate or Not to Laminate, That Is the Question

Laminating your felt pieces means that they will last longer, but it takes away from their "cuddly" feeling and may reflect the glare of the lighting in your program area. For rhymes where children actually touch the felt piece (such as Humpty Dumpty), a piece made purely of felt is recommended. Although unlaminated pieces need to be replaced after a few years, the tactile factor and the cuteness make them a smart choice.

Basic Instructions for Making Felt Pieces

- Make sure your pieces are large enough to be seen. Any piece smaller than your fist is too small. Any piece larger than 7½ × 10½ is too big.
- Although Velcro sticks to felt, it is not recommended for use on the flannelboard because it often pills the felt, leaving the flannelboard looking worn.
- Only use Tacky Glue on your felt pieces. It can be purchased at fabric stores or in the sewing section of most big box stores. When Tacky Glue dries, it is clear. Most other glues do not stick to felt as well.
- Rather than squeezing out the Tacky Glue, pour some on a folded piece of paper, and use a craft stick to spread it on the pieces you would like to glue.
- You may want to decorate your characters with googly eyes, markers, fabric paints, small pom-poms, pieces of fabric, colored pencils, buttons, or anything else you can think of. Don't decorate with glitter glue; it takes a very long time to dry and may make your pieces too heavy.
- Lightweight is best! More than four layers of felt is too heavy and may result in the piece sliding down the flannelboard.
- Give thin pieces a background to ensure durability. For instance, a felt animal with a long, thin tail

may run the risk of the tail coming off. Thin felt can rip easily. Gluing the felt animal to a differently colored, larger piece of felt will create a piece that is esthetically pleasing, easy to handle, and sturdier.

- Less is more! Create only a minimum number of pieces per rhyme. One or two pieces to represent an entire poem are generally plenty! Having too many pieces is unwieldy for the presenter and visually confusing for the audience.
- Pay attention to the color of felt backing on your flannelboard. If the background is red and you've made two red dickey birds, the birds will blend right into the background and not be seen. Always be sure to choose felt that is not the same color as the felt on your flannelboard. If you want to use the same color, use a different color of felt as a background for the piece. Cut out a larger shape (circle, oval, square, etc.), and glue the pieces you have created to that background. Your two red dickey birds, pasted on a white background, will stand out beautifully even though the felt on your easel is red too.

Storing Your Pieces

The first flannel pieces you make will be used regularly, so store them in a stiff file folder and keep it in the storage tub. When setting up for your program, the pieces you need will be right there! Because there is a great amount of repetition, keeping the pieces that will be used over and over again in the same place as your other MGOL equipment will save time.

After the session, take the pieces out of the storage tub where they have been dropped, smooth them out, put them back in the file folder, and place the folder back in the tub. Without doing this, the pieces can get permanently creased. In addition to looking worn, creases make it harder for pieces to stay on the flannelboard.

Once you have built a collection of flannelboard pieces, store them in an accordion file in a way that will make it easy for you to find them. While filed, the felt pieces will not get crunched or wrinkled. Continue leaving your most-used pieces in the storage tub file folder in order to avoid refiling and having to pull them out of the accordion file each week.

Full-size templates for some of the most popular rhymes can be found in part IV, "Mother Goose on the Loose Resources," and resource B, "Some Mother Goose on the Loose Felt Piece Patterns."

Using Rhymes, Felt Pieces, Music, and Books Together

Picture books provide stories for children of all ages as well as a rich selection of illustrations. Felt pieces can be created from some of those illustrations, but they can also be designed in a number of ways to provide multiple visual representations of nursery rhymes. Using books, rhymes, songs, music, and felt pieces to complement each other in MGOL builds visual literacy as well as language and general literacy skills. What a great combination!

Note

1. An instructional CD that includes one complete MGOL session along with directions and developmental tips is available at www.cdbaby.com/cd/bdcohen. Another CD (*Listen, Like Learn with Mother Goose on the Loose*) has 121 songs and is available at www.cdbaby.com/cd/bdcr. "Escucha Y Disfruta con Mama Gansa" at www.cdbaby.com/cd/rembdc has songs in Spanish and English, and there is a CD with songs in English and Hebrew at www.cdbaby.com/cd/bdcr2.

Scheduling and Promoting Your Program

IF NO ONE ATTENDS YOUR PROGRAMS, IT DOESN'T matter how wonderful they might be. Drumming up an audience and scheduling sessions at convenient times for library visitors ensure that as many people as possible can benefit from your program offerings.

Scheduling

Once you are ready to present MGOL, decide when you want the sessions to take place. Keep the following factors in mind:

- In order to go out, parents have to pack up diaper bags with wipes, diapers, bottles, changes of clothing, and other necessary items. It can take quite a while to walk out the door! This means that planning ahead is necessary.
- Parents with newborns generally do not get a full night's sleep and can be overwhelmed with their new responsibilities.
- Birth is a trauma to the body, and it takes time to recover.
- Adjusting to a new being in one's household is not simple. Life is turned upside down when formerly independent adults have to take the needs of a baby into account for just about everything.

All these factors lead to what is sometimes called "baby brain." Because baby brain includes memory loss and muddled thinking, parents may easily forget the date and time of your MGOL sessions if they are not offered regularly. Sessions that occur every other week, once a month, or in a series of six weeks at a time can disappear from the radar screen! For this reason, offering sessions at the same time each week is best.

Ten thirty in the morning seems to be the best time to run programs for families with young babies. Some libraries find that early evening programs work better, enabling working parents to come with their babies. Weekends usually guarantee an audience, but older siblings come along too, so be prepared for a large, multi-aged session.

Registration or Not?

Some libraries ask parents to register their children for a series of sessions, capping the number of attendees. If at all possible for this particular population, limiting via registration is not a good idea because babies are unpredictable.

- When babies are colicky or teething and cannot stop crying, parents may prefer to stay home even if they had planned on attending the session.
- If a baby has had a rough night and has finally fallen asleep, the parent will probably choose to let the baby sleep rather than waking him or her to attend a library program.
- When a baby has a sudden bout of diarrhea, it is not a good time to come to the library!

- Parents may need to keep their babies home due to weather-related concerns.

Parents who register in advance for a certain number of consecutive sessions are agreeing to attend regularly and are possibly depriving others of a place. Even with the best of intentions, because of babies' unpredictability, parents may not be able to keep that commitment. Other parents who did not register might finally be free to come but will not because they haven't registered. Offering weekly MGOL sessions on a drop-in basis means there is no guilt for families who cannot come, and the opportunity remains open for all who wish to attend.

Tickets

Some venues have space limitations and fire codes that allow only a specific amount of people in a room. Giving out tickets on a first-come, first-served basis right before each session ensures that families who have shown up will be able to attend. It also enables you to politely say, "I'm sorry. There are no tickets left. That means the room is full according to the fire code, and we can't let anyone else in." When the counting is done via tickets, entry into the session is clearly not a personal decision. There can be no debate, and conflict is avoided.

Promoting Your Program

Using fliers to describe MGOL, listing the session dates and times, adding the information to your library's online calendar, and individually inviting families with small children to attend may be enough to ensure a decent number of participants for your first sessions. However, sometimes more strenuous efforts are needed to draw an audience. Below are a few suggestions regarding adding website pages, informing local resources, presenting sample programs, doing outreach visits, creating fliers, arranging media coverage, and encouraging word-of-mouth advertising.

Add a Page to Your Website

Create a link on your library website to a page about early literacy (if you don't already have one). List some of the benefits of attending early literacy programs and announce the start of your new MGOL series. Update the site regularly with photos from fun activities during the sessions (with parent permission, of course) and short video testimonials from attendees. You may want to add a "Fingerplay of the Month" and "Developmental Tip of the Month" to keep the page active. Feel free to use the ones on the mgol.net website if you are unable to record your own.

Inform Local Resources

Take stock of the resources in your community that work with or for families with young children. It is in your best interest to tell them about your upcoming program and to ask for their help in encouraging the families they work with to attend. Some local resources might be the following:

- childcare providers
- children's museums
- church, synagogue, and mosque playgroups
- developmental specialists and physical therapists
- Early Head Start and Head Start programs
- the health department
- home health visitors
- parks and recreation departments
- pediatricians and pediatric dentists
- public schools
- social workers

Sample Programs

Sample programs give a taste of the fun activities in MGOL. Choose rhymes that you find exciting and will spark parents' interest. Using colored scarves and bells is often a big draw. Keep it short! Here is a sample script:

"Old Mother Goose"
"Two Little Dickey Birds"
Bells: "We Ring Our Bells Together"
Bells: "Ring Your Bells"
Bells: "Grandfather's Clock Goes Tick Tock"
Bells: "Bells Away"
Scarves: "Wind, Oh Wind"
Scarves: "The Wheels on the Bus"
Scarves: "Scrunch Your Scarf into a Ball"
Scarves: "Scarves Away"
"Can You Kick with Two Feet?"
"It's Time to Say Good-Bye"

If you only have a short time to present, eliminate the bells entirely and just do the above program with fingerplays and colored scarves. The scarves ignite a sense of wonder and are often appreciated most.

Outreach Visits

Sample programs can be presented in shopping malls, at county fairs, at PTA meetings, at playgrounds, and even at stores where baby toys, clothes, and diapers are sold. Any place that parents of very young children visit is fair game. Just make sure to do the following:

- Present a program that you know well, so you don't stumble.
- Choose activities you enjoy because enthusiasm is infectious.
- Have enough supplies to give each attendee one scarf or bell to use.
- Use handouts to invite people to attend MGOL at your library, clearly announcing the location, date, and time of the program. Have your name and contact information on the flier so people can call if they have questions.
- Ask attendees to write their names, e-mail addresses, and cell phone numbers if they would like to be notified of future programs. Create a "group" for e-mail and schedule reminders that can go out two or three days before your sessions. Download an app such as Remind and plug in the phone numbers (www.remind.com). Set a reminder text message and schedule it to be sent to each person on the list one day before the session. The same reminder can be used multiple times.

Childbirth Preparation Classes

Local hospitals may offer childbirth preparation classes for expecting parents. Find out who is in charge of the classes and contact that person. Introduce yourself, explain what MGOL is, and ask if you can schedule a time to visit each class and present ten minutes of a sample program.

Hairdressers and Barbers

Many people get their hair cut or styled regularly. Hair professionals often have conversations with customers while working on their hair. Try forging a relationship with a haircut studio or barbershop and talk to the people who work there about the importance of early literacy. Ask them to pass on the message to parents who come for haircuts and to display your publicity materials.

Fliers

Attractive, colorful fliers draw attention. Present the information as clearly as possible. One glance should tell readers who the session is for, where the session will be held, when it will take place, who to contact for more information, and how to reach that person. A sentence or two about the program's value helps persuade people to attend.

Distribute the fliers to attendees at sample classes. In childbirth classes, give them to parents as well as class instructors. Ask if you can also post fliers on classroom bulletin boards and in maternity wards. Ask hospitals if your flier can become part of each new baby's "welcome package."

Walk around the neighborhoods close to your library, bringing fliers, tape, and a stapler. Visit local stores where new parents might go, such as coffee shops, ice cream parlors, toy stores, places that sell diapers, and so on. Introduce yourself as a local librarian and describe your upcoming program. Ask if you can post your flier in the window or on the bulletin board or if it's okay to leave a stack of fliers on the counter.

Take yourself out for a cup of coffee at a diner or restaurant that is popular with the locals and talk with the manager about posting a flier there. Or ask if you can speak with the serving staff and have them pass on the message to families with babies.

Everyone needs to buy groceries. If your local grocery store has a community bulletin board, ask the store manager if you can post a flier there. Often, items approved for display are stamped or marked in some way. Without this stamp, your flier may be taken down almost as quickly as you put it up. That is why it is always important to ask for permission before posting fliers.

Media Coverage

Send out a press release to local newspapers and radio stations briefly describing the value of MGOL, naming the ages of desired attendees, and including information about place, time, and the contact person. Stress the fact that the program is free. Invite people to bring friends along. Send the press release to online newsgroups and local electronic discussion lists. Shorten the press release so it still contains all relevant information, and post it on Facebook, Twitter, Instagram, and other social media sites that young parents might visit.

Make a funny video advertising your program, upload it to YouTube, and post the link on the library's website.

Invite a photographer to attend a session. Make sure that parents sign release forms allowing the photographer to take pictures of them and their babies and giving you permission to use the photos. Keep copies of the release forms and ask the photographer for copies of the pictures as well. See if your local newspaper would be interested in featuring any of the photographs and supply a brief explanation.

Word of Mouth

Word of mouth is often the best form of advertising. Whenever you see someone with a baby, give them a warm hello and ask if they have heard of MGOL. If not, tell them about it, and invite them to attend a session at your library. New parents generally do not realize there are board books and programs for babies at the library; they will be delighted to hear about a free event where they can socialize with others while building their baby's literacy skills. Keep fliers handy, and follow up every conversation by giving the person a flier.

Asking Parents to Spread the Word

Enthusiastic parents who are media savvy can set up "meetup" groups for MGOL programs. Meetup is an app that connects people who are interested in the same types of activities and alerts them to times and places to meet (http://meetup.com/apps).

Parent bloggers can reach wide audiences. Their glowing reports and enticing photographs appeal to parents in ways that paid advertisements do not. Reading a personal story about a wonderful visit to the public library may inspire others to drop in. Look for the parent bloggers in your area and invite them to attend a session with their children. Give them a flier so they will have all the correct information at their fingertips when writing the article at home.

Before and after Your Program

Preparing to Present

Setting up properly is essential. This preparation is similar to getting ready to present a cooking demonstration on television. Our goals are the same: to carefully arrange all the materials beforehand so there is no distraction from presenting a seamless production. The program flows smoothly only when you are prepared and organized. It is important to be sure you have all the props, know their exact locations, and can find and reach them effortlessly. Being organized focuses children's attention, keeping them from becoming distracted while you search for a missing item. Being properly prepared reduces your presentation butterflies and increases confidence. Knowing exactly which prop you need, when you need it, and where it is lets you focus on the exciting interactions of the program and not on the props that bring the program to life.

This chapter describes how to have an effective MGOL program, including how to set up the room and how to lead each of the ten MGOL sections.

Before the Program Begins

Read through the program again, acquainting yourself with the ten segments, the props, the rhymes, and the sequence of activities. Look at your script outline to make sure you have everything you need. Double-check that you have a book, a felt piece, or a written reminder for each rhyme. If something is missing, get a substitute quickly!

Room Setup

Arrange your presentation space. Set up the following elements in the correct positions.

Setting up the Presentation Area

Place the flannelboard/easel with a chair or low stool next to it at the front of the room. There should be a shelf in the middle of the easel; place your storage tub underneath the shelf of the easel. All your felt pieces and books should still be stacked in the order in which they will be used, safe inside the storage tub. The canvas bags with instruments, scarves, and puppets are also inside the tub. Make sure the cover remains on tightly! This is essential—you don't want to tempt children to play with your props while you are busy greeting people, and you certainly don't want your props to be out of order.

Preparing for Recorded Music

If you are using a tablet, cell phone, or MP3 player for recorded music, prepare your playlist ahead of time so music will play with a simple tap. Place the device on the shelf inside of the easel. If using a CD player, have the

CD loaded and ready in the "pause" position. Position it close to your seat but where curious children who like to press buttons cannot reach it.

Minimize Distractions
If toys or computers are in your program space, remove them or cover them up before the session. A big sheet draped over an early literacy computer works well!

Promote Book Sharing
Scatter some books on the floor. Use board books, nursery rhyme anthologies, or picture books with large illustrations and little text for adults and children to share together until the session starts.

Turn on the Music
Play background music as participants enter the room. Classical music, children's songs, ethnic music, or even rock and roll with clean lyrics will inspire creativity. Choose music that you like and that also has a steady beat. Don't play the music too loudly but be sure that people can hear it.

Prepare for after the Program Ends
If you will be inviting parents and children to stay for a playtime after the program, fill a storage tub with toys (soft balls, wooden puzzles, stacking and nesting toys, etc.), put the lid on securely, and place it in an unobtrusive area. Be sure it is easily accessible and close enough for you to bring out as soon as the program has finished.

Encourage Circulation of Library Materials
You may want to create a display of rhyme books and encourage families to check them out after the program. Give hints regarding playful ways to use the books with children. For instance, "Look at the different illustrations, and see if your child can point out which one is Humpty Dumpty. Learning to recognize shapes can help your child learn to recognize letters later on because letters are made out of shapes. So playing 'Can You Find It?' games with your child actually strengthens literacy skills."

PRESENTATION AREA SETUP AT A GLANCE

- Center: a low stool or small chair where you will sit
- On one side: a five-in-one teacher's easel that has a flannelboard on one side, a shelf in the middle (where you have easy access to the props but the audience cannot see them), and (ideally) a space to tuck a plastic storage tub underneath the shelf
- On the other side: the plastic tub containing the specific program props, *if you don't have room to tuck it underneath the easel's shelf*
- Behind you or to the side when there isn't enough room in the storage tub: the tote bags containing general props—like the farm animals, musical instruments, and scarves—involved in every program

When Participants Arrive

Create a Welcoming Space
MGOL should always take place in an environment that makes both children and their adults feel welcome. The most important part of an optimal learning environment is the welcoming atmosphere and acceptance of everyone. Feeling safe and wanted opens the minds of program participants, enabling them to easily absorb what is going on. Stand at the door and greet everyone personally! A smile and personal hello go a long way toward putting people at ease.

Invite program participants to sit in a semicircle around the flannelboard and encourage them to look at the board books scattered around as they are waiting.

Using Name Tags
Name tags can help you welcome each attendee individually. Put labels and markers by the door, and ask parents to make name tags for themselves and their children as they enter the room. Because children often rip off labels, the parent can write a tag for themselves using their child's name—that is, "Johnny's mom."

For "regulars" who attend weekly, create construction paper name tags, laminate them, and string a long piece of yarn through the top so they can be worn as necklaces and reused each week. Place them on a table by the entrance so participants can pick up their name tags as they enter.

Getting Ready to Begin

Transition into the Program

When the majority of the group has arrived and it's time to start, close the door and turn off the music. You may want to stick a note on the closed door telling latecomers to enter quietly and join the circle. Start singing, "Books away, books away, put your books away today" as you walk around the room with a large basket or canvas bag, inviting children and adults to drop their books inside.

Once the books have been collected, take off the storage tub cover, remove the stack of books and felt characters that are already stacked in their order of use, and place the stack on the shelf inside the easel, facing up (i.e., the felt piece for your first rhyme should be staring you in the face!).

Put the tambourine or small drum on the far side of the easel shelf. Leave any puppets you may be using for the introductory rhymes inside the plastic tub and keep the musical instruments and scarves in baskets or canvas bags on the floor behind you. This keeps them out of sight—and reach—of the children, removing temptation. Place the tub back under the shelf inside the easel or directly behind you and have a seat next to the flannelboard. You now have all your materials where you need them but not where they will distract the children.

By now, all the participants should be sitting in a semicircle around the flannelboard. Infants will be facing their adults; children a bit older will be facing you. It's time to lead your first MGOL session!

Be flexible. Leading MGOL is like learning to play a musical instrument. At the beginning, it's important to follow a score note by note until you feel proficient. Then it's fun to improvise. Feel free to make modifications (as I do) in order to truly make the program your own. If you want to start by following the next five scripts, that's fine. But feel free to add your own voice to the script, and have fun!

Using the Time after Your Session

As soon as the program has finished, replace the lid on the storage tub so your props will remain safe and you are free to talk with everyone in the room. Invite everyone to stay and chat together for about twenty to thirty minutes when the program has finished. Play some music softly in the background. Bring out another plastic storage tub housing toys such as soft building blocks, sensory balls, sturdy wooden puzzles with knobs, and stacking games. Gently dump out the contents on the rug. You may occasionally want to let the children play with the colored scarves, musical instruments, or puppets. Include a few board books along with the toys.

Encourage parents to share stories with each other while children "play" together in whatever way they can. Asking the generic question, "What new thing is your child doing this week?" often starts successful conversations. That particular question does not require that you remember the babies' names or genders. And because babies are always doing something new, parents most likely will have something to say. One parent will hear another's answer and will respond with "My child isn't doing that, but she is doing this…." Parents love talking about their children's accomplishments, so this is a great way to get them to share stories and gel together as a community.

If you see that parents don't seem to know how to play with their children, model play behavior by rolling a ball back and forth with the children, doing puzzles, and talking aloud as you solve the problems: "It doesn't fit in this way. I'm going to try it that way."

Parent Education

Parents of young children are often thirsty for knowledge about their own child's development. They want to know what is best for their child and to have coping strategies for the difficult times of rearing a young child. One of the best ways for parents to get information is by speaking with other parents. Hearing that another child is doing exactly the same thing their child does reassures parents their baby is developing as expected. A parent may pick up many useful tips while listening to different ways parents have coped with certain difficult situations (a child who hates diaper changes, for instance). In addition, being part of a group of parents with young children gives parents a forum through which to meet other people who are going through the same type of things.

After a MGOL session, it is imperative to plan time for parents to remain in the room with their children so they will have unpressured time to talk together. Knowing that there will be socialization time afterward results in parents being less likely to talk together during the session. Also, make an effort to contribute to conversations. Look for parents who have come to the program for the first time and engage them in conversation. Set out a few toys: the babies who are able to crawl can play while their parents chat together.

Once a month in the socialization time after MGOL, try offering a short ten- to fifteen-minute parent education program. This can include anything from showing a video on sign language to giving an update on a conference you recently attended or booktalks on easily readable books by researchers such as Alison Gopnik, Kathy Hirsh-Pasek, and Roberta Golinkoff. You may want to summarize a scientific study or magazine article citing the connection between knowing nursery rhymes and being ready to read. If so, have copies of the article available. Expose parents to the value of baby massage, provide examples of craft activities that help children ease through transitions, or play games that match oft-recited MGOL rhymes with concepts in brain research. You can also bring in a speaker on a relevant topic such as responsible television watching. In each case, a display of books related to the topic that are available for circulation would be greatly appreciated by parents, who often do not have the ability to spend time browsing the shelves for adult reading materials.

If you plan to offer these kinds of parent-education programs, it is important to realize that your audience will not be a quiet, attentive group. The children will be crawling around on the floor, and the parents will be watching them and listening to you with half an ear. You will have to speak loudly over the noise level of a room with children at play and parents on duty. However, although it may seem that the parents are only partially paying attention, it is amazing to discover how many people value the opportunity to hear something geared for adults while they are in a child-friendly atmosphere.

Finishing Up

Five minutes before you want the room emptied, turn off the music and start singing "Toys away, toys away, put the toys away today." Ask everyone to bring the toys up and place them in the storage tub designated for toys. Thank each person as they help. Remind parents to consider checking out books to share with their children until next week's session. And if there is a wastebasket in the room with dirty diapers, be sure to empty it as soon as possible!

Evaluating Your Program

IT IS NO SECRET THAT THERE IS A CONSTANT NEED TO evaluate children's programs in the public library. Internal evaluation is critical because asking program participants about their reactions helps you determine what works and what needs to be changed. External evaluation is important because as municipal budgets are cut nationwide, librarians must justify the existence of their programs and prove they deserve the funding they receive from taxpayers. Positive feedback can be cited in annual reports and publicity, while negative comments can be used to shape and determine the ongoing development of the program. Using a literacy assessment tool will enable you to evaluate the extent to which MGOL supports early literacy development in young children, supports early literacy in families, and engages parents and caregivers in supporting child and family literacy.

Using What You Have Observed

After presenting your first session, think about what occurred, focusing on what you would like to take into account for the next week. Write down your comments in the "observation" area at the bottom of the programming sheet. For instance, you might write "The rhyme about the apple bombed. No one seemed interested" or "Everyone loved 'Zoom, Zoom, Zoom.' Repeat often." You may want to remind yourself to take more time for setting up than you had allotted the previous week. These comments will help refresh your memory, enabling you to use your observations when planning your next session. Save the document on your computer, keeping the same presentation date.

Informal Evaluation

Take note when parents tell you how MGOL has affected their child. Often a child who does not actively participate in programs may sing all the songs and do all the motions to the fingerplays at home. Another child may play "librarian" at home and mimic running the program. Other parents may comment on the growth of attention span, interest in books, or increased vocabulary.

Be sure to record these informal comments for later assessment and evaluation. They are very important indicators for the success of your program. As soon as a parent starts telling you about the impact that attending MGOL has had, ask if the parent or caregiver would be willing to be recorded repeating their comment. Then pull out your phone and start recording. Ask them to sign the permission form once the recording is done. If you can't record an impromptu comment, jot down the comment just after you hear it.

Personal Interviews

If an adult has a few extra moments, find a comfortable space, provide a toy or book for the child to play with, and ask him or her to tell you about the program while you make a video or audio clip of their comments. Start by asking the parent's name, the name and age of the child, the date of the interview, how long they have been attending MGOL programs, and their contact information. Then ask them to tell you what they think about MGOL. Keep the question as broad as possible.

Should a parent find it difficult to speak free form, ask general questions:

- "What do you think about Mother Goose on the Loose?"
- "Why do you come to Mother Goose on the Loose programs at the library?"
- "Would you tell your friends to bring their children to Mother Goose on the Loose? Why or why not?"

Do not ask leading questions such as "Why do you like MGOL?" Instead, ask questions that allow them the broadest possible range of responses. Aim to get answers that are as honest as possible. This entails getting patrons to use their own words to pinpoint what they like or don't like about the program. If you think the comments are especially good for publication, ask them to sign a release form. Be sure to give the child a sticker or some other token of appreciation for his or her patience while the parent has been speaking with you. Both parent and child will appreciate this gesture!

Once the feedback has been recorded, look it over when you can concentrate. If there is any phrase that sticks out, type it out and be sure to note who said it and when they said it. Save these "best quotes." Whenever you need supporting evidence for the program or are trying to prove a particular point about it, you can use the words of actual program attendees to support you.

Send a copy of the video or audio clip to your development department (if you have one) as well as to your immediate supervisor. If a particular librarian is mentioned in a positive light, send a copy to him or her and to the supervisor. If a negative comment is made, think about it carefully and work out a plan for addressing the problem.

Formal Evaluation

To do a full-range, in-house evaluation of your program, participants should be assessed before attending the program and after a specified period of time, which enables you to compare answers. A preassessment is easiest if you are just starting to offer baby programs in your library. If you have ongoing programs, however, target newcomers and ask if they would be willing to participate in a research study on the effectiveness of the program.

Each participant comes with a range of experiences and abilities. By conducting a baseline interview or survey before the participants attend their first MGOL session, you will be able to get a clearer picture of how they grow over the course of their participation in the program. Data generated by this method tends to be far more scientific than that produced by simply asking parents who have attended sessions to fill out an evaluation assessing what their children have learned.

Methods

Because the children attending MGOL are generally too young to make clear comments and evaluations about the program, the adults must be the ones to answer questions and provide feedback. As a rule of thumb, the most effective data-gathering forms are those that solicit necessary information. Keep it brief and clear!

The pre-MGOL survey gives a basis for comparing information before and after attendance at MGOL sessions. Before you begin the survey, do the following:

- Let parents know that there are no right or wrong answers.
- Tell them that all responses will be kept confidential, although the final result as a whole may be publicized without names attached.
- Explain that they do not need to answer any of the questions that might make them feel uncomfortable.
- Present a small gift to the parents or children as a way of saying thank you for participating (this does not have to be expensive; a colorful sticker is fine).

The survey can include questions about child development, parenting methods, and library- or program-related items. Make it easy to fill out, with a number of questions that allow them to circle an answer and only a few open-ended questions at the end. This form can qualitatively assess what program participants are learning or have learned.

Mother Goose on the Loose Participant Survey

Today's date: _____

Name of person filling out this form: _____

Relationship to child: _____

Child's name: _____

Child's date of birth: _____

How old was your child when he or she began attending Mother Goose on the Loose: _____ years, _____ months.

About how many total sessions has your child attended? _____

Please circle the response that best describes your child.

1. My child knows the words to several rhymes or songs.
   1=strongly agree   2=agree   3=neutral   4=disagree   5=strongly disagree

2. My child seems to enjoy combining motions/actions with rhymes or songs.
   1=strongly agree   2=agree   3=neutral   4=disagree   5=strongly disagree

3. My child shows an interest in books.
   1=strongly agree   2=agree   3=neutral   4=disagree   5=strongly disagree

4. My child seems comfortable and confident with other children and adults.
   1=strongly agree   2=agree   3=neutral   4=disagree   5=strongly disagree

5. My child seems to enjoy coming to the public library.
   1=strongly agree   2=agree   3=neutral   4=disagree   5=strongly disagree

6. My child pays attention and follows directions easily.
   1=strongly agree   2=agree   3=neutral   4=disagree   5=strongly disagree

7. My child easily takes turns and shares.
   1=strongly agree   2=agree   3=neutral   4=disagree   5=strongly disagree

8. My child puts toys away when asked.
   1=strongly agree   2=agree   3=neutral   4=disagree   5=strongly disagree

9. My child enjoys playing with others.
   1=strongly agree   2=agree   3=neutral   4=disagree   5=strongly disagree

(continued)

(continued)

Please circle the response that best describes you.

1. I enjoy coming to the library.
   1=strongly agree   2=agree   3=neutral   4=disagree   5=strongly disagree

2. I feel a personal connection with the children's librarian.
   1=strongly agree   2=agree   3=neutral   4=disagree   5=strongly disagree

3. I know what to look for and expect regarding my child's coordination, speech, and memory development.
   1=strongly agree   2=agree   3=neutral   4=disagree   5=strongly disagree

4. I am confident in my parenting skills.
   1=strongly agree   2=agree   3=neutral   4=disagree   5=strongly disagree

5. My child and I sing together regularly.
   1=strongly agree   2=agree   3=neutral   4=disagree   5=strongly disagree

6. My child and I play together regularly.
   1=strongly agree   2=agree   3=neutral   4=disagree   5=strongly disagree

7. I often share books with my child.
   1=strongly agree   2=agree   3=neutral   4=disagree   5=strongly disagree

Thank you for your assistance in the evaluation of this valuable program!

Optional Discussion Questions for Pre-MGOL Survey

1. What is your child's favorite activity?
2. Why did you decide to come to Mother Goose on the Loose?
3. What do you hope you and your child will get out of Mother Goose on the Loose?

Betsy Diamant-Cohen, Mother Goose on the Loose: Updated (Chicago: ALA Editions, 2019).

File away the background questionnaires and the initial survey. After a few months, if this parent and child are still attending your sessions, ask them to fill out a follow-up survey.

The Follow-Up Survey

After families have attended MGOL sessions on a fairly regular basis, you can ask them to complete the follow-up survey immediately following a MGOL session. Explain that feedback is needed to let you know what is working well in the program and what might need improvement. Stress that personal information will remain confidential and that there is no need to answer any questions that make them feel uncomfortable. Because adults will be keeping an eye on their children while filling out the survey, let them know that it should take less than ten minutes to complete.

Use the same survey questions as above but replace the Optional Discussion Questions for the pre-MGOL survey with these:

Optional Discussion Questions for MGOL-Attendee Survey

1. What is your child's (children's) favorite Mother Goose on the Loose activity?
2. How can Mother Goose on the Loose be improved?
3. Would you recommend the program to other parents? Why or why not?
4. What do you think is the most valuable part of Mother Goose on the Loose for you?
5. What do you think is the most valuable part of Mother Goose on the Loose for your child?

Once both presurvey and postsurveys have been completed, compare the results. Has the child's early literacy, social, and emotional skills shown improvement? Have positive interactions between adult and child increased? See if the program met expectations. Look at the survey results, and consider how they can be utilized to support further programs for very young children in the library.

Is there a particular part of the program that people don't like? If so, change it! Is there something people really like that they think isn't done often enough? If so, consider including that activity on a more regular basis. These surveys are not just for directors and funders but also for those who put the program into practice. Use the surveys as a guide to tell you what is working and what is not, and adapt your program to fit the needs and desires of your participants.

Observation and Reflection Survey

Asking adults to document their observations and reflections at the end of a session can be useful. Results can be compared with the pre-MGOL and follow-up surveys, or they can stand on their own. Observation and reflection surveys serve as sources of immediate feedback. They can be formally analyzed after a substantial amount of time and assessed for information about the overall development of the program.

Use a checklist of school readiness skills to give examples of what might fall under the various school readiness categories. Parents may not instinctively recognize their children's achievements. Pointing out some specific skills will help parents recognize their child's growth and appreciate the small changes taking place.

There are a few options for facilitating this.

- Use Survey Monkey to create an online survey asking the questions below and load it on a library tablet. Ask parents to fill it out from time to time directly following a program.
- Set up an area in the program room with a stack of blank survey forms titled "Reflections on Today's Session," pencils, and a box for placing the completed forms. This must be on a table that is high enough that little hands cannot reach the items on top!

Survey: Reflections on Today's Session

Child's name: _____ Date: _____

Please check off the school readiness and STEM skills your child practiced or experienced in the Mother Goose on the Loose activities today. Feel free to elaborate in the comments section below.

Social and emotional well-being	(Check if yes)
Took turns	
Was patient	
Showed appreciation to others	
Received positive reinforcement	
Paid attention	
Followed instructions	
Listened when others spoke	
Sat when asked to sit	
Played with others	
Expressed emotions in a positive way	
Only entered the invisible circle when invited	
Other: _____	

Health and physical well-being	(Check if yes)
Got physical exercise	
Did fingerplays (used fine motor skills)	
Pretended to use a washcloth	
Identified some body parts and what they can do	
Snuggled with a loving adult	
Held onto objects and let go of them	
Laughed	
Stopped when asked to stop	
Other: _____	

Positive approaches to learning	(Check if yes)
Had a positive experience with a book	
Enjoyed interacting with the "teacher"	
Was exposed to different types of books and illustrations	
Saw an adult using a book	
Saw how pictures can tell a story	
Listened to instructions	
Repeated the instructor's physical actions	
Smiled	
Was shown appreciation by others	
Other: _____	

Language development	(Check if yes)
Heard some new words	
"Read" a book	
Repeated sounds	
Connected images to sounds or objects	
Connected illustrations or felt characters to songs and rhymes	
Heard rhymes	
Recited rhymes	
Played a game with syllables	
Noticed the difference between opposites: soft and loud, high and low, quick and slow	
Sang songs	
Other: _____	

General knowledge	(Check if yes)
Saw images of different animals	
Learned animal sounds	
Interacted with people from different backgrounds	
Heard sounds of nature mimicked through the human voice	
Identified colors	

(continued)

(continued)

Saw different shapes named and identified	
Experienced actions and consequences	
Other: _____	

Used STEM skills	**(Check if yes)**
Used sense of observation ("What does it feel like? What does it look like?")	
Tested the properties of objects ("What happens when I shake it?")	
Experimented with cause and effect ("When I shake it softly what happens? When I shake it loudly, what happens?")	
Used numbers	
Used sequencing (first, second, third)	
Heard comparison words (smaller and bigger, taller and shorter)	
Sang songs with repeated patterns (like "The Wheels on the Bus")	
Played games like peek-a-boo	
Was exposed to STEM language comparing size, shape, color, texture, and weight	

Comments: Feel free to describe the impact MGOL has had on you or your child.

Betsy Diamant-Cohen, Mother Goose on the Loose: Updated (Chicago: ALA Editions, 2018).

Stakeholders

When you are considering how to evaluate your MGOL programming, it is important to think about it in terms of the relative investment of those involved.

1. *Children.* The main stakeholders of MGOL are the children who attend the program because it is designed for them and they most directly benefit from participating. While it may be difficult to get information directly from very young children, try to keep them at the forefront in any evaluative process.
2. *Parents.* Parents and caregivers are the secondary MGOL stakeholders and participants. The program endeavors to make adult caregivers aware of "typical" child behavior and development. It provides tools to use with children, such as songs to ease transitions and lullabies to help children calm down. Further, MGOL creates an informal social support group for adults. Finally, benefits to the child (such as improved communication skills, improved ability to follow directions, etc.) can make life easier for parents and caregivers, helping them in their own educational efforts.
3. *Library and library staff.* The third group of stakeholders is the library and the staff hosting and presenting MGOL. Their goal is to run a successful program that brings people into the library and promotes positive feelings about the library, the librarians, the materials inside of the library, and library programs. By running well-attended programs, librarians can prove there is a demand for their services. If documented and presented properly, this data can be used for program funding requests and salaries.

Other Evaluation Tools

While this book was being written, the Public Library Association launched Project Outcome, a website with a free tool kit that includes standardized surveys to measure the effectiveness and impact of library programs and services in different areas, including early childhood literacy (www.projectoutcome.org). This enables librarians to gather and analyze data from library visitors and to present the findings in easily understandable ways. The results can be used to demonstrate the positive impact of library programs and services, to improve what is already being offered, to decide how to allocate limited resources, and to help with long-term planning. All public and state libraries can access Project Outcome online for free.

In addition, many of the behaviors for observation mentioned in *Supercharged Storytimes* can also be applied to the children attending MGOL.

Because Every Child Ready to Read (ECRR) focuses on language skills, you may be looking for a way to see if your programs enable parents to experience all five early literacy practices. To evaluate MGOL in the narrower context of ECRR, a separate survey targeting those practices can be found at www.mgol.net/?page_id=4617&preview=true/.

Self-Evaluation

Whether you are just starting out with MGOL, are a MGOL veteran, or are training staff to run the program, self-evaluation is an important tool. Taking a step back and reviewing your program presentation with a critical eye can help you discover where your strengths (and weaknesses) lie, and you can then take steps to improve.

A lot of time is spent developing skills during our careers, yet we do not always consider our comfort level with the skills. The following self-evaluation focuses on your comfort level with the components of the program. If you find yourself rushing through a section time and time again, it is time to reflect. Oftentimes, improvement is as easy as watching the component being performed by others online or in person or learning new songs, rhymes, or fingerplays for your rotation.

Self-Evaluation for MGOL Facilitators

Interactions with adults and peers are the primary way young children build their literacy skills. While MGOL programs provide environments and materials that encourage literacy development, it is through children's interactions with others that they develop new competencies and understandings. MGOL facilitators should aim to model for parents how to use language playfully with children through nursery rhymes and songs. They can use developmental tips to share information about children's social, emotional, intellectual, and literacy development, fostering an understanding of the significant role parents play in their children's growth. They can also provide resources and opportunities for parents to learn and practice literacy strategies that can be replicated at home while encouraging parents to share books with their children. The facilitators should use rhymes and visual representations that reflect cultural, social, and economic diversity both in the community and beyond. When possible, they should also provide informal play periods before or after the program where adults can engage in informal conversation with each other and with you. Ask yourself, "Am I doing this?"

Celebration

Celebrate your successes! It is sometimes easy to be hard on yourself, and that is the not the purpose of self-evaluation. Use it to see what is already running smoothly and what you can improve so that your program will be even better. Enjoy reading evaluations from parents and caregivers and appreciate knowing that your efforts really do make a difference.

Self-Assessment Survey

If you are facilitating the MGOL program, please take a few minutes to reflect on your programs by completing this assessment.

	Very comfortable	Comfortable	Somewhat comfortable	Not yet comfortable
Joining in children's play				
Encouraging children to play together				
Reciting rhymes and singing songs				
Modeling book-reading behavior				
Modeling playful ways to share a book with a child without actually reading it				
Introducing new words and their meanings to children				
Using rich, descriptive vocabulary when talking and playing with children				
Using felt pieces and book illustrations to build visual literacy				
Being playful with language (playing with sounds, emphasizing fun words)				
Giving developmental tips to adults that explain the skills being built by activities				
Giving developmental tips that describe how to replicate activities at home				
Encouraging parents to talk, sing, share books, and play with their children				

(continued)

(continued)

Additional Questions to Consider

What is your favorite section of Mother Goose on the Loose to present?

How can you improve your comfort level and skill set during your favorite and least favorite sections of Mother Goose on the Loose?

_____ New rhymes

_____ New songs

_____ New fingerplays

_____ New techniques for transitions

_____ Other needs

Betsy Diamant-Cohen, Mother Goose on the Loose: Updated *(Chicago: ALA Editions, 2019).*

Part III

Five Ready-to-Present Mother Goose on the Loose Programs

PROGRAM 1 AT A GLANCE

Section 1: Welcoming comments
Introduce yourself and welcome everyone.
State expectations ("Children this age don't sit perfectly still").
Set guidelines ("If they come within this invisible circle, please come and get them").
Explain how it works ("I'm going to say things twice").

Section 2: Rhymes and reads

Section	Rhyme/read	Prop *(fill in the blanks)*
Opening	"Old Mother Goose"	Mother Goose felt figure
Opening rhyme	"Goosey, Goosey Gander"	Goose on Stairs felt figure
General rhyme	"Two Little Dickey Birds" (DT1)	Two Little Dickey Birds felt figure
Puppet kisses	"Two Little Monkeys"	Monkey puppets or Monkeys Jumping on a Bed felt figure
Book to read aloud	*Freight Train* by Donald Crews	*Freight Train*
Tickle rhyme	"The Little Train Went up the Track"	*Freight Train* or Train felt figure
General rhyme	"We Hit the Floor Together"	Alien felt figure

Section 3: Body rhymes

Head	"Knock on the Door"	Door felt figure
Head	"Eye Winker"	*Baby Faces*
Fingers	"Fingers Like to Wiggle Waggle"	Boy Wiggling Fingers felt figure
Tickle	"'Round and 'Round the Garden"	Corduroy or Teddy Bear felt figure
Hands	"Pat-a-Cake"	Chef's Hat felt figure
Knee bounces	"Seesaw, Scaradown"	What's next card #1
Knee bounces	"To Market, To Market"	*My Very First Mother Goose* (Use a sticky note to mark pages 24–25.)
Knee bounces	"Mother and Father and Uncle John"	*My Very First Mother Goose*

Section 4: The drum sequence

Children tap out names with syllables.		
Drum sequence	"Rum Pum Pum"	Drum, what's next card #2

Section 5: Stand-up / sit-down activities		
Stand-up action 1	Freeze game: "We're Marching to the Drum"	Drum, what's next card #2
Stand-up action 2	Stretch: "Stretch Up High"	What's next card #2
Stand-up action 3	Circle dance: "London Bridge"	What's next card #2
Stand-up action 4	"Handy Spandy"	What's next card #2
Section 6: Animal activities		
Book	"I Went to Visit the Farm One Day"	*The Very Busy Spider*
Puppets	"When the [Cow] Gets Up in the Morning"	Farm animal puppets
Puppets	"Hickory Dickory Dare"	Pig puppet or Pig felt figure
Section 7: Musical instruments and scarves		
Bells	"We Ring Our Bells Together"	Bells, what's next card #3
Bells	"Ring Your Bells"	Bells, what's next card #3
Bells	"Ring Them Up High"	Bells, what's next card #3
Bells	"Grandfather's Clock Goes Tick Tock"	Grandfather's Clock felt figure
Bells	"Bells Away"	Bells, what's next card #4
Colored scarves	"Wind, Oh Wind"	Scarves, what's next card #4
Colored scarves	"Peek-a-Boo"	Scarves, what's next card #4
Colored scarves	"This Is the Way We Wash Our Face"	Hands Washing felt figure, Scarves
Colored scarves	"Scrunch Your Scarf into a Ball"	Scarves, what's next card #5
Colored scarves	"Wind, Oh Wind" / "Scarves Away"	Scarves, what's next card #5
Section 8: Lullabies		
Lullaby	"Twinkle, Twinkle" (DT2)	*Draw Me a Star* or Star felt figure
Section 9: Interactive rhymes		
Interactive rhyme	"Humpty Dumpty"	Humpty Dumpty and Wall felt figures
Section 10: Closing ritual		
Closing rhyme	"Can You Kick with Two Feet?"	What's next card #6
Closing rhyme	"We're So Happy"	What's next card #6

Developmental tip #1: Demonstrate the meanings of the words *soft* and *loud*.

Developmental tip #2: Lullabies help children relax.

Observations: _____

94 Part III: Five Ready-to-Present Mother Goose on the Loose Programs

BELOW IS A SCRIPT FOR A MGOL PROGRAM THAT CONTAINS WORDS TO ALL THE RHYMES, SONGS, AND FINGER-plays you will use. It has the extended welcoming comments to address different situations before they become problems. Included in this script are directions from the librarian to the parents and a few developmental tips.

Section 1: Welcoming Comments

(Smile and speak in a friendly and informal manner.)

"Hello, everyone, and welcome. My name is _____. I am a librarian here at _____. I'm delighted that you are here with me for Mother Goose on the Loose today.

"Mother Goose on the Loose is a brain-based program consisting of thirty minutes of fun skill-building activities. Reciting nursery rhymes in a program like this helps your child build important early literacy skills, and it's lots of fun for everyone.

"Come and sit in a semicircle facing the flannelboard, with your children on your laps, if possible. Children this age are not expected to sit perfectly still. In fact, they are often natural explorers. It is fine for your children to move around. However, please pretend there is an invisible circle around the flannelboard. If your child enters this circle, please come up and physically take him or her back to sit in your lap in the circle.

"A child standing in front of the flannelboard may block everyone else's view, and if a child comes up and takes a felt piece, puppet, or musical instrument from behind the flannelboard, other children are likely to imitate by coming up and handling the props also. All the props are arranged in order for the program, and that is why a swift response is needed if your child ventures into the invisible circle. Otherwise, it's fine for them to wander around.

"If your child starts to cry, feel free to go out of the room until he or she calms down and then come back in. I will not be at all offended if you walk out of the room in the middle of the program, and it is often easier for your child to calm down in a quieter atmosphere. Frankly, it's also easier for us to sing without trying to drown out a screaming child! But please, come back in when your child has settled down. You can go in and out as many times as necessary, but make sure to keep coming back.

"Parents are a child's first and best teacher. Children learn the most by imitating the people they love. In order for your child to get the most out of this program, it's important for you to do all the rhymes and motions with the group in an enthusiastic manner. I made sure to have enough musical instruments and scarves to be able to give one to each adult as well as to each child because your participation is important. So for now, please put your cell phones away and participate fully in the program.

"I will recite each rhyme twice. The first time you can listen; the second time, recite the rhyme along with me. If you already know the rhyme, please feel free to say it both times.

"You are invited to stay afterward for up to thirty minutes for informal play and time to talk with other parents. Don't forget to check out some of the books on display after the program. And now, without further ado, Mother Goose on the Loose."

Section 2: Rhymes and Reads

Put flannel piece of Mother Goose on the flannelboard or put a goose stuffed animal in your lap.

Tap your hands on your legs.

Old Mother Goose when she wanted to wander
Would fly through the air on her very fine gander.

Lift both hands up in the air, move them in an arc over your head, and bring them back down.

Old Mother Goose when she wanted to wander
Would fly through the air on her very fine gander.

When you are done reciting the rhyme, pull the felt piece off of the flannelboard and drop it into the tub.

Put the next felt pieces (a gander on a set of stairs) on the flannelboard and recite:

Goosey, goosey gander, where do you wander?

Lift your hands up and down.

Upstairs, and downstairs,

Give yourself a big hug.

and in my lady's chamber.

Say "Now let's recite the rhyme again. If you'd like, lift your babies up and down in the air at the words upstairs *and* downstairs.*"*

Bounce a pretend baby on your legs.

Goosey, goosey gander, where do you wander?

Lift your arms up and down.

Upstairs, and downstairs,

Give the "baby" a hug.

and in my lady's chamber.

Take the gander and stairs off of the flannelboard and drop them into the tub.

Place the dickey birds felt piece on the flannelboard.

Developmental tip #1: **"This next rhyme introduces the concepts of soft and loud. Notice how we whisper the word** *soft* **and shout the word** *loud***. What a fun way to demonstrate the meaning of words!"**

Make hands into fists with the index fingers sticking out. Bounce both hands up and down in front of you.

Two little dickey birds sitting on a cloud.

Bounce your right hand up and down and whisper this line.

One named "Soft,"

Bounce your left hand up and down and shout this line.

The other named "Loud."

Put your right hand behind your back and whisper this line.

Fly away, Soft!

Put your left hand behind your back and shout this line.

Fly away, Loud!

Bring your right hand back to the front and whisper this line.

Come back, Soft!

Bring your left hand back to the front and shout this line.

Come back, Loud!

"And again…"

Repeat everything a second time.

Remove the felt piece and drop it into the tub. Show an illustration or photograph of a monkey (or monkeys—perhaps the cover of Anne Schreiber's Monkeys*). Then put both hands in front of you in fists and start reciting the rhyme.*

"Look! Here's a monkey!"

Bounce both fists in front of you.

Two little monkeys jumping on the bed.

Drop your right hand down.

One fell off

Lift the hand and tap your head with it.

And bumped his head.

Put the other fist to your left ear as if it is a telephone receiver.

The other called the doctor

Nod your head.

And the doctor said,

Extend your right index finger and shake it back and forth as if you are chastising someone.

"No more monkeys jumping on the bed."

"Oh look! I have some monkeys right here."

Reach into the tub. Put a monkey puppet on each hand and bring them out in front of you.

"Why don't you pretend that you have monkey puppets on your hands also, and we can do the rhyme again?"

Repeat the rhyme with the monkeys on each hand.

Two little monkeys jumping on the bed.
One fell off and bumped his head.
The other called the doctor, and the doctor said.
"No more monkeys jumping on the bed!"

Monkey puppets face each other and converse.

Monkey 1: Hey, they did our rhyme so nicely!
Monkey 2: I know. Let's give everyone a monkey kiss to say thank you.
Monkey 1: Good idea.

Go around the circle giving each child a "kiss" from one of the monkeys.

Give yourself a monkey kiss too and drop monkey puppets into the tub.

Hold up the cover of the book you are going to read aloud.

"Here's the story of *Freight Train* by Donald Crews. Can you make the sound of a train?"

Chug, chug, chug, chug,

Lift up your right hand (with a fist) and make motions as if you are pulling on the cord of train whistle.

Toot! Toot!

"Try that with me."

Chug, chug, chug, chug,

Pretend to pull the train whistle cord.

Toot! Toot!

Read Freight Train *aloud. Before turning each page, recite the chorus with the "toot, toot" movements. Do not recite the chorus after the train has gone.*

Chug, chug, chug, chug,
Toot! Toot!

"And that is the story of *Freight Train* by Donald Crews."

Close the book and put it on the floor with the cover showing, leaning against the easel.

Lean forward. Put your fingers on your toes and "walk" your fingers up to your head.

"Start with your child's toes and work your way up."

A little train went up the track.

Tap your head twice.

It went "Toot Toot"

"Run" fingers back down.

And then it ran back.

Do the same movements, starting with the other foot.

Another train went up the track.
It went "Toot Toot"
And then it ran back.

Place each hand on a foot and repeat with both hands.

Two little trains ran up the track.
They went "Toot Toot"
And then they ran back.

Repeat all three verses and put the book in the tub.

Put the felt piece for "We Hit the Floor Together" on the easel.

Lean forward and hit the floor with the open palms of both hands.

We hit the floor together.
We hit the floor together.
We hit the floor together.
Because it's fun to do.

Use both open hands to smack the upper parts of the legs.

We smack our legs together.
We smack our legs together.
We smack our legs together.
Because it's fun to do.

Clap hands.

We clap our hands together.
We clap our hands together.

**We clap our hands together.
Because it's fun to do.**

Wiggle fingers.

**We wiggle our fingers together.
We wiggle our fingers together.
We wiggle our fingers together.
Because it's fun to do.**

Wave "hello."

**We all wave "hello."
We all wave "hello."
We all wave "hello."
Because it's fun to do.**

Put the felt piece or book into the tub.

Section 3: Body Rhymes

Put door felt piece on the flannelboard.

Start at the head and move down the body.

Knock gently on the baby's head.

Knock on the door.

Lift up a tuft of the baby's hair.

Pull the bell.

Extend your index fingers and point to the furthest end of your eyes.

Peek in.

Put a finger under your nose and lift up.

Lift up the latch.

Walk your finger almost into your open mouth.

Walk in.

Gently pinch one cheek.

Take a chair.

Gently pinch the other cheek.

Sit down.

Grab onto your chin and gently shake it up and down.

How do you do, Mrs. Brown?

"Let's repeat that again."

Repeat and then drop the felt piece into the tub.

Display a felt piece with a large face or a book illustration such as the cover from Margaret Miller's Baby Faces.

"And now, here's a really fun tickle rhyme to try with your baby."

Point to right eye.

Eye winker.

Point to left eye.

Tom Tinker.

Touch nose with both fingers.

Nose smeller.

Touch mouth with both fingers.

Mouth eater.

Tap chin with both fingers.

Chin chopper, chin chopper, chin chopper…

Tap chin with both fingers.

Guzzle whopper!

Tickle your belly all around.

"Give your child a great big tickle in the tummy!"

Repeat.

"And again!"

Put the felt piece or book into the tub.

Now move down to the hands and fingers.

Display the felt piece for "Fingers Like to Wiggle Waggle" on the flannelboard.

Wiggle the fingers of both hands in front of you.

Fingers like to wiggle waggle, wiggle waggle, wiggle waggle.

Continue wriggling fingers while raising hands up. Say "high" in a very high voice.

Fingers like to wiggle waggle, way up high.
Fingers like to wiggle waggle, wiggle waggle, wiggle waggle.

Continue wriggling fingers and lower hands to the floor. Say "low" in a very low voice.

Fingers like to wiggle waggle, way down low.
Fingers like to wiggle waggle, wiggle waggle, wiggle waggle.

Recite in a normal voice while placing fingers on one knee.

Fingers like to wiggle waggle, on my knee.

Repeat motions.

Drop the book or felt piece into the tub.

Display an illustration of a teddy bear (such as on the cover of Don Freeman's Corduroy*) or use a felt piece on the flannelboard.*

"Now take your child's open palm, and with your index finger, make a circle on their palm."

Open your left hand, palm up. Trace circles on the palm with your extended right index finger.

Round and round the garden goes the teddy bear.

Gently pinch your extended left arm once somewhere below the elbow.

One step,

Gently pinch your extended left arm once somewhere above the elbow.

two steps,

Tickle yourself under your left armpit.

TICKLE HIM UNDER THERE!

Extend your right hand, palm up. Trace circles on your right palm with your extended left index finger. (By now, parents should be imitating your movements on their children, or older children will be doing it on themselves.)

'Round about, 'round about goes the wee mouse.

Gently pinch your extended right arm somewhere below the elbow.

Up a step,

Gently pinch your extended right arm somewhere above the elbow.

up a step,

Tickle under your left armpit.

all around the house.

Repeat.

Drop the book or felt piece into the tub.

Display an illustration of a chef's hat or a cake or use a felt piece.

Clap and tap to the beat.

Pat-a-cake, pat-a-cake, baker's man.
Bake me a cake as fast as you can.
Roll it, and knead it,

Write B in the air with a finger.

and mark it with a *B*.

Open oven door and place cake inside.

And put it in the oven

Point to baby, then yourself.

for baby and me.

"When repeating that, use your child's initial and say your child's name."

Repeat, but use a different initial and name other than B and Baby.

Pat-a-cake, pat-a-cake, baker's man.
Bake me a cake as fast as you can.

Mime rolling and kneading.

Roll it, and knead it, and mark it with a B
And put it in the oven for baby and me.

Put chef's hat away.

Knee Bounces:

Give knee bounce instructions to the parents. Put your legs out straight in front of you (as best as you can if you are sitting in a chair).

"Now we're going to do some knee bounces. Parents, put your legs out in front of you, and put your child on your legs facing me. Those of you with infants, position them so they can look directly into your eyes rather than out to the circle."

An illustration with a seesaw would work well here. If you don't have an illustration or felt pieces, what's next card #1 will remind you what to do.

"We're going to start by moving one foot up and one foot down, as if you were riding a bicycle."

Start by slightly moving one knee up and one knee down.

Seesaw, Scaradown,
This is the way to Londontown.
One knee up and the other knee down,
This is the way to Londontown.

Repeat and personalize by filling in the name of the local city, town, or neighborhood.

Seesaw, Scaradown,
This is the way to Baltimoretown.
One knee up and the other knee down,
This is the way to Baltimoretown.

Drop what's next card #1 into the tub.

Display My Very First Mother Goose *(edited by Iona Opie and illustrated by Rosemary Wells). Open it to pages 24–25, marked with a sticky note. Lean the book against the flannelboard to show the illustration.*

Bounce your knees up and down together to the steady rhythm of the rhyme until you get to the last line.

To market, to market, to buy a fat pig.
Home again, home again, jiggety jig.
To market, to market, to buy a fat hog.
Home again, home again, jiggety jog.

To market, to market, to buy a currant bun.
Home again, home again, market is done.
To market, to market, to buy a brand-new mop,
Home again, home again,
Oh no, it's going to drop!

Lift your arms up high in the air to show parents that they can lift their babies up high and then bring them back down again.

Repeat.

Keep the same illustration displayed for the next rhyme.

Bounce both legs together.

Mother and Father and Uncle John went to town
one by one.

Lean to one side as far as you can.

Mother fell off.

Lean to the other side as far as you can.

And father fell off.

Sit upright, bounce. Recite as quickly as you can while bouncing faster and faster!

But Uncle John went
on and on and on and on and on…

Recite as quickly as you can while bouncing faster and faster.

Repeat.

Place the book in the tub.

Section 4: The Drum Sequence

Stand up, take the tambourine off of the easel's shelf, and hit it in rhythm to your words in a singsong voice.

> **Rum pum pum. This is my drum.**
> **Rum pum pum. This is my drum.**
> **My name is Betsy. What's your name?**

Recite your name, hitting the drum with each syllable.

"Now I am going to go around the room. I'd like each child to tap his or her name on the drum with syllables. For instance, Joe would just be Joe, but Shaniqua would be Sha-ni-qua with three syllables."

Tap "Joe" with just one tap.

Tap "Shaniqua" with three syllables, one tap for each syllable.

"And parents, if your child is too young to tap out his or her name, please take a hand and help him or her tap with his or her hands."

Walk around the circle. Approach the first child and chant.

"What's your name?"

Hold out the tambourine, and let the child hit his or her name. Answer with a personal welcome such as "Hello" or "Welcome," "Good morning," "Good afternoon," or "I'm glad you're here" after each child taps the name. If the name was clearly understandable to you, repeat it after the greeting, such as "Welcome, Tyrone."

"Good morning.

Welcome, Jennifer.

Glad to see you, Finn.

Stand in the middle of the circle and tap the drum on "Stand up."

Everybody, stand up!"

Section 5: Stand-Up / Sit-Down Activities

Stand in the middle of the circle and point out the direction in which you want people to march. Sing the next song to the tune of "The Farmer in the Dell." Hit the tambourine in beat to the song. March around the inside of the circle as you are singing.

"Make a circle. We are going to march around the room in this direction."

> **We're marching to the drum.**
> **We're marching to the drum.**
> **Hi-ho the derri-o,**
> **We're marching to the drum.**
>
> **We're marching 'round the room.**
> **We're marching 'round the room.**
> **Hi-ho the derri-o,**
> **We're marching 'round the room.**
>
> **We're marching to the drum.**
> **We're marching to the drum.**
> **Hi-ho the derri-o,**
> **We're marching to the drum.**

And the drum says, "*Stop!*"

Go up to a child and ask: "Can you hit 'stop'?"

Hold out the tambourine and encourage the child to hit it. As soon as she does, say a positive word.

"Good."

Do the same thing with the next child.

"Great."

And the next.

"Marvelous."

And the next.

"Super."

Continue around the circle.

"Fantastic. Now we are going to run around the room."

Tap the drum as you run around the inside of the circle.

> We're running to the drum.
> We're running to the drum.
> Hi-ho the derri-o,
> We're running to the drum.
>
> We're running 'round the room.
> We're running 'round the room.
> Hi-ho the derri-o,
> We're running 'round the room.
>
> We're running to the drum.
> We're running to the drum.
> Hi-ho the derri-o,
> We're running to the drum.

And the drum says, "*Stop!*"

Repeat the earlier step of having each child hit the tambourine and saying a positive word.

"Now we are going to tiptoe to the drum."

Tap the drum lightly as you tiptoe around the inside of the circle.

> We'll tiptoe to the drum.
> We'll tiptoe to the drum.
> Hi-ho the derri-o,
> We'll tiptoe to the drum.
>
> We'll tiptoe 'round the room.
> We'll tiptoe 'round the room.
> Hi-ho the derri-o,
> We'll tiptoe 'round the room.
>
> We'll tiptoe to the drum.
> We'll tiptoe to the drum.
> Hi-ho the derri-o,
> We'll tiptoe to the drum.

And the drum says, "Stop!"

"Can you hit 'stop'?"

Use positive words to encourage each child.

Return the tambourine to the shelf for the next song.

"Get ready to stretch!"

> Stretch up high.

Reach up as high as you can.

> Stretch down low.

Bend over and touch the floor with your hands.

> Stretch your arms in the middle so.

Put your arms out to the side as widely as you can.

"Let's try that one again!"

> Stretch up high.
> Stretch down low.
> Stretch your arms in the middle so.

Ask everyone to form a circle for "London Bridge." Point in the direction you want the circle to move.

"Let's make a big circle. Everyone hold hands. We are going to walk around the circle in this direction while we sing."

Walk around the circle.

> London Bridge is falling down, falling down,
>   falling down.
> London Bridge is falling down, my fair lady.

Kneel down.

Down!

Tap the floor to a steady beat while in the kneeling position.

> Build her up with sticks and stones, sticks and
>   stones, sticks and stones.
> Build her up with sticks and stones, my fair lady.

Stand up.

Up!

Hold hands and repeat.

Use the tambourine for the next rhyme, tapping to the beat. This turns sitting back down into a fun activity.

Give a steady tap.

> **Handy Spandy, sugar and candy,
> we all jump in.**

Jump into the center of the circle.

> **Handy Spandy, sugar and candy,
> we all jump out.**

Jump back to your starting point.

> **Handy Spandy, sugar and candy,
> we all jump up.**

Jump up.

> **Handy Spandy sugar and candy,
> we all sit down.**

Go back to your chair next to the flannelboard.

Section 6: Animal Activities

Once everyone is seated back in the circle after some exercise, they can be more attentive. Put the what's next card #2 in the tub. You are now going to model using a book in a fun way without reading it.

Display the cover of Eric Carle's The Very Busy Spider.

"Please join along in this song about the animals and the sounds they make."

Open to the picture of the horse and sing:

> **I went to visit the farm one day.
> I saw a horse across the way.
> And what do you think the horse did say?
> "Neigh, neigh, neigh."**

Turn to the next page with the picture of the cow.

> **I went to visit the farm one day.
> I saw a cow across the way.
> And what do you think the cow did say?
> "Moo, moo, moo."**

Turn to the next page with a picture of a sheep.

> **I went to visit the farm one day.
> I saw a sheep across the way.
> And what do you think the sheep did say?
> "Baa, baa, baa."**

Skip the next page because a goat's sound is too much like a sheep's sound. You can continue singing the song about all the following animals or skip around and just sing about one or two. If you decide to use the last page with the picture of the owl in the nighttime, sing this verse:

> **I went to visit the farm one night.
> I saw an owl by the moonlight.
> And what do you think the owl did say?
> "Hooo, hooo, hooo."**

Close the book and drop it in the tub. Pick up the duffel bag filled with stuffed animals or puppets and hold it on your lap.

Go directly into the next activity.

"Everyone, I am going to need your help with this song. Please sing along with me. Oh, look what I have here! Who is inside this bag?"

Slowly pull out one of the animals (a hen, for instance).

"It's a hen—a hen who says, 'Cluck!'"

Sing the song while holding the puppet.

> **When the hen gets up in the morning,
> She always says, "Cluck."
> When the hen gets up in the morning,
> She says, "Cluck, cluck."**

When you finish a verse, drop the animal back into the tub so curious hands will not be able to take the animal.

Pull out another animal and sing another verse. For instance, if it is a cow:

> **When the cow gets up in the morning,
> She always says, "Moo."
> When the cow gets up in the morning,
> She says, "Moo, moo."**

Continue pulling out animals and singing the songs about them. You can vary the types of animals but use about four to five animals for this activity. Save the pig for the last one, and sing:

> **When the pig gets up in the morning,**
> **She always says, "Oink."**
> **When the pig gets up in the morning,**
> **She says, "Oink, oink."**

Hold the pig and recite:

> **Hickory dickory dare.**
> **The pig flew up in the air.**

Throw the pig up in the air.

> **Farmer Brown soon brought her down.**

Catch the pig on its way down.

> **Hickory dickory dare.**

Give instructions regarding the next activity.

"Now I'm going to give each child a chance to throw the pig up in the air. If your child is too young to do it on his or her own, please use his or her hands to hold the pig and throw it up in the air. As each child throws the pig up, I'd like everyone to give a big round of applause so he or she can feel appreciation for a job well done."

Give the pig to the first child. When he throws the pig up in the air, give a big clap and say: "Yay!"

Pass the pig to the next child and repeat.

If a child is hesitant about throwing the pig, assist by counting: "One, two, three… Yay!"

If you have an older child, some encouragement might be needed: "What fabulous pig-throwing skills!"

If a child is shy and does not even want to touch the pig, legitimize her feelings and move on to the next child: "That's okay if she is shy; maybe next time."

When the pig has been passed all the way around the circle, repeat the rhyme one last time with the motion.

> **Hickory dickory dare.**
> **The pig flew up in the air.**
> **Farmer Brown soon brought her down.**
> **Hickory dickory dare.**

Drop the pig into the tub.

Section 7: Musical Instruments and Scarves

"Time for musical instruments!"

Lift up the canvas bag with bells in it. Walk around the circle giving a bell to each child and adult. It is important to give the bells directly to the children; sometimes the adults will try to take them from you to give to the child, but you want to build up a bond with the child, and directly handing the instrument to her is one way to do so.

When everyone has a bell, sit back down on your chair and start singing and ringing:

> **We ring our bells together.**
> **We ring our bells together.**
> **We ring our bells together.**
> **Because it's fun to do.**

Repeat.

Sing to the tune of "Jingle Bells". Ring to the beat.

> **Ring your bells, ring your bells,**
> **Ring your bells today.**
> **Oh what fun it is to ring,**
> **To ring your bells today-ay!**

Ring up high for "today-ay!"

> **Ring your bells, ring your bells.**
> **Ring your bells today.**
> **Oh what fun it is to ring,**
> **To ring your bells today.**

Repeat

Sing "high" in a high voice and ring the bells above you.

> **Ring them up high.**

Sing "low" in a low voice and ring the bells below you.

> **Ring them down low.**

Sing in a normal voice and ring the bells in front of you.

> **Ring them in the middle.**

Drop the what's next card #3 into the tub, and put the clock felt piece on the flannelboard.

Ring your bells slowly to the beat.

> **Grandfather's clock goes tick tock, tick tock.**

Ring at a medium tempo.

> **Mother's kitchen clock goes tick tock, tick tock, tick tock, tick tock.**

Ring very quickly.

> **Brother's little watch goes tick tick, tick tick, tick tick, tick tick, tick tick, tick tick,**

Stop ringing!

> **Stop!**

Hold open the canvas bag with one handle in each hand. Walk around the circle singing "Bells Away" as children and parents drop their bells in the bag.

> **Bells away, bells away, put your bells away today.**
> **Bells away, bells away, put your bells away today.**
> **Bells away, bells away, put your bells away today.**
> **Bells away, bells away, put your bells away today.**

Let parents know that they can give the instrument directly to you for washing if it has been put into a mouth. Be ready to hold the instrument in the hand holding the canvas bag rather than letting it drop inside.

> **"If your child put the bells in her mouth, please put it in my hand rather than in the bag so I can clean it after the program."**

Put the bag of bells down behind the flannelboard and take out the bag of colored scarves.

The Scarf Portion

Walk around the circle, handing out a scarf to each child and adult. Take a scarf for yourself and sit back down on your chair.

Wave your scarf from side to side.

> **Wind, oh wind, oh wind, I say.**
> **What are you blowing away today?**
> **Scarves, oh scarves, oh scarves I say.**
> **I am blowing the scarves away.**

Hold the scarf in front of your face. Blow at it and let go at the same time. Watch it float away!

> **"Blow and let go!"**

Repeat.

Put the scarf over your head.

> **"Now let's play peek-a-boo!"**

Start singing the song while lifting up the scarf and putting it back down again.

> **Peek-a-boo**
> **I see you.**
> **I see you hiding there.**
> **Peek-a-boo**
> **I see you.**
> **I see you smiling there.**
> **Peek-a-boo!**

Repeat the song while standing up and walking around the circle, squatting in front of each child and lifting up your scarf to play peek-a-boo with each child. Continue singing the song until you have gone around the entire circle.

Return to your seat. Put the hands washing felt piece on the easel. Scrunch your scarf into a ball as you give the next set of instructions.

> **"Scrunch your scarf up. Pretend it is a washcloth, and let's start washing our necks."**

Rub the scrunched-up scarf against your neck.

This is the way we wash our neck,
Wash our neck,
Wash our neck.
This is the way we wash our neck,
So early in the morning.

"What else can we wash?"

Ask what body part can be washed next. Use the suggestions for the next verse, naming different body parts. For instance, if someone suggests knees, start rubbing your knees with the scarf while singing.

Sing about three more verses, asking for body part suggestions. If you don't have any suggestions, use belly, arms, legs, and ears. Try not to use nose because you don't want to get mucus on the scarves!

Tell everyone to scrunch their scarves into balls.

"Scrunch your scarf into a ball. On the count of three, we'll throw them up in the air and watch all the beautiful colors come floating down."

Scrunch your scarves into a ball.
Make them very, very small.
Are you ready?
One, two, three…Oooh!
"Let's try that again."

Repeat "Wind, Oh Wind" and then pick up the scarves canvas bag and drop your scarf in. Without giving any verbal directions, begin singing the cleanup song.

Walk around with the open bag, and let children drop their scarves into the bag. Take wet scarves into your hand to be washed after the program. In between verses of "Scarves Away," say "thank you" to the children as they put their scarves into the bag.

Wind, oh wind, oh wind, I say.
What are you blowing away today?
Scarves, oh scarves, oh scarves I say.
I am blowing the scarves away.
Scarves away.
Scarves away.
Put your scarves away today.

Scarves away.
Scarves away.
Put your scarves away today.

Put the bag into the tub under the flannelboard along with tip card #5 and sit down on your chair.

Section 8: Lullabies

Ask parents to put their children on their laps, snuggle, rock, and sing a lullaby.

Developmental tip #2: "**Holding your children closely enables them to hear your heartbeat. They associate the sound with being a fetus in the womb, and it helps them relax. It's good to learn lullabies to keep in your 'parenting toolbox.' Use them with your children the next time they have a meltdown by holding, rocking, and singing to them softly.**"

Show a large star illustration from Eric Carle's Draw Me a Star. *Lean the book against the base of the flannelboard so everyone can see the star.*

Hug yourself and rock gently from side to side while singing "Twinkle, Twinkle" twice through.

"Now let's sing a lullaby. Hold your child close for a snuggle."

Twinkle, twinkle, little star.
How I wonder what you are.
Up above the world so high.
Like a diamond in the sky.
Twinkle, twinkle, little star.
How I wonder what you are.

Repeat.

Put the book into the tub.

"Time to go back into active mode!"

Section 9: Interactive Rhymes

Sit down on your chair. Put the felt Humpty Dumpty and wall on the flannelboard. Recite the rhyme.

Humpty Dumpty sat on a wall
Humpty Dumpty had a great fall.

> All the king's horses
> And all the king's men.
> **Couldn't put Humpty together again.**

Pull Humpty off of his wall and drop him on the floor.

Important: Give instructions to the parents and children. (1) Parents need to know that if their baby is very small, they can still participate. (2) Instead of the parent pulling Humpty off for the child, he should hold onto the child's hand and use the child's hand to do it. (3) Many children want more than one turn. Setting the scene by giving directions lets parents know that it is perfectly normal for a child to want more than one turn but that in this particular activity, everyone only gets one turn. And (4) it is fine for the parent to physically bring the child back to his seat in the circle if he is having difficulty going back on his own. These instructions are as much for the parents as they are for the children.

"Now I'd like to invite each child to have a turn to come up and pull Humpty off of the wall. If your child is too young to do it on his own, please take his hand gently, and use his hand to pull Humpty off. Because everyone gets one turn, the children should go back to their seats when they are done, making room for the other children to come up. If your child has trouble moving back, please feel free to come up and physically bring him back to your lap. Again, I'd like everyone to give a big round of applause for each child as they pull Humpty off of his wall."

Do not recite the rhyme over and over as each child pulls Humpty off; you could get hoarse! Clap as each child pulls Humpty off and say something affirmative like "Good job!"

Then pick Humpty off of the floor and put him back on the wall, waiting for the next child to pull him off.

You may need to ask, "Who is next?"

If you have a child who has been waiting patiently while other children zip in front of him, say in a cheerful, affirming voice, "You have been waiting so patiently! Now it is your turn."

If a child comes up but doesn't know quite what to do, help him by moving his hand to pull Humpty off.

If a child comes up and then is scared to do anything, say, "That's fine. You don't need to pull Humpty off if you don't want to." This is very important because some parents feel that their child is supposed to do what everyone else does and may try to force their child to perform the action, even when they are clearly uncomfortable.

Observe the faces of the children at the flannelboard. It is wonderful to see the looks of determination as they try pulling Humpty off and the looks of triumph and pride when they receive applause for succeeding.

Once everyone has pulled Humpty off, repeat the rhyme for a last time and put Humpty (and his wall) straight into the tub.

"One last time, let's say it all together."

> **Humpty Dumpty sat on a wall.**
> **Humpty Dumpty had a great fall.**
> All the king's horses
> And all the king's men
> **Couldn't put Humpty together again.**

Section 10: Closing Ritual

It is important to announce that this is your ending song; otherwise, parents might start leaving because their children may get restless after pulling off Humpty and waiting patiently for everyone else to do so. If they know this is the closing song and the program is almost over, they will generally join in.

Put your feet out in front of you and follow the song's directions.

"And now for our ending song…put your feet out in front of you."

> **Can you kick with two feet?**
> Two feet, two feet?
> **Can you kick with two feet?**
> Kick, kick, kick, kick, kick.

Clap your hands.

> **Can you clap with two hands,**
> Two hands, two hands?
> **Can you clap with two hands?**
> Clap, clap, clap, clap, clap.

Wiggle your fingers.

Can you wiggle with ten fingers?
Ten fingers, ten fingers?
Can you wiggle with ten fingers?
Wiggle, wiggle, wiggle, wiggle, wiggle.

Sway from side to side.

Can you sway from side to side?
Side to side, side to side?
Can you sway from side to side?
Sway, sway, sway, sway, sway.

After each line, pause and kiss the air. Parents usually take this opportunity to give their children a kiss. Give five kisses in a row after reciting the last line.

Can you kiss with two lips?
Two lips, two lips?
Can you kiss with two lips?
Kiss, kiss, kiss, kiss, kiss.

Wave bye-bye.

Can you wave "bye-bye"?
Bye-bye, bye-bye?
Can you wave "bye-bye"?
Bye-bye, bye-bye, bye-bye.

"It's time to say good-bye, but…"

We're so happy,
We're so happy,
We're so happy that everyone is here.

We're so happy,
We're so happy,
We're so happy that everyone is here.

If you have a small group and you know the names of all the children or they are wearing name tags, you can substitute each child's name for the word everyone as you go around the circle. For the final verse, use everyone.

Recite this in a singsong voice.

Good-bye, everyone.

Thank you for coming.

See you next week.

Put the what's next card #6, the bags of musical instruments, scarves, and puppets in the plastic tub. Put the cover on the tub, and you are now ready to speak with parents and children.

PROGRAM 2 AT A GLANCE

Section 1: Welcoming comments
Introduce yourself and welcome everyone.
State expectations ("Children this age don't sit perfectly still").
Set guidelines ("If they come within this invisible circle, please come and get them").
Explain how it works ("I'm going to say things twice").

Section 2: Rhymes and reads		
Section	**Rhyme/read**	**Prop** *(fill in the blanks)*
Opening	"Old Mother Goose"	Mother Goose felt figure
Opening rhyme	"Goosey, Goosey Gander"	Goose on Stairs felt figure
General rhyme	"Two Little Dickey Birds"	Two Little Dickey Birds felt figure
Puppet kisses	"Good Morning, Mrs. Perky Bird"	Bird puppet
Book to read aloud	*Busy Fingers* by C. W. Bowie	*Busy Fingers*
Tickle rhyme	"Pizza, Pizza, Hot"	Pizza felt figure
General rhyme	"I Hear Thunder"	Rain Cloud felt figure

Section 3: Body rhymes		
Head	"Knock on the Door"	Door felt figure
Head	"Eye Winker"	*Baby Faces*
Fingers	"Fingers Like to Wiggle Waggle"	Boy Wiggling Fingers felt figure
Tickle	"'Round and 'Round the Garden"	*Corduroy* or Teddy Bear felt figure
Hands	"Open Them, Shut Them"	
Knee bounces	"Seesaw, Scaradown"	
Knee bounces	"To Market, To Market"	
Knee bounces	"Mother and Father and Uncle John"	
Knee bounces	"The Grand Old Duke of York"	Duke of York felt figure

Section 4: The drum sequence		
Children tap out names with syllables.		
Drum sequence	"Rum Pum Pum" (DT1)	Tambourines or drum

Section 5: Stand-up / sit-down activities		
Stand-up action 1	Freeze game: "We're Marching to the Drum"	Drum
Stand-up action 2	"And We Walk"	
Stand-up action 3	"Handy Spandy"	
Section 6: Animal activities		
Book	"I Went to Visit the Farm One Day"	*The Very Busy Spider*
Puppets	"When the [Cow] Gets Up in the Morning"	Farm animal puppets
Puppets	"Hickory Dickory Dare"	Pig puppet or Pig felt figure
Section 7: Musical instruments and scarves		
Bells	"We Ring Our Bells Together"	Bells
Bells	"Ring Your Bells"	Bells
Bells	"Are You Sleeping Brother John / Frère Jacques"	Bed felt figure
Bells	"Bells Away" (DT2)	Bells
Colored scarves	"Wind, Oh Wind"	Scarves
Colored scarves	"Peek-a-Boo"	Scarves
Colored scarves	"This Is the Way We Wash Our Face"	Hands Washing felt figure
Colored scarves	"Oh Where, Oh Where Has My Little Head Gone?"	Scarves
Colored scarves	"Wind, Oh Wind" / "Scarves Away"	Scarves
Section 8: Lullabies		
Lullaby	"Twinkle, Twinkle"	*Draw Me a Star* or Star felt figure
Section 9: Interactive rhymes		
Interactive rhyme	"Humpty Dumpty" (DT3)	Humpty Dumpty and Wall felt figures
Section 10: Closing ritual		
Closing rhyme	"Can You Kick with Two Feet?"	
Closing rhyme	"We're So Happy"	

Developmental tip #1: Tapping on the drum builds phonemic awareness.

Developmental tip #2: Songs make clearing-up time fun.

Developmental tip #3: Build self-regulation skills.

Observations: _____

Everyone should be sitting in a circle surrounding the flannelboard/easel. Invite parents to put their children on their laps.

Section 1: Welcoming Comments

Be sure to smile and speak in a friendly and informal manner.

Section 2: Rhymes and Reads

Put a felt piece on the flannelboard, show a book illustration, or use a stuffed animal goose.

> **Old Mother Goose when she wanted to wander**
> **Would fly through the air on her very fine gander.**

"Now take your hands and move them with me as we say the rhyme again."

Repeat.

Drop the visual representation of the rhyme into the tub.

Display the visual representation for "Goosey, Goosey Gander."

> **Goosey, goosey gander, where do you wander?**
> **Upstairs, and downstairs,**
> **And in my lady's chamber.**

"Now let's recite the rhyme again. If you'd like, lift your babies up and down in the air at the words *upstairs* and *downstairs*. Don't forget to give a great big hug at the end!"

Repeat.

Drop the visual representation of the rhyme into the tub.

Display the visual representation for "Two Little Dickey Birds." Put both fists in front of you with index fingers extended.

> **Two little dickey birds sitting on a cloud.**
> **One named "Soft,"**
> **the other named "Loud."**
> **Fly away, Soft!**
> **Fly away, Loud!**
> **Come back, Soft!**
> **Come back, Loud!**

Repeat.

Drop the visual representation of the rhyme into the tub.

Introduce the bird puppet for "Good Morning, Mrs. Perky Bird."

"Oh, look, here is Mrs. Perky Bird! Good morning, Mrs. Perky Bird!"

> **Good morning, Mrs. Perky Bird, Perky Bird, Perky Bird.**
> **Good morning, Mrs. Perky Bird, where are you?**

"Fly" the bird puppet in the air. Give puppet kisses to the children seated around the circle.

> **I'm flying in the air, the air.**
> **The air, the air, the air, the air.**
> **I'm flying in the air, the air.**
> **And down to the ground.**

Bring the bird puppet down to the floor. Repeat singing until each child has gotten a puppet kiss.

Drop the bird puppet into the storage tub.

Display the visual representation for "We Hit the Floor Together."

> **We hit the floor together.**
> **We hit the floor together.**
> **We hit the floor together.**
> **Because it's fun to do.**

Repeat the refrain, replacing "we hit the floor together" with the following variations:

> **We smack our knees together.**
> **We clap our hands together.**
> **We wave our arms together.**
> **We wiggle our fingers together.**
> **We sway from side to side.**
> **And we all wave "hello."**

Drop the visual representation of the rhyme into the tub.

Show the book cover of Busy Fingers.

"Here's the story of *Busy Fingers* by C. W. Bowie, illustrated by Fred Willingham. See if your fingers can do what the fingers in the book are doing."

Read the story aloud then drop the book into the tub.

Display the visual representation for "Pizza, Pizza, Hot."

> **Pizza, pizza, hot. Pizza, pizza, cold.**
> **Pizza, pizza in the box, nine days old.**
> **Some like it hot. Some like it cold.**
> **Some like it in the box, nine days old. Yuck!**

Repeat.

Drop the visual representation of the rhyme into the tub.

Display the visual representation for "I Hear Thunder." You may want to take out an umbrella as well!

"Do you hear thunder? I do!"

> **I hear thunder. I hear thunder.**
> **Hark, don't you? Hark, don't you?**
> **Pitter, patter raindrops. Pitter, patter raindrops.**
> **I'm wet through, I'm wet through.**

Repeat.

Drop the visual representation of the rhyme into the tub.

Section 3: Body Rhymes

Head Rhymes:

Display the visual representation for "Knock on the Door."

> **Knock on the door.**
> **Pull the bell.**
> **Peek in!**
> **Lift up the latch.**
> **Walk in.**

> **Take a chair.**
> **Sit down.**
> **"How do you do, Mrs. Brown?"**

Repeat.

Drop the visual representation of the rhyme into the tub.

Display the visual representation for "Eye Winker."

"And now, for a really fun tickle rhyme!"

> **Eye winker.**
> **Tom Tinker.**
> **Nose smeller.**
> **Mouth eater.**
> **Chin chopper, chin chopper, chin chopper…**
> **Guzzle whopper!**

"Give your child a great big tickle in the tummy!"

"And again…"

Repeat.

Drop the visual representation of the rhyme into the tub.

Finger Rhymes:

Display the visual representation for "Fingers Like to Wiggle Waggle."

> **Fingers like to wiggle waggle, wiggle waggle, wiggle waggle.**
> **Fingers like to wiggle waggle, way up high.**
> **Fingers like to wiggle waggle, wiggle waggle, wiggle waggle.**
> **Fingers like to wiggle waggle, way down low.**
> **Fingers like to wiggle waggle, wiggle waggle, wiggle waggle.**
> **Fingers like to wiggle waggle, on my knee.** *(Place fingers on your knee. Don't change tone of voice.)*

Repeat to a much quicker beat.

Drop the visual representation of the rhyme into the tub.

Display the visual representation for "'Round and 'Round the Garden."

"Now take your child's open palm, and with your index finger, draw a circle there."

> 'Round and 'round the garden goes the teddy bear.
> One step, two steps, tickly under there!

"Now on your child's other hand."

> 'Round about, 'round about goes the wee mouse.
> Up a step, up a step, all around the house.

Repeat.

Drop the visual representation of the rhyme into the tub.

Hand Rhymes:

Display the visual representation for "Open Them, Shut Them."

> **Open them, shut them. Open them, shut them.
> Give a little clap.
> Open them, shut them. Open them, shut them,
> Put them in your lap.
> Creep them, creep them. Creep them, creep them,
> Right up to your chinny chin chin.
> Open up your little mouth
> But do not let them in!**

Repeat.

Drop the visual representation of the rhyme into the tub.

Knee Bounces:

"Now we're going to do some knee bounces. Parents, sit up straight. Put your legs out in front of you and place your child on your legs. Position your infants to face you so they can have eye-to-eye contact with one of the people they love most. Place children who are a bit older on your outstretched knees facing me so they can see the other children around the circle. Gently move your legs up and down one at a time, as if you are riding a bicycle."

Display the visual representation for "Seesaw, Scaradown."

Extend your feet in front of you. Raise and lower one knee and then the other.

> **Seesaw, Scaradown,
> This is the way to Londontown.
> One knee up and the other knee down,
> This is the way to Londontown.**

> **Seesaw, Scaradown,
> This is the way to _____ town.
> One knee up and the other knee down.
> This is the way to _____ town.**

Drop the visual representation of the rhyme into the tub.

Display the visual representation for "To Market, To Market." This can be the cover of Anne Miranda's book, To Market, To Market. *Bounce knees up and down.*

> **To market, to market, to buy a fat pig.
> Home again, home again, jiggety jig.
> To market, to market, to buy a fat hog.
> Home again, home again, jiggety jog.**

> **To market, to market, to buy a currant bun.
> Home again, home again, market is done.
> To market, to market, to buy a brand-new mop.
> Home again, home again, oh no, it's going to drop!**

Repeat.

Drop the visual representation of the rhyme into the tub.

Display the visual representation for "Mother and Father and Uncle John."

> **Mother and Father and Uncle John went to market, one by one.** *(Gently bounce your outstretched legs as your child sits on them.)*
> **Mother fell off.** *(Lean to one side.)*
> **And father fell off.** *(Lean to the other side.)*
> **But Uncle John went on and on and on and on and on…** *(Sit up straight and bounce very quickly.)*

Repeat.

Drop the visual representation of the rhyme into the tub.

Display the visual representation for "The Grand Old Duke of York."

"Keep your children on your knees facing me. For this song, when the men go up, bring your knees up; when they go down, bring your legs back down to the floor; and for halfway up, just go halfway up."

> Oh, the Grand Old Duke of York. He had ten thousand men.
> He marched them up to the top of the hill,
> And he marched them down again.
> And when they were up, they were up.
> And when they were down, they were down.
> And when they were only halfway up,
> They were neither up nor down.

Repeat.

Drop the visual representation of the rhyme into the tub.

Section 4: The Drum Sequence

Developmental tip #1: "By tapping out their names on the drum, children become aware of syllables and sounds (called phonemic awareness). When learning to read, children often find it easiest to 'sound out' the word, so hearing the sounds in words is an important prereading skill."

Take out tambourine or hand drum.

> Rum pum pum. This is my drum. *(Tap to the beat.)*
> Rum pum pum. This is my drum.
> My name is _____. What's your name?
>   *(Tap your name with syllables on the drum.)*

"Now I am going to go around the room. I'd like each child to tap his or her name on the drum with syllables. For instance, Joe would just be Joe, but Shaniqua would be Sha-ni-qua with three syllables. And parents, if your children are too young to tap out their names on their own, please take their hands and help them tap out their names with their own hands."

What's your name?

Hello.

Good morning.

Welcome, Jennifer.

Glad to see you, Finn.

"Everybody, stand up!"

Section 5: Stand-Up / Sit-Down Activities

"Make a circle! We are going to march around the room together in this direction." *(Point in the direction you will be moving.)*

> We're marching to the drum.
> We're marching to the drum.
> Hi-ho the derri-o,
> We're marching to the drum.
>
> We're marching 'round the room.
> We're marching 'round the room.
> Hi-ho the derri-o,
> We're marching 'round the room.
>
> We're marching to the drum.
> We're marching to the drum.
> Hi-ho the derri-o,
> We're marching to the drum.

And the drum says, "Stop!"

Can you hit "stop"?

Good.

Can you hit "stop"?

Marvelous.

Can you hit "stop"?

Extraordinary. (Continue using positive words.)

"Now let's run to the drum."

Repeat the refrain above, substituting run *for* march.

"Now let's tiptoe to the drum."

Repeat the refrain above, substituting tiptoe *for* march.

"Here's another freeze game. Walk around the circle in this direction."

> And we walk, and we walk, and we walk, and we stop.
> And we walk, and we walk, and we walk, and we stop.
> And we walk, and we walk, and we walk, and we stop.
> And we all turn around—Woo!
>
> And we run, and we run, and we run, and we stop.
> And we run, and we run, and we run, and we stop.
> And we run, and we run, and we run, and we stop.
> And we all turn around—Woo!
>
> Now let's bend down and creep very quietly.
> And we creep, and we creep, and we creep, and we stop.
> And we creep, and we creep, and we creep, and we stop.
> And we creep, and we creep, and we creep, and we stop.
> And we all turn around—Woo!

> Handy Spandy, sugar and candy, we all jump in.
> Handy Spandy, sugar and candy, we all jump out.
> Handy Spandy, sugar and candy, we all jump up.
> Handy Spandy, sugar and candy, we all sit down.

Sit down and put tambourine or drum into the tub.

Section 6: Animal Activities

Take out Eric Carle's The Very Busy Spider *and show the cover.*

"Everyone, please join in and help me sing this song about the sounds the animals make."

> I went to visit the farm one day.
> I saw a horse across the way.
> And what do you think the horse did say?
> "Neigh, neigh, neigh."
>
> I went to visit the farm one day.
> I saw a cow across the way.
> And what do you think the cow did say?
> "Moo, moo, moo."
>
> I went to visit the farm one day.
> I saw a sheep across the way.
> And what do you think the sheep did say?
> "Baa, baa, baa."
>
> I went to visit the farm one night.
> I saw an owl by the moonlight.
> And what do you think the owl did say?
> "Hooo, hooo, hooo."

Close the book and put it into the tub.

Lift up your tote bag with farm animal puppets inside. Show one part of an animal peeking over the front tip of the tote bag. This could be an ear, a tail, or a foot.

"Oh, look what I have here! Who is inside this bag?"

Give children time to guess which animal you have in the bag. Then pull it out.

"It's a hen. A hen who says, 'Cluck!'"

> When the hen gets up in the morning,
> She always says, "Cluck."
> When the hen gets up in the morning,
> She says, "Cluck, cluck."

Place animals in the tub after each verse.

> When the cow gets up in the morning,
> She always says, "Moo."
> When the cow gets up in the morning,
> She says, "Moo, moo."
>
> When the pig gets up in the morning,
> She always says, "Oink."
> When the pig gets up in the morning,
> She says, "Oink, oink."

Do not place the pig in the storage tub. Instead, hold the pig and recite the next rhyme.

> Hickory dickory dare.
> The pig flew up in the air. (*Throw pig puppet up in the air and catch it coming down.*)
> Farmer Brown soon brought her down.
> Hickory dickory dare.

"Now I'm going to give each child a chance to throw the pig up in the air. If your child is too young to do it on her own, please use her hands to hold the pig and then throw it up in the air. As each child throws the pig up, let's all give a big round of applause so they will feel our appreciation for a job well done."

Yay!

Yay!

One, two, three… Yay!

What fabulous pig-throwing skills!

That's okay if she is shy; maybe next time.

Section 7: Musical Instruments and Scarves

Walk around the circle with a tote bag full of bells. Hand one bell to each child and one to each adult. If the bells are different colors, you can name the colors as you are passing them out.

Bells

> We ring our bells together,
> We ring our bells together.
> We ring our bells together.
> Because it's fun to do.

Repeat.

> Ring them up high.
> Ring them down low.
> Ring them in the middle!

Sing to the tune of "Jingle Bells"

> Ring your bells, ring your bells,
> Ring your bells today.
> Oh what fun it is to ring,
> To ring your bells today-ay!

> Ring your bells, ring your bells,
> Ring your bells today.
> Oh what fun it is to ring,
> To ring your bells today.

> Ring your bells, ring your bells,
> Ring your bells today.

> Ring them up high.
> Ring them down low.
> Ring them in the middle!

Repeat.

> Are you sleeping, are you sleeping?
> Brother John? Brother John?
> Morning bells are ringing. Morning bells are ringing.
> Ding dang dong. Ding dang dong.

> Frère Jacques, Frère Jacques,
> Dormez-vous? Dormez-vous?
> Sonnez les matines, sonnez les matines,
> Din, din, don! Din, din, don!

> Ring them up high.
> Ring them down low.
> Ring them in the middle!

"If your child put the bell in her mouth, please put it in my hand rather than in the bag so I can clean it after the program. Thanks."

Collect bells in the tote bag.

> Bells away, bells away, put your bells away today.
> Bells away, bells away, put your bells away today.

Repeat until all the bells have been collected.

Developmental tip #2: "Singing a cleanup song makes cleaning up a fun activity for children and teaches them what behavior you expect when it is time to put something away. Cleaning up with a song is gentle and loving and makes the activity seem much more like fun than a chore. Try singing cleanup songs with your child at home!"

Scarves

Walk around the circle with the scarf-filled tote bag. Hand each child and adult a scarf. You may want to name the color of the scarf you are handing out.

> Wind, oh wind, oh wind, I say.
> What are you blowing away today?
> Scarves, oh scarves, oh scarves, I say.
> I am blowing the scarves away.

Place scarf over your head. Sing the first verse of this song. Then walk over to the child sitting closest to you in the circle and sing a line of the song while looking directly into the child's eyes and playing peek-a-boo. Move to the next child and sing the next line, doing the same thing. Continue all the way around the circle until all children have had a chance to play peek-a-boo with you.

> Peek-a-boo, I see you, I see you hiding there.
> Peek-a-boo, I see you, I see you hiding there.
>   (Peek-a-boo!)

Repeat as much as needed.

"Scrunch your scarf into a ball. Pretend it's a washcloth, and let's wash our faces."

> This is the way we wash our face, wash our face, wash our face.
> This is the way we wash our face, so early in the morning.

Wash hands, belly, knees, etc.

Place your scarf over your head.

"Now place your scarves over your heads once again."

> Oh where, oh where has my little head gone? Oh where, oh where can it be?
> Oh where, oh where has my little head gone? Oh where, oh where can it be?
> One…Two…Three…Here it is!

Repeat using knee or other body parts.

"Now take your scarves and squish them into tiny balls. On the count of three, let's throw them all into the air, and watch the beautiful colors come floating down. Ready? One, two, three…Oooh! Let's try that again. Ready? One, two, three…Oooh!"

> Wind, oh wind, oh wind, I say.
> What are you blowing away today?

> Scarves, oh scarves, oh scarves, I say.
> I am blowing the scarves away.

Walk around the circle holding the tote bag open in front of each child (and adult, if necessary). Sing the cleanup song, and watch the children put their scarves into the bag. In between verses, say, "Thank you."

> Scarves away, scarves away,
> Put your scarves away today.

Drop the bag with scarves into the storage tub.

Section 8: Lullabies

"Now it's lullaby time. Last week, we mentioned that any song can be a lullaby as long as it is sung softly and slowly. Let's repeat the song we sang last week, 'Twinkle, Twinkle.' Let's hold our children close as we rock gently from side to side while we sing."

> Twinkle, twinkle, little star,
> How I wonder what you are.
> Up above the world so high,
> Like a diamond in the sky.
> Twinkle, twinkle, little star,
> How I wonder what you are.

Repeat.

Section 9: Interactive Rhymes

Display the visual representation for "Humpty Dumpty"—the egg and his wall.

> Humpty Dumpty sat on a wall.
> Humpty Dumpty had a great fall.
> All the king's horses
> And all the king's men
> Couldn't put Humpty together again.

"Now I'd like to invite each child to have a turn to come up and pull Humpty off of the wall. If your child is too young to do it on his own, please take his hand gently and use his hand to pull Humpty off. Because everyone gets one turn, the children should go back to their seats when they are done, making room for the other children to come up. If your child has trouble moving back, please feel free to come up and physically bring your child back to your lap. Again, I'd like everyone to give a big round of applause for each child as Humpty is pulled off of his wall."

Developmental tip #3: "This rhyme is a great way to help your child build what is called 'self-regulation skills.' Social and emotional skills like learning to listen, to be patient, and to take turns will help your children do well in a classroom when they enter school. A good way to teach these skills is by giving children practice listening and taking turns and then reinforcing their successes with a smile, a clap, or a word of encouragement."

Remember to give positive reinforcement every time a child completes the requested task. Your phrases might include the following:

Good job!

You have been waiting so patiently! Now it is your turn.

That's fine. You don't need to pull Humpty off if you don't want to.

"One last time, let's say it all together."

> Humpty Dumpty sat on a wall.
> Humpty Dumpty had a great fall.
> All the king's horses
> And all the king's men
> Couldn't put Humpty together again.

Put the felt pieces in the tub.

Section 10: Closing Ritual

"And now for our ending song, put your feet out in front of you."

Display the visual representation for "Can You Kick with Two Feet?"

> Can you kick with two feet?
> Two feet, two feet?
> Can you kick with two feet?
> Kick, kick, kick, kick, kick.
>
> Can you clap with two hands?
> Two hands, two hands?
> Can you clap with two hands?
> Clap, clap, clap, clap, clap.
>
> Can you wiggle with ten fingers?
> Ten fingers, ten fingers?
> Can you wiggle with ten fingers?
> Wiggle, wiggle, wiggle, wiggle, wiggle.
>
> Can you sway from side to side?
> Side to side, side to side?
> Can you sway from side to side?
> Sway, sway, sway, sway, sway.
>
> Can you kiss with two lips?
> Two lips, two lips?
> Can you kiss with two lips?
> Kiss, kiss, kiss, kiss, kiss.
>
> Can you wave "bye-bye"?
> Bye-bye, bye-bye?
> Can you wave "bye-bye"?
> Bye-bye, bye-bye, bye-bye.

"It's time to say good-bye, but…"

> We're so happy,
> We're so happy,
> We're so happy that everyone is here.
> We're so happy,
> We're so happy,
> We're so happy that everyone is here.

"Good-bye, everyone. Thank you for coming. See you next week."

Put the cover on the storage tub. Remind everyone that they are welcome to stay and play after the program. Bring out toys for the children and engage in conversation with the parents.

PROGRAM 3 AT A GLANCE

Section 1: Welcoming comments
Introduce yourself and welcome everyone.
State expectations ("Children this age don't sit perfectly still").
Set guidelines ("If they come within this invisible circle, please come and get them").
Explain how it works ("I'm going to say things twice").

Section 2: Rhymes and reads

Section	Rhyme/read	Prop *(fill in the blanks)*
Opening	"Old Mother Goose"	Mother Goose felt figure
Opening rhyme	"Goosey, Goosey Gander"	Goose on Stairs felt figure
General rhyme	"Two Little Dickey Birds"	Two Little Dickey Birds felt figure
General rhyme	"Good Morning, Mrs. Perky Bird"	Bird puppet
Book to read aloud	*Stripes of All Types* by Susan Stockdale	*Stripes of All Types*
Tickle rhyme	"If You're Happy and You Know It"	
Puppet kisses	"The Eency Weency Spider"	Spider and Rain Cloud felt figures

Section 3: Body rhymes

Section	Rhyme/read	Prop
Head	"My Face Is Round"	
Head	"Eye Winker"	*Baby Faces*
Fingers	"Fingers Like to Wiggle Waggle"	Boy Wiggling Fingers felt figure
Hands	"Open Them, Shut Them"	
Tickle	"The Little Train Went up the Track"	Train felt figure
Knee bounces	"Seesaw, Scaradown"	
Knee bounces	"See the Ponies Galloping"	Horseshoe felt figure
Knee bounces	"Mother and Father and Uncle John"	
Knee bounces	"The Grand Old Duke of York"	Duke of York and Men of York felt figures

Section 4: The drum sequence

Children tap out names with syllables.		
Drum Sequence	"Rum Pum Pum"	Drum

Section 5: Stand-up / sit-down activities		
Stand-up action 1	"And We Walk" (DT1)	
Stand-up action 2	"The Hokey Pokey"	Three Children Dancing felt figure
Stand-up action 3	"Jack-in-the-Box"	
Stand-up action 4	"Handy Spandy"	
Section 6: Animal activities		
Book	"I Went to Visit the Farm One Day" (DT2)	*The Very Busy Spider*
Puppets	"When the [Cow] Gets Up in the Morning"	Farm animal puppets
Section 7: Musical instruments and scarves		
Chick-itas	"We Shake Our Shakers Together"	Maracas
Chick-itas	"Grandfather's Clock Goes Tick Tock"	Mother's Kitchen Clock felt figure
Chick-itas	"Shake Your Rattles like the Leaves"	Maracas
Chick-itas	"Shakers Away"	Maracas
Colored scarves	"Wind, Oh Wind"	Scarves
Colored scarves	"Peek-a-Boo"	Scarves
Colored scarves	"Oh Where, Oh Where Has My Little Head Gone?"	Scarves
Colored scarves	"This Is the Way We Wash Our Face"	Hands Washing felt figure
Colored scarves	"Scrunch Your Scarf into a Ball"	Scarves
Colored scarves	"Scarves Away"	Scarves
Section 8: Lullabies		
Lullaby	"ABC Song"	ABC felt figure
Section 9: Interactive rhymes		
Interactive rhyme	"Humpty Dumpty"	Humpty Dumpty and Wall felt figures
Section 10: Closing ritual		
Closing rhyme	"Can You Kick with Two Feet?"	
Closing rhyme	"We're So Happy"	

Developmental tip #1: Practice stopping when hearing the word *stop*.

Developmental tip #2: Discuss the value of sharing books without reading them.

Observations: _____

Everyone should be sitting in a circle surrounding the flannelboard/easel. Invite parents to put their children on their laps.

Section 1: Welcoming Comments

Be sure to smile and speak in a friendly and informal manner.

Section 2: Rhymes and Reads

Put a felt piece on flannelboard, show a book illustration, or use a stuffed animal goose.

> **Old Mother Goose when she wanted to wander**
> **Would fly through the air on her very fine gander.**

"Now take your hands and move them with me as we say the rhyme again."

Repeat.

Drop the visual representation of the rhyme into the tub.

Display the visual representation for "Goosey, Goosey Gander."

> **Goosey, goosey gander, where do you wander?**
> **Upstairs, and downstairs,**
> **and in my lady's chamber.**

Repeat.

Drop the visual representation of the rhyme into the tub.

Display the visual representation for "Two Little Dickey Birds."

> **Two little dickey birds sitting on a cloud.**
> **One named "Soft,"**
> **The other named "Loud."**
> **Fly away, Soft!**
> **Fly away, Loud!**
> **Come back, Soft!**
> **Come back, Loud!**

Repeat.

Drop the visual representation of the rhyme into the tub.

Display a bird puppet for "Good Morning, Mrs. Perky Bird."

"Let's welcome Mrs. Perky Bird! Good morning, Mrs. Perky Bird!"

> **Good morning, Mrs. Perky Bird, Perky Bird, Perky Bird.**
> **Good morning, Mrs. Perky Bird, where are you?**

"Fly" the bird puppet in the air.

> **I'm flying in the air, the air.**
> **The air, the air, the air, the air.**
> **I'm flying in the air, the air.**
> **And down to the ground.**

Bring the bird puppet down to the floor.

Repeat and drop the bird puppet into the storage tub.

Show the book cover of Stripes of All Types.

*"Here's the story **Stripes of All Types** by Susan Stockdale."*

Read the book aloud.

*"And that's **Stripes of All Types** by Susan Stockdale."*

Drop the book into the tub.

Display the visual representation for "If You're Happy and You Know It," and sing the first verse twice.

> **If you're happy and you know it, clap your hands.**
> **If you're happy and you know it, clap your hands.**
> **If you're happy and you know it and you really**
>   **want to show it,**
> **If you're happy and you know it, clap your hands.**

Drop the visual representation of the rhyme into the tub.

Display the visual representation for "The Eency Weency Spider."

> The eency weency spider went up the waterspout.
> Down came the rain and washed the spider out.
> Out came the sun and dried up all the rain.
> And the eency weency spider went up the spout again.

Bring out a spider puppet, and use a deep voice as he talks:

"Wait a minute! That's not fair. Everyone is always singing songs about my brother, Eency Weency, but no one ever sings a song about me, Great Big Spider. I am so sad I think I am going to cry. Boo-hoo-hoo."

Respond in your own voice: "Don't cry, Great Big Spider. We can sing a song about you too. Can't we boys and girls? *(Pause for reply.)* Okay! Spider, come here on top of the easel and watch us. Everyone let's get ready to use our great big hands *(spread your arms as wide as possible)* and our deep, deep, voices *(say this in a very deep voice)*."

"Here we go!" *(Sing with wide hand movements and deep voices.)*

> The great big spider went up the waterspout.
> Down came the rain and washed the spider out.
> Out came the sun and dried up all the rain.
> And the great big spider went up the spout again.

Spider puppet responds: "That was so wonderful! I loved hearing a song about me. Thank you so much. I think you all deserve a nice spider kiss for singing my song."

Walk around the circle with spider puppet, giving puppet kisses to children on their arms, legs, or cheeks. If a child seems afraid of the puppet, ask the adult if you can give them the spider kiss instead. You may want the puppet to occasionally remark "Yum!" or "Delicious!" After every child has gotten a spider kiss, have the spider give you a kiss too, and then drop him into the tub.

Section 3: Body Rhymes

Head:

Display the visual representation for "My Face Is Round."

> My face is round.
> I have two eyes,
> A nose,
> And a mouth!

Repeat.

Drop the visual representation of the rhyme into the tub.

Display the visual representation for "Eye Winker."

> Eye winker.
> Tom Tinker.
> Nose smeller.
> Mouth eater.
> Chin chopper, chin chopper, chin chopper…
> Guzzle whopper!

"Give your child a great big tickle in the tummy!"

Repeat.

Drop the visual representation of the rhyme into the tub.

Fingers:

Display the visual representation for "Fingers Like to Wiggle Waggle."

> Fingers like to wiggle waggle, wiggle waggle, wiggle waggle.
> Fingers like to wiggle waggle, way up high.
> Fingers like to wiggle waggle, wiggle waggle, wiggle waggle.
> Fingers like to wiggle waggle, way down low.
> Fingers like to wiggle waggle, wiggle waggle, wiggle waggle.
> Fingers like to wiggle waggle, on my knee. *(Place your fingers on your knee. Don't change your tone of voice.)*

Repeat using a much quicker pace.

Drop the visual representation of the rhyme into the tub.

Hands:

Display the visual representation for "Open Them, Shut Them."

> **Open them, shut them. Open them, shut them.**
> **Give a little clap.**
> **Open them, shut them, open them, shut them,**
> **Put them in your lap.**
> **Creep them, creep them, creep them, creep them,**
> **Right up to your chinny, chin, chin.**
> **Open up your little mouth**
> **But do not let them in!**

Repeat.

Drop the visual representation of the rhyme into the tub.

Tickle Rhymes:

Display the visual representation for "The Little Train."

> **The little train ran up the track.**

Walk fingers up one of the baby's arms.

> **It went "toot, toot,"**

Knock gently on the baby's head.

> **And then it ran back.**

Quickly tickle the baby's tummy.

Repeat going up baby's other arm. Then "Two Little Trains" up both arms.

Knee Bounces:

"For the knee bounces, sit up straight, and put your legs out straight in front of you. Place your child on your legs, positioning infants to face you so they can have eye-to-eye contact with you. Place children a bit older to face me so they can see the other children around the circle. Gently move your legs up and down."

Display the visual representation for "Seesaw, Scaradown."

Extend your feet in front of you. Raise and lower one knee and then the other.

> **Seesaw, Scaradown,**
> **This is the way to Londontown.**
> **One knee up and the other knee down,**
> **This is the way to Londontown.**
>
> **Seesaw, Scaradown,**
> **This is the way to _____ town.**
> **One knee up and the other knee down.**
> **This is the way to _____ town.**

Drop the visual representation of the rhyme into the tub.

Display the visual representation for "See the Ponies Galloping."

> **See the ponies galloping, galloping,**
> **Down the county lane.**
> **See the ponies galloping, galloping,**
> **Down the county lane.**
> **See the ponies coming home,**
> **All tired out! All tired out!**

Drop the visual representation of the rhyme into the tub.

Display the visual representation for "Mother and Father and Uncle John."

> **Mother and Father and Uncle John went to market, one by one.**
> **Mother fell off.**
> **And father fell off.**
> **But Uncle John went on and on and on and on and on...**

Repeat.

Drop the visual representation of the rhyme into the tub.

Display the visual representation for "The Grand Old Duke of York."

"Keep your children on your knees, facing me. For this song, when the men go up, bring your knees up;

when they go down, bring your legs back down to the floor; and for halfway up, just go halfway up."

> Oh, the Grand Old Duke of York. He had ten thousand men.
> He marched them up to the top of the hill,
> And he marched them down again.
> And when they were up, they were up.
> And when they were down, they were down.
> And when they were only halfway up,
> They were neither up nor down.

Repeat.

Drop the visual representation of the rhyme into the tub.

Section 4: The Drum Sequence

Take out a tambourine or hand drum.

> **Rum pum pum. This is my drum.** *(Tap to the beat.)*
> **Rum pum pum. This is my drum.**
> **My name is _____. What's your name?**
> *(Tap your name with syllables on the drum.)*

"Now I am going to go around the room. I'd like each child to tap his or her name on the drum with syllables. For instance, Joe would just be Joe, but Shaniqua would be Sha-ni-qua with three syllables. And parents, if your children are too young to tap out their names on their own, please take their hands and help them tap out their names with their own hands."

What's your name?

Hello.

Good morning.

Welcome, Jennifer.

Glad to see you, Finn.

"Everybody, stand up!"

Section 5: Stand-Up / Sit-Down Activities

"Make a circle! We are going to walk around the room together in this direction." *(Point in the direction you will be moving.)*

> And we walk, and we walk, and we walk, and we stop.
> And we walk, and we walk, and we walk, and we stop.
> And we walk, and we walk, and we walk, and we stop.
> And we all turn around—Woo!
>
> And we jump, and we jump, and we jump, and we stop.
> And we jump, and we jump, and we jump, and we stop.
> And we jump, and we jump, and we jump, and we stop.
> And we all turn around—Woo!

Developmental tip #1: "What word do all children need to learn?" *(Pause for an answer.)* "That's right, stop. Rather than waiting to teach stop in situations that are urgent or when you are angry, try playing games that teach stop in a loving manner. Then when you need your children to instantly respond to the stop command, they will be able to stop immediately without scared or negative feelings. To reinforce this, play freeze games together at home."

"It's time for the 'The Hokey Pokey'! Because young children don't know the difference between right and left, we're just going to say hand, foot, and head."

Put hand in.

> You put your hand in.

Take hand out.

> You take your hand out.

Put hand in.

> You put your hand in,

Shake it all about.

And you shake it all about.

Point index finger in each hand and sway slightly from side to side while shrugging shoulders.

You do the hokey pokey

Turn around.

And you turn yourself around.

Clap to the beat.

That's what it's all about.

Jump up.

Hey!

Repeat with your foot, head, backside, and whole self.

"Now let's pretend that we are jack-in-the-boxes. Follow the directions!"

**Let's climb into our boxes,
Push ourselves down,
And close the lid.
Now let's wind ourselves up…
And here we go.**

**Jack-in-the-box sitting so still, won't you come out?
Yes, I will!**

Jump out.

Repeat.

**Handy Spandy, sugar and candy, we all jump in.
Handy Spandy, sugar and candy, we all jump out.
Handy Spandy, sugar and candy, we all jump up.
Handy Spandy, sugar and candy, we all sit down.**

Sit down and put the tambourine or drum into the tub.

Section 6: Animal Activities

Show the cover of Eric Carle's The Very Busy Spider.

Developmental tip #2: **"You don't need to read books aloud in order to share them with your children. You can simply sing songs about the pictures and imitate the sounds the animals make. It's a great way to build a positive connection between your child and books. Naming the animals and imitating the sounds they make is fun, and it increases your children's knowledge of the world around them."**

"Everyone, please help me sing this song about the sounds the animals make."

Sing using the animal illustrations.

**I went to visit the farm one day.
I saw a horse across the way.
And what do you think the horse did say?
"Neigh, neigh, neigh."**

**I went to visit the farm one day.
I saw a cow across the way.
And what do you think the cow did say?
"Moo, moo, moo."**

**I went to visit the farm one day.
I saw a sheep across the way.
And what do you think the sheep did say?
"Baa, baa, baa."**

Close the book and put it into the tub.

Lift up your tote bag with farm animal puppets inside. Show one part of an animal peeking over the front tip of the tote bag. This could be an ear, a tail, or a foot.

"Oh, look what I have here! Who is inside this bag?"

Give children time to guess which animal you have in the bag. Then pull it out.

"It's a hen. A hen who says, 'Cluck!'"

**When the hen gets up in the morning,
She always says, "Cluck."
When the hen gets up in the morning,
She says, "Cluck, cluck."**

Place animals in the tub after each verse.

> When the cow gets up in the morning,
> She always says, "Moo."
> When the cow gets up in the morning,
> She says, "Moo, moo."
>
> When the pig gets up in the morning,
> She always says, "Oink."
> When the pig gets up in the morning,
> She says, "Oink, oink."

Section 7: Musical Instruments and Scarves

Walk around the circle with a tote bag full of shakers. Hand one shaker to each child and adult. If the shakers are different colors, you can name the colors as you distribute them.

Shakers

> We shake our shakers together,
> We shake our shakers together.
> We shake our shakers together.
> Because it's fun to do.

Repeat.

> Shake them up high.
> Shake them down low.
> Shake them in the middle!

Display the visual representation for "Grandfather's Clock Goes Tick Tock."

> Grandfather's clock goes "Tick tock, tick tock, tick tock."
> Mother's kitchen clock goes "Tick tock, tick tock, tick tock, tick tock."
> Brother's little watch goes "Tick tick tick tick, tick tick tick tick, tick tick tick tick, stop!"

Repeat.

Drop the visual representation into the tub.

Display the visual representation for "Shake Your Rattles."

> Shake your rattles, shake your rattles,
> Like the leaves.
> That are growing, that are growing,
> on the trees.
> Shake them high, and
> Shake them low.
> 'Round about
> And to and fro.
> Shake your rattles, shake your rattles,
> Like the leaves.

Repeat.

Drop the visual representation into the tub.

> Shake them up high.
> Shake them down low.
> Shake them in the middle!
>
> Shakers away, shakers away, put your shakers away today.
> Shakers away, shakers away, put your shakers away today.

Repeat until all the shakers have been collected.

Scarves

Walk around the circle with the scarf-filled tote bag. Hand each child and adult a scarf. You may want to name the color of the scarf you are handing out.

> Wind, oh wind, oh wind, I say.
> What are you blowing away today?
> Scarves, oh scarves, oh scarves, I say.
> I am blowing the scarves away.

Display the visual representation for "Peek-a-Boo."

Place the scarf over your head. Sing the first verse of this song. Then walk over to the child sitting closest to you in the circle and sing a line of the song while looking directly into the child's eyes and playing peek-a-boo. Move to the next child and sing the next line, doing the same thing. Continue all the way around the circle until all children have had a chance to play peek-a-boo with you.

> Peek-a-boo, I see you, I see you hiding there.
> Peek-a-boo, I see you, I see you smiling there.
>   (Peek-a-boo!)

Repeat as much as needed.

Drop the visual representation into the tub.

Display the visual representation for "Oh Where, Oh Where Has My Little Head Gone?" and put your scarf over your head.

> Oh where, oh where has my little head gone?
>   Oh where, oh where can it be?
> Oh where, oh where has my little head gone?
>   Oh where, oh where can it be?

One…two…three…Here it is!

Repeat using your knees or other body parts.

Drop the visual representation into the tub.

Display the visual representation for "This Is the Way We Wash Our Belly."

"Scrunch up your scarves and pretend that they are washcloths."

> This is the way we wash our belly, wash our belly, wash our belly.
> This is the way we wash our belly, so early in the morning.

(Wash hands, neck, knees, etc.)

Drop the visual representation into the tub.

"Now take your scarves and squish them into a tiny ball."

> Scrunch your scarf into a ball.
> Make it very, very small.

Recite rather than sing the following lines.

On the count of three, throw them in the air, and watch all the beautiful colors fly down.

One, two, three, throw!

Throw the scarves into the air; watch them float down.

> Wind, oh wind, oh wind, I say.
> What are you blowing away today?
> Scarves, oh scarves, oh scarves, I say.
> I am blowing the scarves away.

Go directly into the cleanup song, walking around the circle holding the tote bag open in front of each child (and adult, if necessary). Sing as the children put their scarves into the bag. In between verses, say "Thank you."

> Scarves away, scarves away,
> Put your scarves away today.

Drop the bag with scarves into the storage tub.

Section 8: Lullabies

"Now it's lullaby time. I've mentioned that any song can be a lullaby as long as it is sung softly and slowly. Hold your child closely and rock gently from side to side while we sing the "ABC Song" as our lullaby for today."

Display the visual representation for "ABC Song."

> A B C D E F G.
> H I J K L M N O P.
> Q R S T U V…W X Y and Z.
> Now I've learned my ABCs.
> Next time won't you sing with me?

Repeat.

Drop the visual representation into the tub.

Section 9: Interactive Rhymes

Display the visual representation for "Humpty Dumpty"—the egg and his wall.

> Humpty Dumpty sat on a wall.
> Humpty Dumpty had a great fall.

All the king's horses
And all the king's men
Couldn't put Humpty together again.

"Now I'd like to invite each child to have a turn to come up and pull Humpty off of the wall. If your child is too young to do it on his own, please take his hand gently and use his hand to pull Humpty off. Because everyone gets one turn, your child should go back to his or her seat when done, making room for other children to come up. When a child has trouble leaving the flannelboard, please come up and physically help him or her back to your lap. Again, let's give a big round of applause for each child as they pull Humpty off his wall."

Remember to give positive reinforcement every time a child completes the requested task. Your phrases might include the following:

Good job!

You have been waiting so patiently! Now it is your turn.

That's fine. You don't need to pull Humpty off if you don't want to.

"One last time, let's say it all together."

Humpty Dumpty sat on a wall.
Humpty Dumpty had a great fall.
All the king's horses
And all the king's men.
Couldn't put Humpty together again.

Put the felt pieces in the tub.

Section 10: Closing Ritual

"And now for our ending song, put your feet out in front of you."

Display the visual representation for "Can You Kick with Two Feet?"

Can you kick with two feet?
Two feet, two feet?
Can you kick with two feet?
Kick, kick, kick, kick, kick.

Can you clap with two hands?
Two hands, two hands?
Can you clap with two hands?
Clap, clap, clap, clap, clap.

Can you wiggle with ten fingers?
Ten fingers, ten fingers?
Can you wiggle with ten fingers?
Wiggle, wiggle, wiggle, wiggle, wiggle.

Can you sway from side to side?
Side to side, side to side?
Can you sway from side to side?
Sway, sway, sway, sway, sway.

Can you kiss with two lips?
Two lips, two lips?
Can you kiss with two lips?
Kiss, kiss, kiss, kiss, kiss.

Can you wave "bye-bye"?
Bye-bye, bye-bye?
Can you wave "bye-bye"?
Bye-bye, bye-bye, bye-bye.

"It's time to say good-bye, but…"

We're so happy,
We're so happy,
We're so happy that everyone is here.
We're so happy,
We're so happy,
We're so happy that everyone is here.

"Good-bye, everyone. Thank you for coming. See you next week."

Drop the visual representation into the tub.

Put the cover on the storage tub. Remind everyone that they are welcome to stay and play after the program. Bring out toys for the children and engage in conversation with the parents.

Program 4

PROGRAM 4 AT A GLANCE

Section 1: Welcoming comments
Introduce yourself and welcome everyone.
State expectations ("Children this age don't sit perfectly still").
Set guidelines ("If they come within this invisible circle, please come and get them").
Explain how it works ("I'm going to say things twice").

Section 2: Rhymes and reads		
Section	**Rhyme/read**	**Prop** *(fill in the blanks)*
Opening	"Old Mother Goose"	Mother Goose felt figure
Opening rhyme	"Two Little Dickey Birds"	Two Little Dickey Birds felt figure
General rhyme	"Zoom, Zoom, Zoom"	Rocket Ship felt figure
Book to read aloud	*Opposite Surprise* by Agnese Baruzzi	*Opposite Surprise*
General rhyme	"I Hear Thunder"	Rain Cloud felt figure
General rhyme	"Five Fat Sausages"	Sausage and Pan felt figures

Section 3: Body rhymes		
Head	"My Face Is Round"	
Head	"Knock on the Door"	Door felt figure
Tickle	"The Garden Snail"	
Hands	"Open Them, Shut Them"	
Hands	"If You're Happy and You Know It"	
Knee bounces	"See the Ponies Galloping"	
Knee bounces	"Mother and Father and Uncle John" (DT1)	
Knee bounces	"The Grand Old Duke of York"	Duke of York and Men of York felt figures

Section 4: The drum sequence		
Children tap out names with syllables.		
Drum sequence	"Rum Pum Pum"	Drum

Section 5: Stand-up / sit-down activities		
Stand-up action 1	"The Hokey Pokey"	Three Children Dancing felt figure
Stand-up action 2	"And We Walk"	
Stand-up action 3	"I'm a Little Teapot"	
Stand-up action 4	"Handy Spandy"	
Section 6: Animal activities		
Book	"I Went to Visit the Farm One Day"	*The Very Busy Spider*
Puppets	"When the [Cow] Gets Up in the Morning"	Farm animal puppets
Puppet kisses	"The Eency Weency Spider"	Spider felt figure, Spider puppet
Section 7: Musical instruments and scarves		
Shakers	"We Shake Our Shakers Together"	Maracas
Shakers	"Hickory Dickory Dock"	Mouse felt figure
Shakers	"I'm Driving in My Car"	
Shakers	"Grandfather's Clock Goes Tick Tock"	Grandfather's Clock, Mother's Kitchen Clock, Brother's Watch felt figures
Shakers	"Shakers Away"	
Colored scarves	"Wind, Oh Wind"	
Colored scarves	"Oh Where, Oh Where Has My Little Head Gone?"	
Colored scarves	Wave scarves	Recorded music
Colored scarves	"Wind, Oh Wind" / "Scarves Away"	
Section 8: Lullabies		
Lullaby	"ABC Song"	ABC felt figure
Section 9: Interactive rhymes		
Interactive rhyme	"Jack Be Nimble"	Jill Jumping felt figure
Section 10: Closing ritual		
Closing rhyme	"Can You Kick with Two Feet?" (DT2)	
Closing rhyme	"We're So Happy"	

Developmental tip #1: Connect words with movements via context.

Developmental tip #2: Discuss the benefits of naming body parts.

Observations: _____

Everyone should be sitting in a circle surrounding the flannelboard/easel. Invite parents to put their children on their laps.

Section 1: Welcoming Comments

Be sure to smile and speak in a friendly and informal manner.

Section 2: Rhymes and Reads

Put a felt piece on flannelboard, show a book illustration, or use a stuffed animal goose.

> **Old Mother Goose when she wanted to wander
> Would fly through the air on her very fine gander.**

Repeat.

Drop the rhyme's visual representation into the tub.

Display the visual representation for "Two Little Dickey Birds."

> **Two little dickey birds sitting on a cloud.
> One named "Soft,"
> The other named "Loud."
> Fly away, Soft!
> Fly away, Loud!
> Come back, Soft!
> Come back, Loud!**

Repeat.

Drop the visual representation of the rhyme into the tub.

Display the visual representation for "Zoom, Zoom, Zoom."

Rub hands together with flat palms.

> **Zoom, zoom, zoom, we're going to the moon.
> Zoom, zoom, zoom, we're going very soon.**

Bend your elbow to lift one arm; fingers from the other hand "crawl" up the lifted arm.

> **If you want to take a trip,
> Climb aboard my rocket ship.**

Rub hands together.

> **Zoom, zoom, zoom, we're going to the moon.**

Hold up fingers and count down.

> **Five, four, three, two, one…blastoff!**

Throw your empty hands into the sky or lift a baby into the air.

> **Blastoff!**

Repeat with variations like "Fun, fun, fun, we're going to the sun" and "Far, far, far, we're going to the stars."

Drop the visual representation of the rhyme into the tub.

Show the book cover of Opposite Surprise.

"Here's the story of Opposite Surprise by Agnese Baruzzi."

Read the book aloud.

"And that's Opposite Surprise by Agnese Baruzzi."

Drop the book into the tub.

Display the visual representation for "I Hear Thunder." You may want to take out an umbrella as well!

> **I hear thunder. I hear thunder.
> Hark, don't you? Hark, don't you?
> Pitter, patter raindrops. Pitter, patter raindrops.
> I'm wet through, I'm wet through.**

Repeat.

Drop the visual representation of the rhyme into the tub.

Display the visual representation for "Five Fat Sausages." If you have older children, start with five sausages. With only very young children, start with three sausages.

> **Five fat sausages, frying in a pan.
> All a sudden,
> One went bang.**

Four fat sausages…
Three fat sausages…
Two fat sausages…
One fat sausage frying in a pan.

All a sudden, (spread arms out) it went bang.
And there were no sausages left!

Drop the visual representation of the rhyme into the tub.

Section 3: Body Rhymes

Head:

Display the visual representation for "My Face Is Round."

**My face is round.
I have two eyes,
A nose,
And a mouth!**

Repeat.

Drop the visual representation of the rhyme into the tub.

Display the visual representation for "Knock on the Door."

**Knock on the door.
Pull the bell.
Peek in!
Lift up the latch.
Walk in.
Take a chair.
Sit down.
"How do you do, Mrs. Brown?"**

Repeat.

Drop the visual representation of the rhyme into the tub.

Tickle:

Display the visual representation for "The Garden Snail."

Slowly walk your fingers up the baby's body from right toe to head.

Slowly, slowly, very slowly creeps the garden snail.

Slowly walk your fingers up the baby's body from left toe to head.

Slowly, slowly, very slowly, up the garden rail.

Repeat the same actions quickly.

Quickly, quickly, very quickly goes the little mouse.

End with a tummy tickle.

Quickly, quickly, very quickly, all around the house!

Repeat.

Drop the visual representation of the rhyme into the tub.

Hands:

Display the visual representation for "Open Them, Shut Them."

**Open them, shut them. Open them, shut them.
Give a little clap.
Open them, shut them, open them, shut them,
Put them in your lap.
Creep them, creep them, creep them, creep them,
Right up to your chinny, chin, chin.
Open up your little mouth
But do not let them in!**

Repeat.

Drop the visual representation of the rhyme into the tub.

Display the visual representation for "If You're Happy and You Know It," and sing the first verse twice.

**If you're happy and you know it, clap your hands.
If you're happy and you know it, clap your hands.
If you're happy and you know it and you really
    want to show it,
If you're happy and you know it, clap your hands.**

Drop the visual representation of the rhyme into the tub.

Knee Bounces:

"**For the knee bounces, sit up and put your legs out straight in front of you. Place your child on your legs, positioning infants so they can have eye-to-eye contact with you. Place babies and older children facing the circle so they can see the other children.**"

Display the visual representation for "See the Ponies Galloping."

> See the ponies galloping, galloping,
> Down the county lane.
> See the ponies galloping, galloping,
> Down the county lane.
> See the ponies coming home,
> All tired out! All tired out!

Repeat.

Drop the visual representation of the rhyme into the tub.

Display the visual representation for "Mother and Father and Uncle John."

Developmental tip #1: "**By repeating 'Mother and Father and Uncle John' each week, even the youngest children learn to connect the words with the leaning motions. They often correctly anticipate the upcoming lean and may even start leaning before mother falls off. This ability to connect words in context with knowing how to respond is a beginning literacy skill. It also means that your child is listening and following the unspoken directions!**"

> Mother and Father and Uncle John went to market,
>   one by one.
> Mother fell off.
> And father fell off.
> But Uncle John went on and on and on and on
>   and on.

Repeat.

Drop the visual representation of the rhyme into the tub.

Display the visual representation for "The Grand Old Duke of York."

"**Keep your children on your knees facing me. Bring your knees up and down according to the words of the song.**"

> Oh, the Grand Old Duke of York. He had ten
>   thousand men.
> He marched them up to the top of the hill,
> And he marched them down again.
> And when they were up, they were up.
> And when they were down, they were down.
> And when they were only halfway up,
> They were neither up nor down.

Repeat.

Drop the visual representation of the rhyme into the tub.

Section 4: The Drum Sequence

Take out a tambourine or hand drum

> **Rum pum pum. This is my drum.** *(Tap to the beat.)*
> **Rum pum pum. This is my drum.**
> **My name is _____. What's your name?**
>   *(Tap your name with syllables on the drum.)*

"Now I am going to go around the room. I'd like each child to tap his or her name on the drum with syllables. For instance, Joe would just be Joe, but Shaniqua would be Sha-ni-qua with three syllables. And parents, if your children are too young to tap out their names on their own, please take their hands and help them tap out their names with their own hands."

Follow the same routine from previous weeks. Put the tambourine or drum into the tub.

Section 5: Stand-Up / Sit-Down Activities

"**Make a circle!**"

"It's time for the 'The Hokey Pokey'! Because young children don't know the difference between 'right' and 'left,' we're just going to say 'hand, foot, and head.'"

> You put your hand in.
> You take your hand out.
> You put your hand in,
> And you shake it all about.
> You do the hokey pokey
> And you turn yourself around.
> That's what it's all about.
> Hey!

Repeat with your foot, head, backside, and whole self.

"We are going to march around the room together in this direction." *(Point in the direction you will be moving.)*

> And we march, and we march, and we march, and we stop.
> And we march, and we march, and we march, and we stop.
> And we march, and we march, and we march, and we stop.
> And we all turn around—Woo!
> And we tiptoe, and we tiptoe, and we tiptoe, and we stop.
> And we tiptoe, and we tiptoe, and we tiptoe, and we stop.
> And we tiptoe, and we tiptoe, and we tiptoe, and we stop.
> And we all turn around—Woo!

"Now let's use our imaginations and pretend that we are teapots. Follow the directions!"

> I'm a little teapot short and stout.
> Here is my handle, here is my spout.
> When I get all steamed up, hear me shout,
> "Just tip me over and pour me out."

Repeat.

> Handy Spandy, sugar and candy, we all jump in.
> Handy Spandy, sugar and candy, we all jump out.
> Handy Spandy, sugar and candy, we all jump up.
> Handy Spandy, sugar and candy, we all sit down.

Sit down.

Section 6: Animal Activities

Show the cover of Eric Carle's The Very Busy Spider.

"Everyone, please help me sing this song about the sounds the animals make."

Sing using the animal illustrations.

> I went to visit the farm one day.
> I saw a horse across the way.
> And what do you think the horse did say?
> "Neigh, neigh, neigh."

Repeat with other animal illustrations and sounds.

Close the book and put it into the tub.

Lift up your tote bag with farm animal puppets inside. Show one part of an animal peeking over the front tip of the tote bag. This could be an ear, a tail, or a foot.

"Oh, look what I have here! Who is inside this bag?"

Give children time to guess which animal you have in the bag. Then pull it out.

"It's a cow. A cow who says 'Moo!'"

> When the cow gets up in the morning,
> She always says, "Moo."
> When the cow gets up in the morning,
> She says, "Moo, moo."

Repeat with other animal puppets and sounds.

Display the visual representation for "The Eency Weency Spider."

> The eency weency spider went up the waterspout.
> Down came the rain and washed the spider out
> Out came the sun and dried up all the rain.
> And the eency weency spider went up the spout again.

Bring out spider puppet and use a deep voice as he talks:

"Wait a minute! That's not fair. Everyone is always singing songs about my brother, Eency Weency, but no one ever sings a song about me, Great Big Spider. I am so sad I think I am going to cry. Boo-hoo-hoo."

Respond in your own voice: "Don't cry, Great Big Spider. We can sing a song about you too. Can't we boys and girls? *(Pause for reply.)* Okay! Spider, come here on top of the easel and watch us. Everyone let's get ready to use our great big hands *(spread your arms as wide as possible)* and our deep, deep, voices *(say this in a very deep voice).*"

"Here we go!" *(Sing with wide hand movements and deep voices.)*

> The great big spider went up the waterspout.
> Down came the rain and washed the spider out
> Out came the sun and dried up all the rain.
> And the great big spider went up the spout again.

Spider puppet responds: "That was so wonderful! I loved hearing a song about me. Thank you so much. I think you all deserve a nice spider kiss for singing my song."

Walk around the circle with the puppet, giving puppet kisses to children on their arms, legs, or cheeks. If a child seems afraid of the puppet, ask the adult if you can give them the spider kiss instead. You may want the puppet to occasionally remark "Yum!" or "Delicious!" After every child has gotten a spider kiss, have the spider give you a kiss too, and then drop him into the tub.

Section 7: Musical Instruments and Scarves

Walk around the circle with a tote bag full of shakers. Hand one shaker to each child and adult. If the shakers are different colors, you can name the colors as you are passing them out.

Shakers

> We shake our shakers together,
> We shake our shakers together.
> We shake our shakers together.
> Because it's fun to do.

Repeat.

> Shake them up high.
> Shake them down low.
> Shake them in the middle!

Display the visual representation for "Hickory Dickory Dock."

> Hickory dickory dock,
> The mouse ran up the clock.
> The clock struck one,
> And down she run.
> Hickory dickory dock.

Repeat.

Drop the visual representation into the tub.

Display the visual representation for "I'm Driving in My Car."

> I'm driving in my car, I'm driving in my car,
> Beep beep, toot toot, I'm driving in my car.
> I'm driving very slowly…
> I'm driving very fast…
> The lights are turning red, and I must stop my car…
> The lights are turning green, and I can go again…

Drop the visual representation into the tub.

Display the visual representation for "Grandfather's Clock Goes Tick Tock."

> Grandfather's clock goes "Tick tock, tick tock, tick tock."
> Mother's kitchen clock goes "Tick tock, tick tock, tick tock, tick tock."
> Brother's little watch goes "Tick tick tick tick, tick tick tick tick, tick tick tick tick, Stop!"

Repeat.

Drop the visual representation into the tub.

Shake them up high.
Shake them down low.
Shake them in the middle!

Shakers away, shakers away,
    put your shakers away today.
Shakers away, shakers away,
    put your shakers away today.

Repeat until all the shakers have been collected.

Scarves

Walk around the circle with the scarf-filled tote bag. Hand each child and adult a scarf. You may want to name the color of the scarf you are handing out.

Display the visual representation for "Wind, Oh Wind."

Wind, oh wind, oh wind, I say.
What are you blowing away today?
Scarves, oh scarves, oh scarves, I say.
I am blowing the scarves away.

Drop the visual representation into the tub.

Display the visual representation for "Oh Where, Oh Where Has My Little Head Gone," and put your scarf over your head.

Oh where, oh where has my little head gone? Oh where, oh where can it be?
Oh where, oh where has my little head gone? Oh where, oh where can it be?

One…two…three… (pull scarf off) Here it is!

Continue covering different body parts such as a hand, knee, and leg.

Drop the visual representation into the tub.

Do some creative movement with the scarves. Show a photo or use a felt piece like a snake and have your scarf slither on the ground. Then show a photo of a butterfly and have your scarf flutter. Try imitating a jumping kangaroo with your scarf.

After a maximum of five animals, play recorded music and wave your scarves to the music. Watch to see what the children are doing with the scarves and follow their lead.

Help everyone transition into cleanup by singing that well-known song…

Wind, oh wind, oh wind, I say.
What are you blowing away today?
Scarves, oh scarves, oh scarves, I say.
I am blowing the scarves away.

Go directly into the cleanup song.

Scarves away, scarves away,
Put your scarves away today.

Drop the bag with scarves into the storage tub.

Section 8: Lullabies

"Now it's lullaby time. Hold your child closely and rock gently from side to side while we sing."

Display the visual representation for "ABC Song."

A B C D E F G.
H I J K L M N O P.
Q R S T U V…W X Y and Z.
Now I've learned my ABCs.
Next time won't you sing with me?

Repeat.

Drop the visual representation into the tub.

Section 9: Interactive Rhymes

Display the visual representation for "Jack Be Nimble."

Place a candlestick on the floor. Invite children to take turns standing in front of the candlestick. When they hear the word jump, *they should jump over the candlestick.*

> **Jack be nimble. Jack be quick.**
> **Jack jump over the candlestick.**

Invite children to turn around and recite the female version of the rhyme. Again, ask them to jump over the candlestick when they hear jump.

> **Jill be nimble. Jill be quick.**
> **Jill jump over the candlestick.**

Remember to give positive reinforcement every time a child completes the requested task. Your phrases might include:

Good job!

You have been waiting so patiently! Now it is your turn.

Repeat until each child has had a turn. Put the candlestick into the tub.

Section 10: Closing Ritual

Display the visual representation for "Can You Kick with Two Feet?"

Developmental tip #2: "**This song shows children how parts of the body can develop movement. They learn that feet kick, hands clap, and fingers wiggle. Children who enter kindergarten knowing more words usually have an easier time learning how to read. Being able to name their body parts also helps them tell you if something is hurting and needs attention.**"

Can you kick with two feet?
Two feet, two feet?
Can you kick with two feet?
Kick, kick, kick, kick, kick.

Can you clap with two hands?...
Can you wiggle with ten fingers?...
Can you sway from side to side?...
Can you kiss with two lips?...
Can you wave "Bye-bye"?...

"It's time to say good-bye, but..."

> We're so happy,
> We're so happy,
> We're so happy that everyone is here.

> We're so happy,
> We're so happy,
> We're so happy that everyone is here.

"Good-bye, everyone. Thank you for coming. See you next week."

Drop the visual representation into the tub.

Put the cover on the storage tub. Remind everyone that they are welcome to stay and play after the program. Bring out toys for the children and engage in conversation with the parents.

Program 5

PROGRAM 5 AT A GLANCE

Section 1: Welcoming comments
Introduce yourself and welcome everyone.
State expectations ("Children this age don't sit perfectly still").
Set guidelines ("If they come within this invisible circle, please come and get them").
Explain how it works ("I'm going to say things twice").

Section 2: Rhymes and reads		
Section	**Rhyme/read**	**Prop** *(fill in the blanks)*
Opening	"Old Mother Goose"	Mother Goose felt figure
Puppet kisses	"Good Morning, Mrs. Perky Bird"	Bird puppet
General rhyme	"Two Little Monkeys"	Monkey puppets or Bed felt figure
General rhyme	"Five Fat Sausages"	Sausage and Pan felt figures
Book to read aloud	*Zoom, Zoom, Baby* by Karen Katz	*Zoom, Zoom, Baby*
General rhyme	"I Hear Thunder"	*In the Rain* by Elizabeth Spurr
General rhyme	"We Hit the Floor Together"	Alien felt figure

Section 3: Body rhymes		
Head	"My Face Is Round"	Book illustration
Fingers	"This Little Piggy"	Pig felt figure
Hands	"If You're Happy and You Know It"	Illustration from *Sing with Me!* by Naoko Stoop
Hands	"Zoom, Zoom, Zoom"	Rocket Ship felt figure
Knee bounces	"Row, Row, Row Your Boat"	Rowboat felt figure
Knee bounces	"Humpty Dumpty"	Use a book illustration
Knee bounces	"The Grand Old Duke of York"	Duke of York and Men of York felt figures
Feet/toes	"Shoe the Little Horse"	Horseshoe felt figure

Section 4: The drum sequence		
Children tap out names with syllables.		
Drum sequence	"Rum Pum Pum"	Drum or tambourine

Section 5: Stand-up / sit-down activities

Stand-up action 1	Freeze game: "We're Marching to the Drum"	Drum or tambourine
Stand-up action 2	"I'm a Little Teapot"	
Stand-up action 3	"Jack-in-the-Box"	Jack-in-the-Box prop
Stand-up action 4	"Handy Spandy"	
Section 6: Animal activities		
Book	"I Went to Visit the Farm One Day"	*The Very Busy Spider*
Puppets	"When the [Cow] Gets Up in the Morning"	Farm animal puppets
Puppets	"Hickory Dickory Dare" (DT1)	Pig puppet or Pig felt figure
Section 7: Musical instruments and scarves		
Bells	"We Ring Our Bells Together"	Bells
Bells	"Hickory Dickory Dock"	Mouse felt figure; Grandfather's Clock felt figure
Bells	"Ring Them Up High" (DT2)	Bells
Bells	"Jack-in-the-Box"	Picture from the Internet
Bells	"Bells Away"	Bells
Colored scarves	"Wind, Oh Wind"	Scarves
Colored scarves	"Peek-a-Boo"	Scarves
Colored scarves	"The Wheels on the Bus"	Bus felt figure
Colored scarves	"Scrunch Your Scarf into a Ball"	Scarves
Colored scarves	"Scarves Away"	Scarves
Section 8: Lullabies		
Lullaby	"You Are My Sunshine"	Sun felt figure
Section 9: Interactive rhymes		
Interactive rhyme	"Humpty Dumpty"	Humpty Dumpty and Wall felt figures
Section 10: Closing ritual		
Closing rhyme	"Can You Kick with Two Feet?"	
Closing rhyme	"We're So Happy"	

Developmental tip #1: Positive self-esteem leads to willingness to try.

Developmental tip #2: Use high, low, and middle for word understanding.

Observations: _____

Everyone should be sitting in a circle surrounding the flannelboard/easel. Invite parents to put their children on their laps.

Section 1: Welcoming Comments

Be sure to smile and speak in a friendly and informal manner.

Section 2: Rhymes and Reads

Put a felt piece on flannelboard, show a book illustration, or use a stuffed animal goose.

> **Old Mother Goose when she wanted to wander**
> **Would fly through the air on her very fine gander.**

Repeat.

Drop the visual representation of the rhyme into the tub.

Display a bird puppet for "Good Morning, Mrs. Perky Bird."

"Here's Mrs. Perky Bird! Good morning, Mrs. Perky Bird!"

> **Good morning, Mrs. Perky Bird, Perky Bird, Perky Bird.**
> **Good morning, Mrs. Perky Bird, where are you?**

"Fly" the bird puppet around the circle, giving puppet kisses to the children.

> **I'm flying in the air, the air.**
> **The air, the air, the air, the air.**
> **I'm flying in the air, the air.**
> **And down to the ground.**

Bring the bird puppet down to the floor. Repeat singing until each child has gotten a puppet kiss.

Drop the bird puppet into the storage tub.

Display the visual representation for "Two Little Monkeys."

> **Two little monkeys jumping on the bed.**
> **Two little monkeys jumping on the bed.**
> **One fell off and bumped his head.**
> **The other called the doctor, and the doctor said,**
> **"No more monkeys jumping on the bed."**

Repeat.

Drop the visual representation into the storage tub.

Display the visual representation for "Five Fat Sausages." If you have older children, start with five sausages. With only very young children, start with three sausages.

> **Five fat sausages, frying in a pan.**
> **All a sudden,**
> **One went bang.**
>
> **Four fat sausages…**
> **Three fat sausages…**
> **Two fat sausages…**
> **One fat sausage frying in a pan.**
>
> **All a sudden, (spread arms out) it went bang.**
> **And there were no sausages left!**

Drop the visual representation of the rhyme into the tub.

Show the book cover of Zoom, Zoom Baby.

"Here's the story of *Zoom, Zoom, Baby* by Karen Katz."

Read the book aloud.

"And that's *Zoom, Zoom, Baby* by Karen Katz."

Drop the book into the tub.

Display the visual representation for "I Hear Thunder." Try showing the cover of In the Rain *by Elizabeth Spurr (Peachtree, 2018). You may want to take out an umbrella as well!*

> **I hear thunder. I hear thunder.**
> **Hark, don't you? Hark, don't you?**
> **Pitter, patter raindrops. Pitter, patter raindrops.**
> **I'm wet through, I'm wet through.**

Repeat.

Drop the visual representation of the rhyme into the tub.

Display the visual representation for "We Hit the Floor Together."

> **We hit the floor together.**
> **We hit the floor together,**
> **We hit the floor together.**
> **Because it's fun to do!**
>
> **We hit the floor together.**
> **We hit the floor together.**
> **We hit the floor together.**
> **Because it's fun to do!**
>
> **We smack our knees together…**
> **We clap our hands…**
> **We wave our arms…**
> **We wiggle our fingers…**
> **We sway from side to side…**
> **We all wave hello…**

Drop the visual representation of the rhyme into the tub.

Section 3: Body Rhymes

Head:

Display a visual representation for "My Face Is Round."

> **My face is round.**
> **I have two eyes,**
> **A nose,**
> **And a mouth!**

Repeat.

Drop the visual representation of the rhyme into the tub.

Fingers:

Display the visual representation for "This Little Piggy."

> **This little piggy went to market,**
> **This little piggy stayed home.**
> **This little piggy had roast beef.**
> **This little piggy had none.**
> **And this little piggy cried,**
> **Wee wee wee wee—all the way home!**

Repeat.

Drop the visual representation of the rhyme into the tub.

Hands:

Display the visual representation for "If You're Happy and You Know It," and sing the first verse twice. Naoko Stoop's illustration in Sing with Me *(Henry Holt, 2016) is lovely!*

> **If you're happy and you know it, clap your hands.**
> **If you're happy and you know it, clap your hands.**
> **If you're happy and you know it and you really**
> **   want to show it,**
> **If you're happy and you know it, clap your hands.**

Drop the visual representation of the rhyme into the tub.

Display the visual representation for "Zoom, Zoom, Zoom."

> **Zoom, zoom, zoom, we're going to the moon.**
> **Zoom, zoom, zoom, we're going very soon.**
> **If you want to take a trip,**
> **Climb aboard my rocket ship.**
> **Zoom, zoom, zoom, we're going to the moon.**
> **Five, four, three, two, one . . .**
> **Blastoff!**

Drop the visual representation of the rhyme into the tub.

Knee Bounces:

Display the visual representation for "Row, Row, Row Your Boat."

> **Row, row, row your boat, gently down the stream.**
> **Merrily, merrily, merrily, merrily, life is but a dream.**

"Put your child on your outstretched legs facing you. Hold each hand in one of your hands. Lean back and forth, pulling in a gentle rocking motion. Sing at normal speed, then very quickly, then slowly, and then back at normal speed. Match your movements to the tempo."

Repeat.

Drop the visual representation of the rhyme into the tub.

Display a different visual representation for "Humpty Dumpty" than your typical one. Use an illustration! Do this as a knee bounce. Bounce legs, "fall back," and continue bouncing.

> **Humpty Dumpty sat on a wall.**

Lean gently from side to side.

> **Humpty Dumpty had a great fall…**

Fall over onto one side.

> **All the king's horses and all the king's men**

Bounce your legs up and down rapidly.

> **Couldn't put Humpty together again.**

Drop the visual representation of Humpty Dumpty into the tub.

Display the visual representation for "The Grand Old Duke of York."

> **Oh, the Grand Old Duke of York. He had ten thousand men.**
> **He marched them up to the top of the hill,**
> **And he marched them down again.**
> **And when they were up, they were up.**
> **And when they were down, they were down.**
> **And when they were only halfway up,**
> **They were neither up nor down.**

Repeat.

Drop the visual representation of the rhyme into the tub.

Foot Patting:

Display the visual representation for "Shoe the Little Horse."

> **Shoe the little horse.**
> **Shoe the little mare.**
> **But let the little colt run bare, bare, bare!**

Drop the visual representation of the rhyme into the tub.

Section 4: The Drum Sequence

Take out a tambourine or hand drum.

> **Rum pum pum. This is my drum.** *(Tap to the beat.)*
> **Rum pum pum. This is my drum.**
> **My name is _____. What's your name?**
>   *(Tap your name with syllables on the drum.)*

"Now I am going to go around the room. I'd like each child to tap his or her name on the drum with syllables. For instance, Joe would just be Joe, but Shaniqua would be Sha-ni-qua with three syllables. And parents, if your children are too young to tap out their names on their own, please take their hands and help them tap out their names with their own hands."

Follow the same routine from previous weeks. Put the tambourine or drum into the tub.

Section 5: Stand-Up / Sit-Down Activities

"Make a circle! We are going to march around the room together in this direction." *(Point in the direction you will be moving.)*

> We're marching to the drum.
> We're marching to the drum.
> Hi-ho the derri-o, we're marching to the drum.
>
> We're marching 'round the room.
> We're marching 'round the room.
> Hi-ho the derri-o, we're marching 'round the room.
>
> We're marching to the drum.
> We're marching to the drum.
> Hi-ho the derri-o, we're marching to the drum.

And the drum says, "Stop!"

Can you hit "stop"?

Good. *(Continue repeating until all children have had a turn.)*

Now let's run to the drum.

> We're running to the drum…
> We're tiptoeing to the drum…
> We're creeping to the drum…

Drop the visual representation of the rhyme into the tub.

Display the visual representation for "I'm a Little Teapot."

"Now let's use our imaginations and pretend that we are teapots. Follow the directions!"

> I'm a little teapot short and stout.
> Here is my handle, here is my spout.
> When I get all steamed up, hear me shout,
> "Just tip me over and pour me out."

Repeat.

Drop the visual representation of the rhyme into the tub.

Display the visual representation for "Jack-in-the-Box" or show the actual toy.

"Now let's pretend that we are jack-in-the-boxes. Follow the directions! Let's climb into our boxes, push ourselves down, and close the lid. Now let's wind ourselves up…and here we go."

> Jack-in-the-box sitting so still, won't you come out?
> Yes, I will!

Jump out.

Repeat.

Drop the visual representation of the rhyme into the tub.

> Handy Spandy, sugar and candy, we all jump in.
> Handy Spandy, sugar and candy, we all jump out.
> Handy Spandy, sugar and candy, we all jump up.
> Handy Spandy, sugar and candy, we all sit down.

Sit down.

Section 6: Animal Activities

Show the cover of Eric Carle's The Very Busy Spider.

"Everyone, please help me sing this song about the sounds the animals make."

Sing using the animal illustrations.

> I went to visit the farm one day.
> I saw a horse across the way.
> And what do you think the horse did say?
> "Neigh, neigh, neigh."

Repeat with other animal illustrations and sounds.

Close the book and put it into the tub.

Lift up your tote bag with farm animal puppets inside. Show one part of an animal peeking over the front tip of the tote bag. This could be an ear, a tail, or a foot.

"Oh, look what I have here! Who is inside this bag?"

Give children time to guess which animal you have in the bag. Then pull it out.

"It's a cow. A cow who says, 'Moo!'"

> When the cow gets up in the morning,
> She always says, "Moo."
> When the cow gets up in the morning,
> She says, "Moo, moo."

Repeat with other animal puppets and sounds.

Display the visual representation for "Hickory Dickory Dare."

> Hickory dickory dare.
> The pig flew up in the air. (*Throw pig puppet up in the air and catch it coming down.*)
> Farmer Brown soon brought her down.
> Hickory dickory dare.

Give each child a turn throwing the pig up into the air (see p. 103 for more detailed instructions).

Repeat the rhyme once more after each child has had a turn.

Developmental tip #1: "Notice how I don't say 'good job' after every rhyme; that's because I expect everyone to recite the rhymes with me. But when I ask the children to do something specific, like throwing the pig up in the air, we all give applause in recognition of each child's successful turn-taking, patience, and following of directions. The children are also learning how to show appreciation to others and to accept praise for doing what has been asked of them. Children who believe that they are capable of succeeding are more likely to embrace new challenges. Believing in yourself is a powerful motivator, and it's easy to give verbal recognition when children do what they have been asked to do."

Drop the visual representation into the tub.

Section 7: Musical Instruments and Scarves

Walk around the circle with a tote bag full of bells. Hand one bell to each child and adult. If the bells are different colors, you can name the colors as you are passing them out.

Bells

> We ring our bells together.
> We ring our bells together.
> We ring our bells together.
> Because it's fun to do.
> Ring them up high.
> Ring them down low.
> Ring them in the middle!

Repeat.

Display the visual representation for "Hickory Dickory Dock."

> Hickory dickory dock,
> The mouse ran up the clock.
> The clock struck one,
> And down she run.
> Hickory dickory dock.

Repeat.

Drop the visual representation into the tub.

Developmental tip #2: "Adding the variation in tone of voice increases your child's understanding of the words *high, low,* and *middle.* When we sing this song, each word is experienced as a tone as well as a physical space. And experience is what strengthens brain connections!"

> Ring up high.
> Ring down low.
> Ring your bells in the middle so!

Repeat.

Display the visual representation for "Jack-in-the-Box."

"Let's use our imaginations and pretend that our bells are Jack. To put him into the box, place your bell gently on the ground in front of you. Now close the lid, wind him up, and here we go!"

> Jack-in-the-box
> Sitting so still. Won't you come out?
> Yes, I will!

Repeat.

"Isn't this a great way to teach our children how to practice self-regulation skills? If they weren't pretending the bell was Jack, do you think they'd be able to leave it on the floor without touching it while we recite the rhyme?"

Drop the visual representation into the tub.

Walk around with the tote bag, collecting bells.

> Bells away, bells away, put your bells away today.
> Bells away, bells away, put your bells away today.

Repeat until all the bells have been collected.

Scarves

Walk around the circle with the scarf-filled tote bag. Hand each child and adult a scarf. You may want to name the color of the scarf you are handing out.

Display the visual representation for "Wind, Oh Wind."

> Wind, oh wind, oh wind, I say.
> What are you blowing away today?
> Scarves, oh scarves, oh scarves, I say.
> I am blowing the scarves away.

Drop the visual representation into the tub.

Display the visual representation for "Peek-a-Boo."

> Peek-a-boo, I see you, I see you hiding there.
> Peek-a-boo, I see you, I see you smiling there.
>   (Peek-a-boo!)

Repeat as much as needed.

Drop the visual representation into the tub.

Display the visual representation for "The Wheels on the Bus."

"Here's a song that everyone knows. But look how different it is when we do the actions using our scarves. Notice how colorful our circle becomes."

> The wheels on the bus go 'round and 'round,
> 'Round and 'round, 'round and 'round.
> The wheels on the bus go 'round and 'round,
> On our way to the library.
>
> Horn goes "beep-beep"…
> Babies go "waah-waah"…
> Parents go "shhh"…

Drop the visual representation into the tub.

"Now take your scarves and squish them into a tiny ball."

> Scrunch your scarf into a ball.
> Make it very, very small.

On the count of three, throw them in the air, and watch all the beautiful colors fly down.

One, two, three, throw!

Throw the scarves into the air; watch them float down.

Repeat.

Collect scarves with the tote bag.

> Scarves away, scarves away,
> Put your scarves away today.

Drop bag with scarves into the storage tub.

Section 8: Lullabies

"Now it's lullaby time. Hold your child closely and rock gently from side to side while we sing."

Display the visual representation for "You Are My Sunshine."

> You are my sunshine, my only sunshine.
> You make me happy, when skies are gray.
> You'll always know, dear, how much I love you.
> So I'll hug my sunshine today.

Repeat.

Drop the visual representation into the tub.

Section 9: Interactive Rhymes

Display the visual representation for "Humpty Dumpty."

> Humpty Dumpty sat on a wall.
> Humpty Dumpty had a great fall.
> All the king's horses
> And all the king's men
> Couldn't put Humpty together again.

Invite children to pull Humpty off of his wall.

Repeat the rhyme when everyone has had a turn and put felt pieces into the tub.

Section 10: Closing Ritual

Display the visual representation for "Can You Kick with Two Feet?"

> Can you kick with two feet?
> Two feet, two feet?
> Can you kick with two feet?
> Kick, kick, kick, kick, kick.
>
> Can you clap with two hands?…
> Can you wiggle with ten fingers?…
> Can you sway from side to side?…
> Can you kiss with two lips?…
> Can you wave "Bye-bye"?…

"It's time to say good-bye, but…"

Drop the visual representation into the tub.

Display the visual representation for "We're So Happy."

> We're so happy,
> We're so happy,
> We're so happy that everyone is here.
> We're so happy,
> We're so happy,
> We're so happy that everyone is here.

"Good-bye, everyone. Thank you for coming. See you next week."

Drop the visual representation into the tub.

Put the cover on the storage tub. Remind everyone that they are welcome to stay and play after the program. Bring out toys for the children and engage in conversation with the parents.

Part IV

Mother Goose on the Loose Resources

The Mother Goose on the Loose Songbook and Rhyme Book

HERE IS A COMPREHENSIVE LIST OF SIXTY-SIX RHYMES and songs that appear in the five programs. Stage directions are italicized throughout. All songs are traditional, public-domain songs unless otherwise noted.

A

ABC Song (This can be sung slowly and softly as a lullaby.)
>A B C D E F G.
>H I J K L M N O P.
>Q R S T U V…W X Y and Z.
>Now I've learned my ABCs.
>Next time won't you sing with me?

And We Walk
>And we walk and we walk and we walk and we stop.
>*Tap tambourine in beat. Give a hard whack for "stop," and pause before resuming.*
>And we walk and we walk and we walk and we stop. And we walk and we walk and we walk and we stop. And we all turn around—Woo!
>*Shake the tambourine vigorously while everyone turns around.*
>(*Substitute walk with words and motions: run, creep, tiptoe, jump, march, etc.*)
>—Betsy Diamant-Cohen

Are You Sleeping Brother John / Frère Jacques
>Are you sleeping, are you sleeping, Brother John, Brother John?
>Morning bells are ringing, morning bells are ringing. Ding ding dong. Ding ding dong.
>Frère Jacques, Frère Jacques, Dormez-vous? Dormez-vous?
>Sonnez les matines, Sonnez les matines. Ding ding dong. Ding ding dong.

B

Bells Away
>Bells away, bells away,
>Put your bells away today.
>(*Walk around with an open canvas bag, and sing this song while children put their bells back into the bag. This song can be used to clean up many items!*)
>—Barbara Cass-Beggs

C

Can You Kick with Two Feet?
>Can you kick with two feet, two feet, two feet?
>Can you kick with two feet? Kick, kick, kick, kick, kick…
>(*Continue with more verses: wave with two arms, nod with one head, kiss with two lips, and sway from side to side.*)
>—Words and music by Barbara Cass-Beggs

E

The Eency Weency Spider

The eency weency spider went up the waterspout.
Put your thumb to your index finger on the other hand and vice versa; "walk" them up in the air.
Down came the rain and washed the spider out.
Push down and out with your hands.
Out came the sun and dried up all the rain.
Raise your hands above your head and touch your fingers together to form a circle.
So the eency weency spider climbed up the spout again.
Put your thumb to your index finger on the other hand and vice versa; "walk" them up into the air.
The great big spider went up the waterspout…
Repeat the song using a deep voice and large hand movements.

Eye Winker

Eye winker,
Point to one eye.
Tom Tinker,
Point to the other eye.
Nose smeller,
Tap finger on nose.
Mouth eater,
Tap finger on lips.
Chin chopper, chin chopper, chin chopper,
Tap finger on chin.
Guzzle whopper!
Give child a big tummy tickle.

F

Fingers Like to Wiggle Waggle

Fingers like to wiggle waggle, wiggle waggle, wiggle waggle.
Wiggle the fingers of both hands in front of you.
Fingers like to wiggle waggle way up high!
Wiggle your fingers as you raise your hands, saying "up high" in a very high voice.
Fingers like to wiggle waggle, wiggle waggle, wiggle waggle.
Wiggle the fingers of both hands in front of you.
Fingers like to wiggle waggle way down low!
Wiggle your fingers as you lower hands to the floor, saying "way down low" in a very low voice.
Fingers like to wiggle waggle, wiggle waggle, wiggle waggle.
Wiggle the fingers of both hands in front of you.
Fingers like to wiggle waggle on my knee!
Place your fingers on your knee without changing your tone of voice.
—Barbara Cass-Beggs

Five Fat Sausages

Five fat sausages, frying in a pan.
Hold five fingers and bounce them up and down.
All a sudden,
Spread arms out.
One went bang.
Give a big clap on "bang."
Four fat sausages…
Three fat sausages…
Two fat sausages…
One fat sausage, frying in a pan.
Hold up one finger and bounce it up and down.
All a sudden, *(spread arms out)* it went bang.
Give a big clap on "bang."
And there were no sausages left!

G

The Garden Snail

Slowly, slowly, very slowly creeps the garden snail.
Slowly walk your fingers up the baby's body from right toe to head.
Slowly, slowly, very slowly, up the garden rail.
Slowly walk your fingers up the baby's body from left toe to head.
Quickly, quickly, very quickly goes the little mouse.
Repeat the same actions quickly.
Quickly, quickly, very quickly, all around the house!
End with a tummy tickle.

Good Morning, Mrs. Perky Bird

Good morning, Mrs. Perky Bird, Perky Bird, Perky Bird.
Take a brightly colored bird puppet out of the plastic tub. Wave the bird around.
Good morning, Mrs. Perky Bird, where are you?
I'm flying in the air—the air, the air—the air, the air.

Fly the bird around up high in the air. You may want to walk around the circle and have the puppet give "kisses" to each child.

I'm flying in the air—the air—and down to the ground.

Bring the bird slowly down to the ground.

—*Words and music by Barbara Cass-Beggs*

Goosey, Goosey Gander

Goosey, goosey gander.
Tap hands on top of your legs.
Where do you wander? Upstairs
Lift your arms up.
and downstairs
Bring your arms down.
and in my lady's chamber.
Hug yourself.

The Grand Old Duke of York

Oh, the Grand Old Duke of York,
Bounce legs up and down.
He had ten thousand men.
He marched them up to the top of the hill,
Bring legs up, bending your knees.
And marched them down again.
Bounce legs straight on the floor.
And when they were up, they were up.
Bring legs up bending your knees.
And when they were down, they were down.
Bounce legs straight on the floor.
And when they were only halfway up,
Bring knees halfway up.
They were neither up nor down.
Bounce knees up and then fully down.

Grandfather's Clock Goes Tick Tock

Grandfather's clock goes tick tock, tick tock.
Ring bells slowly.
Mother's kitchen clock goes tick tock, tick tock, tick tock, tick tock.
Ring bells at a medium tempo.
Brother's little watch goes tick tock, tick tock, tick tock, tick tock, tick tock, tick tock, tick tock, tick tock.
Ring bells very, very quickly.
Stop!
Stop tapping.
—*Words and music by Barbara Cass-Beggs*

H

Handy Spandy (This song helps everyone sit down after standing up.)

Handy Spandy, sugar and candy, we all jump in.
Jump into circle.
Handy Spandy, sugar and candy, we all jump out.
Jump out of circle.
Handy Spandy, sugar and candy, we all jump up.
Jump up.
Handy Spandy, sugar and candy, we all sit down.
Sit down.

Hickory Dickory Dare (This can be used with puppets or scarves.)

Hickory dickory dare.
The pig flew up in the air.
Farmer Brown soon brought her down.
Hickory dickory dare.
—*Traditional, words adapted by Betsy Diamant-Cohen*

Hickory Dickory Dock

Standing straight, dangle your hands down and clasp them together like a pendulum.
Hickory dickory dock,
Swing the pendulum from side to side.
The mouse ran up the clock.
Starting at your toes, walk your fingers up your body to your head.
The clock struck one,
Clap your hands together over your head.
And down she run.
Run your fingers back down your body.
Hickory dickory dock.
Swing your pendulum again.

The Hokey Pokey

You put your hand in.
Put hand in.
You take your hand out.
Take hand out.
You put your hand in,
Put hand in.
And you shake it all about.
Shake your hand.
You do the hokey pokey
Point the index finger of each hand, and sway slightly from side to side while shrugging shoulders.

And you turn yourself around.
Turn around.
That's what it's all about.
Clap to the beat.
Hey!
Jump up.
(Repeat with your foot, head, backside, and whole self.)

Humpty Dumpty
Humpty Dumpty sat on a wall.
Lean gently from side to side.
Humpty Dumpty had a great fall…
Fall backward gently.
All the king's horses and all the king's men
Bounce your legs up and down rapidly.
Couldn't put Humpty together again.
Recite the rhyme and invite children to take turns pulling the felt Humpty off of his wall.

I

I Hear Thunder (Use tune to "Frère Jacques.")
I hear thunder, I hear thunder.
Put one hand over an ear as if listening for something.
Hark, don't you? Hark, don't you?
Put the other hand over the other ear.
Pitter patter raindrops, pitter patter raindrops.
Lift both of your hands. Wiggle your fingers while bringing them down.
I'm wet through, I'm wet through.
Hug yourself.
—Words by Barbara Cass-Beggs

I Went to Visit a Farm One Day
I went to visit a farm one day. I saw a [cow] along the way.
And what do you think the [cow] did say? [Moo, moo, moo]
(Suggest other animals and their sounds.)

If You're Happy and You Know It
If you're happy and you know it, clap your hands.
Clap twice.
If you're happy and you know it, clap your hands.
Clap twice.
If you're happy and you know it and you really want to show it,
If you're happy and you know it, clap your hands.
Clap twice.
(One verse is fine for infants and babies. With toddlers, continue with additional verses: "If you're happy and you know it, stamp your feet"; "If you're happy and you know it, shout 'Hooray!'"; or "If you're happy and you know it, do all three.")

I'm Driving in My Car
I'm driving in my car, I'm driving in my car,
Beep beep, toot toot, I'm driving in my car.
Hold a pretend steering wheel. Turn both hands slightly from side to side.
I'm driving very fast…
Use quick movements.
I'm driving very slowly…
Use slow movements.
The lights are turning red, and I must stop my car…
Put out a hand to signal stop.
The lights are turning green, and I can go again…
Drive car again.
—Traditional, words and music adapted by Barbara Cass-Beggs

I'm a Little Teapot
I'm a little teapot, short and stout.
Stand up straight.
Here is my handle.
Bend your right arm, and put it on your hip.
Here is my spout.
Bring your left arm up, and flop your hand down.
When I get all steamed up, hear me shout,
"Just tip me over and pour me out."
Lean over to the left.

J

Jack Be Nimble
Place a candlestick on the floor. Invite children to take turns standing in front of the candlestick. When they hear the word jump, *they should jump over the candlestick.*

Jack be nimble. Jack be quick. Jack jump over the candlestick.
Recite the female version of the rhyme.
Jill be nimble. Jill be quick. Jill jump over the candlestick.

Jack-in-the-Box

Before you begin reciting this rhyme, pretend to climb into a box and shut the lid.
Jack-in-the-box
Recite the rhyme while squatting.
Sitting so still. Won't you come out?
Yes, I will!
Jump up.
(*Instead of pretending to climb into a box, you can mime shutting the lid and turning the handle. Recite the rhyme, and during the last line, lift up the prop and vigorously shake it.*)

K

Knock on the Door

Knock on the door.
Knock gently on top of a baby's head.
Pull the bell.
Lift a tuft of hair.
Peek in.
Extend an index finger and point to the furthest end of the baby's eyes.
Lift up the latch.
Put a finger under the baby's nose and lift up.
Walk in.
"Walk" fingers toward the baby's open mouth.
Take a chair.
Gently pinch one cheek.
Sit down.
Gently pinch the other cheek.
"How do you do, Mrs. Brown?"
Grab the baby's chin and gently shake it up and down.

L

The Little Train

The little train ran up the track.
Walk your fingers up one of a baby's arms or legs.
It went toot, toot,
Knock gently on the baby's head.
And then it ran back.
Quickly tickle the baby's tummy.
(*Repeat going up the baby's other arm or leg. Then "Two Little Trains" go up both arms or legs.*)

London Bridge

London Bridge is falling down, falling down, falling down.
Hold hands and walk around in a circle.
London Bridge is falling down, my fair lady.
Down!
Drop hands and squat or kneel on the floor.
Build it up with sticks and stones, sticks and stones, sticks and stones.
Tap the floor with your hands.
Build it up with sticks and stones, my fair lady.
Up!
Stand up.

M

Mother and Father and Uncle John

Mother and Father and Uncle John went to market one by one.
Gently bounce your outstretched legs as your child sits on them.
Mother fell off!
Lean to one side as far as you can.
Father fell off!
Lean to the other side as far as you can.
But Uncle John went on and on and on…
Sit up straight and bounce as quickly as you can.

My Face Is Round

My face is round.
Outline your face using an index finger.
I have two eyes,
Point at your eyes.
a nose,
Point at your nose.
and a mouth!
Point at mouth.
—Regina Wade

O

Oh Where, Oh Where Has My Little Head Gone?

(Tune: "Oh Where, Oh Where Has My Little Dog Gone?")
Place a scarf over your head.
Oh where, oh where has my little head gone? Oh where, oh where can it be?

Oh where, oh where has my little head gone? Oh where, oh where can it be?
One…two…three… *(pull scarf off)* Here it is!
(Continue covering different body parts such as your hand, knee, and leg.)

Old Mother Goose

Old Mother Goose when she wanted to wander
Tap your hands on the top of your legs.
Would fly through the air on a very fine gander.
Lift both hands up in the air and move them in an arc over your head.

Open Them, Shut Them

Open them, shut them, open them, shut them,
Put your closed fists in front of you, and open and shut them.
Give a little clap.
Give one clap.
Open them, shut them, open them, shut them,
Put your closed fists in front of you, and open and shut them.
Put them in your lap.
Put your hands in your lap.
Creep them, creep them, creep them, creep them
Walk your fingers up your body from your knees.
Right up to your chinny-chin-chin.
Stop creeping when your fingers get up to your chin.
Open up your little mouth,
Open your mouth with your fingers still on your chin.
But
Pause.
Do not let them in!
Quickly move both hands behind your back.

P

Pat-a-Cake

Pat-a-cake, pat-a-cake, baker's man,
Clap your hands together and then clap palms with your child's palms.
Bake me a cake as fast as you can.
Roll it and pat it and mark it with a B,
And put it in the oven for baby and me.
Before reciting this rhyme, tell adults that they can substitute their baby's first initial and name in place of the B and baby.

Peek-a-Boo

Place a scarf over your head and play peek-a-boo.
Peek-a-boo, I see you. I see you hiding there.
Peek-a-boo, I see you. I see you smiling in there.

Pizza, Pizza, Hot

Pizza, pizza, hot. Pizza, pizza, cold.
Tap knees and clap hands to a steady beat.
Pizza, pizza in the box, nine days old.
Some like it hot. Some like it cold.
Some like it in the box, nine days old. Yuck!

R

Ring Them Up High

Ring up high,
Ring bells up high.
Ring down low,
Ring bells down low.
Ring your bells in the middle so.
Ring bells in the middle.
—Barbara Cass-Beggs
(Substitute another word for other props—that is, shake rattles, tap sticks, wave scarves, etc.)

Ring Your Bells

(Tune: "Jingle Bells")
Ring your bells, ring your bells, ring your bells today.
Oh, what fun it is to ring, to ring your bells today-ay [2×].
—Music by James Pierpont; words by Barbara Cass-Beggs

'Round and 'Round the Garden

'Round and 'round the garden goes the teddy bear.
Open your child's hand, palm up. Use your extended right index finger to trace circular motions on your child's palm.
One step,
Gently pinch your child's left arm somewhere below the elbow.
Two steps,

Gently pinch your child's left arm somewhere above the elbow.
Tickly under there.
Tickle your child under the left armpit.
'Round about, 'round about goes the wee mouse,
Use your extended left index finger to trace circular motions on your child's right palm.
Up a step,
Gently pinch your child's right arm somewhere below the elbow.
Up a step,
Gently pinch your child's right arm somewhere above the elbow.
All around the house.
Give a great big tickle!

Row, Row, Row Your Boat
Row, row, row your boat, gently down the stream.
Merrily, merrily, merrily, merrily, life is but a dream.
Put your child on your outstretched legs facing you. Hold each hand in one of your hands. Lean back and forth, pulling in a gentle rocking motion. Sing at normal speed, then very quickly, then slowly, and then back at normal speed. Match your movements to the tempo.

Rum Pum Pum
Rum pum pum, this is my drum.
Hit a drum to the beat.
Rum pum pum, this is my drum.
My name is [Betsy]. What's your name?
Tap your name with syllables on the drum. Then take the drum around the circle and let each child tap out his or her own name with syllables. Give a personal greeting after each name.
—Barbara Cass-Beggs

S

Scarves Away
Scarves away, scarves away.
Put your scarves away today.
Use this song to collect scarves in tote bags or baskets.
—Words and music by Barbara Cass-Beggs

Scrunch Your Scarf into a Ball
Scrunch your scarf into a ball.
Scrunch your scarf into a tiny ball.
Make it very, very small.
Recite rather than sing the following lines.
On the count of three, throw them in the air, and watch all the beautiful colors fly down.
One, two, three, throw!
Throw the scarves into the air and watch them float down.
—Regina Wade

See the Ponies Galloping
See the ponies galloping, galloping down the country lane [2×]
Bounce knees quickly.
See the ponies coming home,
All tired out! All tired out!
Bounce knees slowly.

Seesaw, Scaradown
Seesaw, Scaradown,
This is the way to Londontown.
Bounce one leg at a time so baby moves up and down in a "seesaw" motion.
One knee up and the other knee down,
This is the way to Londontown.
(Sing this song first using Londontown. When you sing it a second time, substitute the name of your particular town, city, or neighborhood.)

Shake Your Rattles like the Leaves
Shake your rattles, shake your rattles,
Shake your rattles in front of you in an up-and-down motion.
Like the leaves
Shake your rattles in front of you in a side-to-side motion.
That are growing, that are growing
Shake your rattles in front of you in an up-and-down motion.
On the trees.
Shake your rattles in front of you in a side-to-side motion.
Shake them high and
Shake rattles up high.
Shake them low.

Shake rattles down low.
'Round about
Shake rattles in a circle.
And to and fro.
Shake rattles from side to side.
Shake your rattles, shake your rattles,
Shake your rattles in front of you in an up-and-down motion.
Like the leaves!
Shake your rattles in front of you in a side-to-side motion.
—Barbara Cass-Beggs

Shakers Away
Shakers away, shakers away,
Put your shakers away today.
—Barbara Cass-Beggs
(Walk around with an open tote bag, and sing this song while children put their shakers back into the bag. This song can be used to clean up many items!)

Shoe the Little Horse
Shoe the little horse.
Pat the soles of your baby's feet together.
Shoe the little mare.
But let the little colt run bare, bare, bare!

Stretch Up High
Stretch up high,
Reach up as high as you can.
Stretch down low.
Bend over and touch the floor.
Stretch your arms in the middle so.
Put your arms out to the sides as widely as you can.
—Words and music by Barbara Cass-Beggs

T

This Is the Way We Wash Our Legs
This is the way we wash our legs, wash our legs, wash our legs.
Gently rub the scrunched-up scarf on your legs.
This is the way we wash our legs, so early in the morning.
(Sing more verses substituting other body parts.)

This Little Piggy
This little piggy went to market.
Gently tug on the child's pinky.
This little piggy stayed home.
Gently tug on the child's ring finger.
This little piggy had roast beef.
Gently tug on the child's middle finger.
This little piggy had none.
Gently tug on the child's index finger.
And this little piggy cried,
Gently tug on the child's thumb.
Wee wee wee wee—all the way home!
Give the child a big tummy tickle!
(Repeat using the other hand or toes.)

To Market, To Market
To market, to market, to buy a fat pig,
Home again, home again, jiggety jig!
Bounce child gently on your outstretched legs.
To market, to market, to buy a fat hog,
Home again, home again jiggety jog!
To market, to market, to buy a currant bun,
Home again, home again, market is done.
To market, to market, to buy a brand-new mop,
Home again, home again, oh no, it's going to drop!
Lift the child up in the air and bring the child gently to the floor between your legs.

Twinkle, Twinkle
Twinkle, twinkle, little star.
How I wonder what you are.
Up above the world so high.
Like a diamond in the sky.
Twinkle, twinkle, little star.
How I wonder what you are.
—Jane Taylor

Two Little Dickey Birds
Two little dickey birds sitting on a cloud.
Make two fists, each index finger pointing out. Bounce both hands up and down in front of you.
One named "Soft,"
Whisper this as you bounce one hand up and down.
and the other named "Loud"!

Shout this as you bounce your other hand up and down.
Fly away, Soft,
Whisper as you put your first hand behind your back.
Fly away, Loud!
Shout as you put your other hand behind your back.
Come back, Soft,
Whisper as you bring your first hand to the front.
Come back, Loud!
Shout as you bring your other hand to the front.
—Words adapted by Barbara Cass-Beggs
(Some people prefer to use "pretty birds" rather than the British "dickey birds.")

Two Little Monkeys
Two little monkeys jumping on the bed.
Bounce two fists up and down.
One fell off
Drop a fist.
And bumped his head.
Tap your head with a hand.
The other called the doctor, and the doctor said,
Put your other fist next to your ear.
"No more monkeys jumping on the bed."
Shake your head and wag your finger.

W

We Hit the Floor Together
We hit the floor together.
We hit the floor together.
We hit the floor together.
Because it's fun to do!
Hit the floor with your hands.
(Sing more verses with other movements such as smack our knees, clap our hands, wave our arms, wiggle our fingers, wiggle our toes, nod our heads, and sway from side to side. "Wiggle toes" can only be sung if the children are barefoot; "nod heads" only works with older children who have muscle control of their heads.)
—Traditional; words by Barbara Cass-Beggs

We're Marching to the Drum
(Tune: "The Farmer in the Dell")
Hit the drum to a steady beat while everyone marches around in a circle.
We're marching to the drum, we're marching to the drum.
Hi-ho the derri-o, we're marching to the drum.
We're marching 'round the room. We're marching 'round the room.
Hi-ho the derri-o, we're marching 'round the room.
We're marching to the drum, we're marching to the drum.
Hi-ho the derri-o, we're marching to the drum.
And the drum says, "Stop!"
Can you hit "stop"?
(Walk around the circle asking each individual child to hit the drum you are holding. Try to use a different positive word each time a child hits the drum. Repeat, substituting running, creeping, marching, or other movement words.)
—Traditional; words by Barbara Cass-Beggs

We're So Happy
We're so happy,
We're so happy,
We're so happy that everybody's here!
—Barbara Cass-Beggs

We Ring Our Bells Together
We ring our bells together [3×]
Ring bells.
Because it's fun to do.
Ring them up high,
Ring bells up high.
Ring them down low,
Ring bells down low.
And ring them in the middle.
Ring bells in the middle.
—Traditional; words by Barbara Cass-Beggs
(You can substitute "shake our shakers," "tap our sticks," "play our instruments," etc.)

We Shake Our Shakers Together

We shake our shakers together [3×]
Because it's fun to do!
—*Barbara Cass-Beggs*
(This can also be used with rattles, maracas, Chick-itas, shaker eggs, etc.)

The Wheels on the Bus

The wheels on the bus go 'round and 'round,
'round and 'round, 'round and 'round.
The wheels on the bus go 'round and 'round,
on our way to the library.
(Variation: Hold a musical instrument or scarf and follow the traditional hand motions to this song. Add verses: "horn goes 'beep-beep,'" "babies go 'waah-waah,'" "parents go 'shhh,'" etc.)

When the [Cow] Gets Up in the Morning

When the [cow] gets up in the morning, she always says, ["Moo"].
When the [cow] gets up in the morning, she says, ["Moo, Moo"].
(Suggest other animals and their sounds.)

Wind, Oh Wind

Wind, oh wind, oh wind, I say,
What are you blowing away today?
Scarves, oh scarves, oh scarves I say.
I am blowing the scarves away.
Wave scarves from side to side.
—*Barbara Cass-Beggs*

Y

You Are My Sunshine

You are my sunshine, my only sunshine.
You make me happy when skies are gray.
You'll always know, dear, how much I love you.
So I'll hug my sunshine today.
—*Traditional, adapted by Betsy Diamant-Cohen*

Z

Zoom, Zoom, Zoom

Zoom, zoom, zoom, we're going to the moon.
Rub your hands together with flat palms.
Zoom, zoom, zoom, we're going very soon.
If you want to take a trip,
Bend your elbow to lift one arm; fingers from the other hand "crawl" up the lifted arm.
Climb aboard my rocket ship.
Repeat using other hand.
Zoom, zoom, zoom, we're going to the moon.
Rub hands together.
Five, four, three, two, one…blastoff!
Hold up fingers and count down.
Blastoff!
Throw your empty hands into the sky or lift a baby into the air.
(Try "Fun, fun, fun, we're going to the sun" and "Far, far, far, we're going to the stars.")

Some Mother Goose on the Loose Felt Piece Patterns

THIS SOURCE CONTAINS ILLUSTRATIONS FOR RHYMES used often in the Mother Goose on the Loose (MGOL) programs, drawn by Celia Yitzhak. Make them the size that you want by using a photocopier to resize and print them. Cut around the outside line of each character. Then you have some choices:

- Glue each cutout to a piece of colored felt, and it becomes a flannelboard character.
- Color in the piece, and then glue it to a piece of felt.
- Use colored paper when you are photocopying!
- Staple or pin the printed copy to a piece of felt and cut along the black line to get the correct outside shape. Remove the paper and use a permanent marker to fill in the details directly onto the felt. (It takes longer, but this is my favorite way to use templates.)
- Cut out the outline and use Tacky Glue to attach the paper picture to a felt shape that is larger than the picture. Once the glue has dried, color in the picture.

ABC

Resource B: Some Mother Goose on the Loose Felt Piece Patterns 161

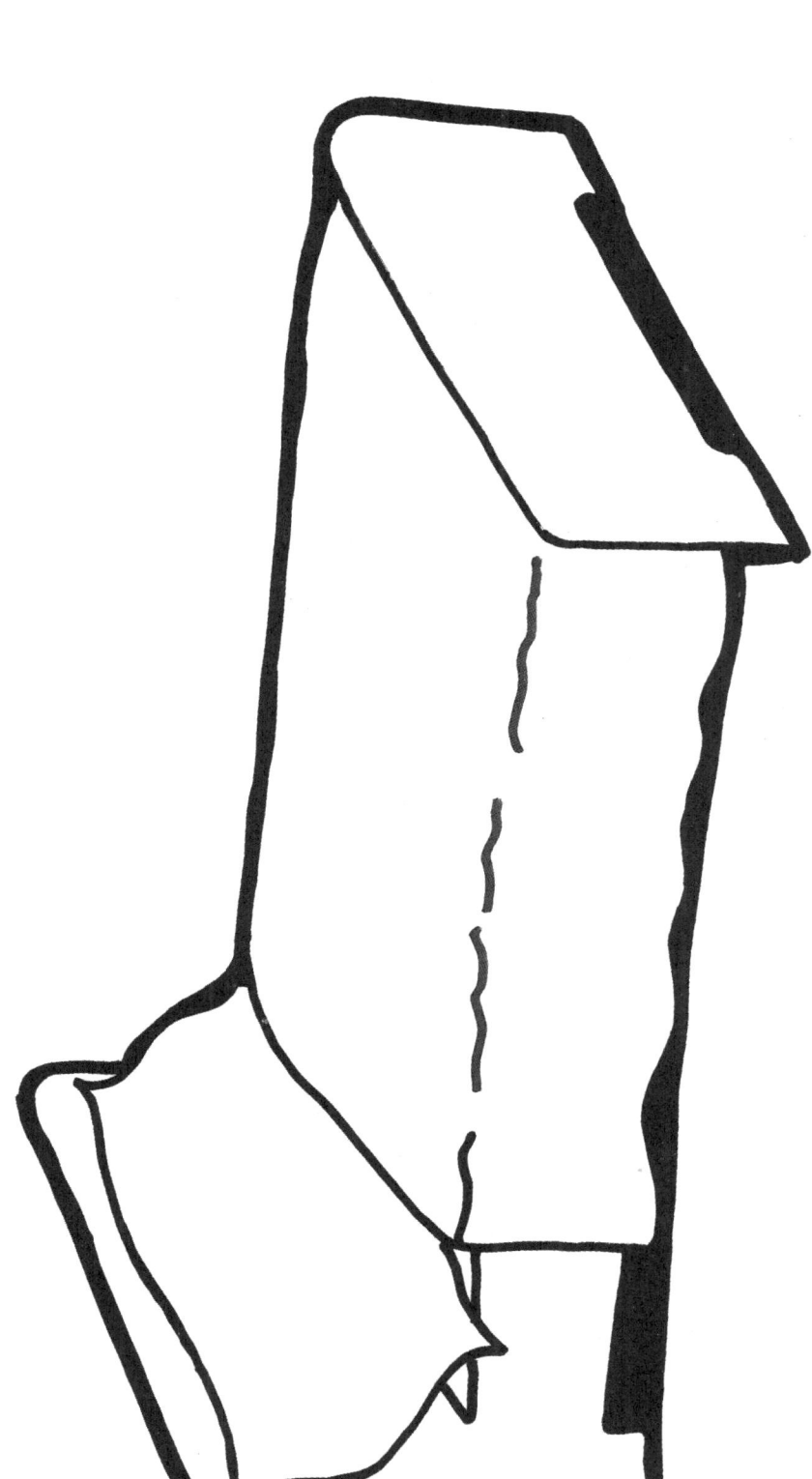

Bed

162   Part IV: Mother Goose on the Loose Resources

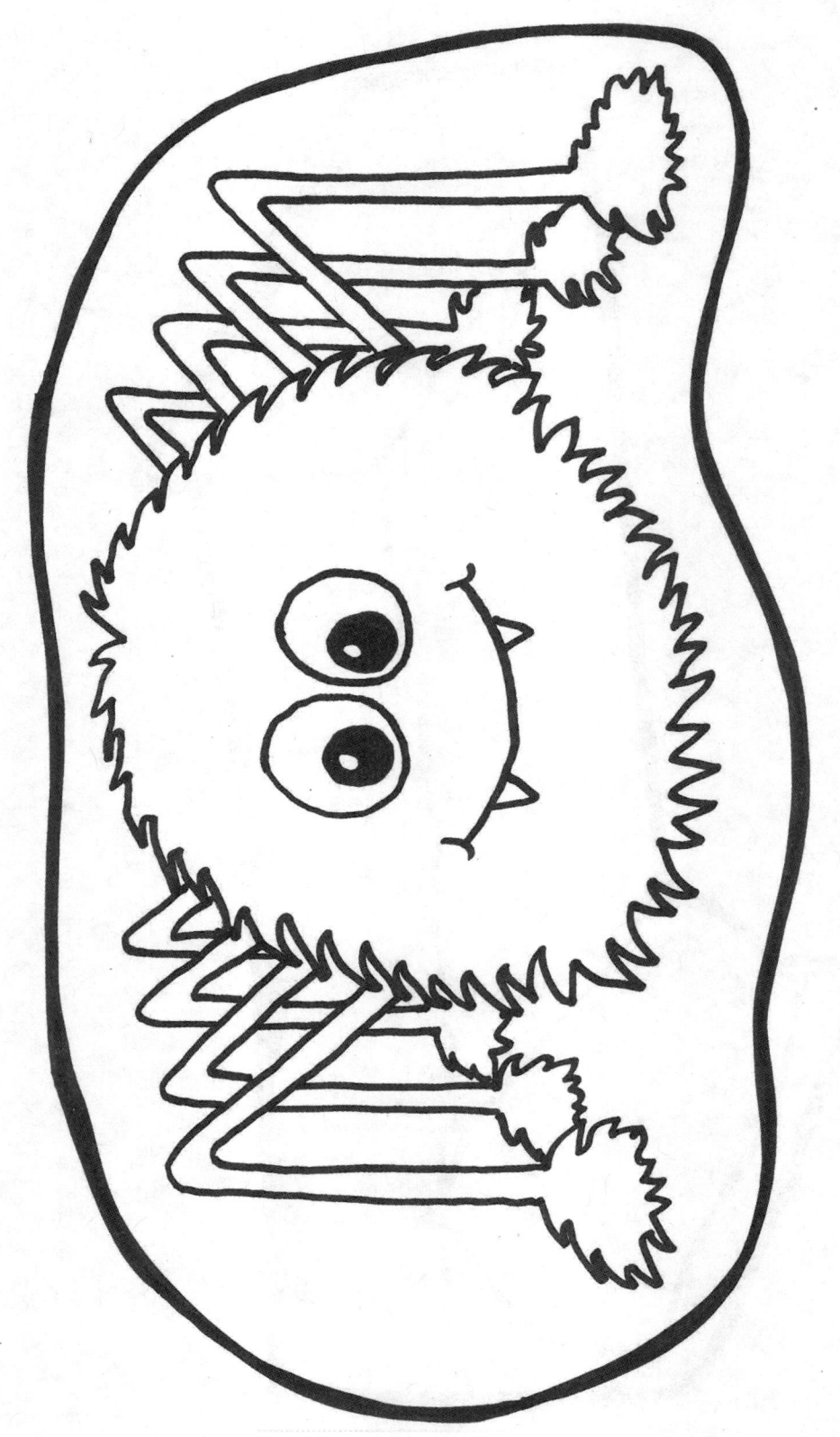

Spider

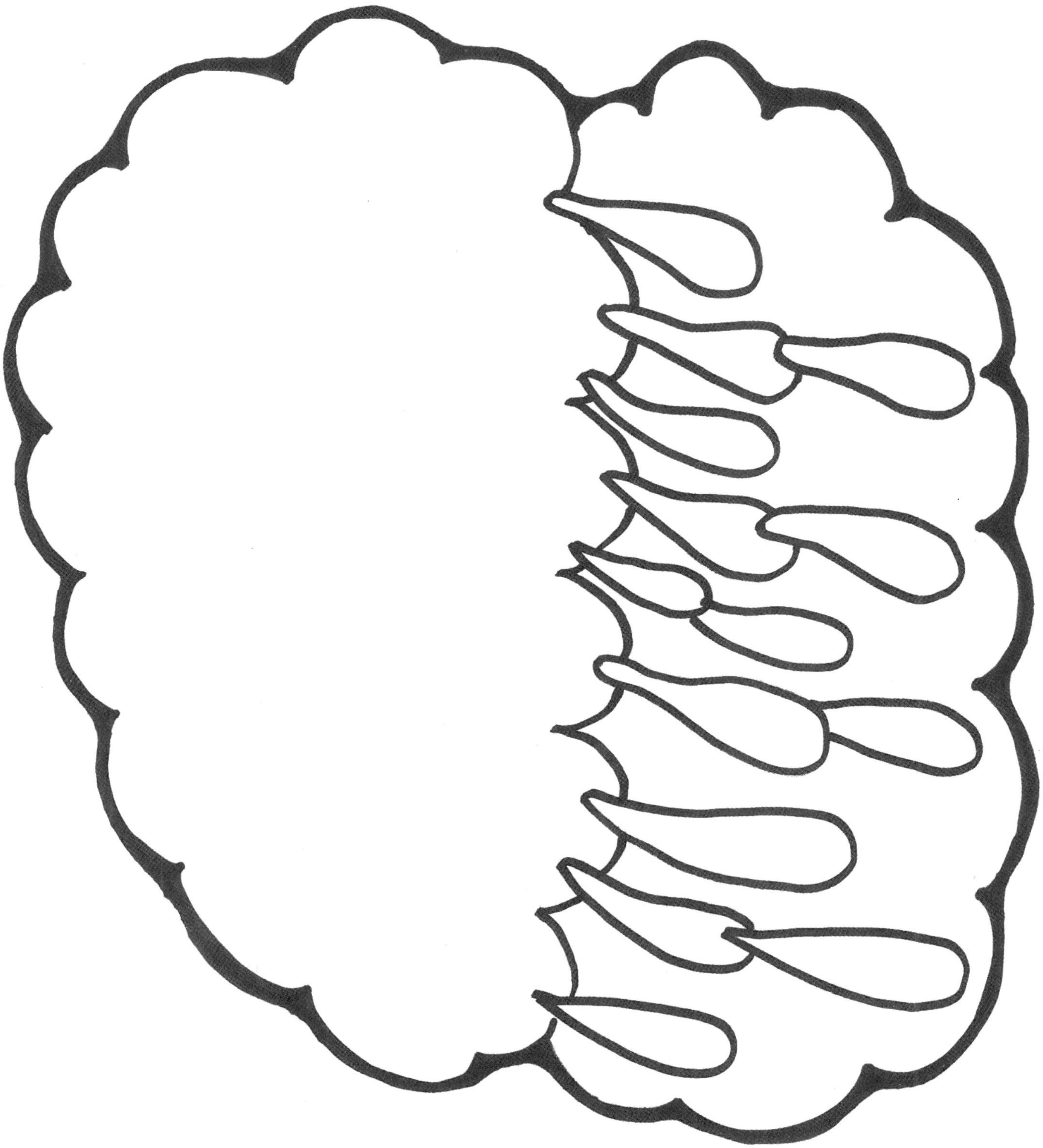

Resource B: Some Mother Goose on the Loose Felt Piece Patterns

Rain Cloud

164 *Part IV: Mother Goose on the Loose Resources*

Boy Wiggling Fingers

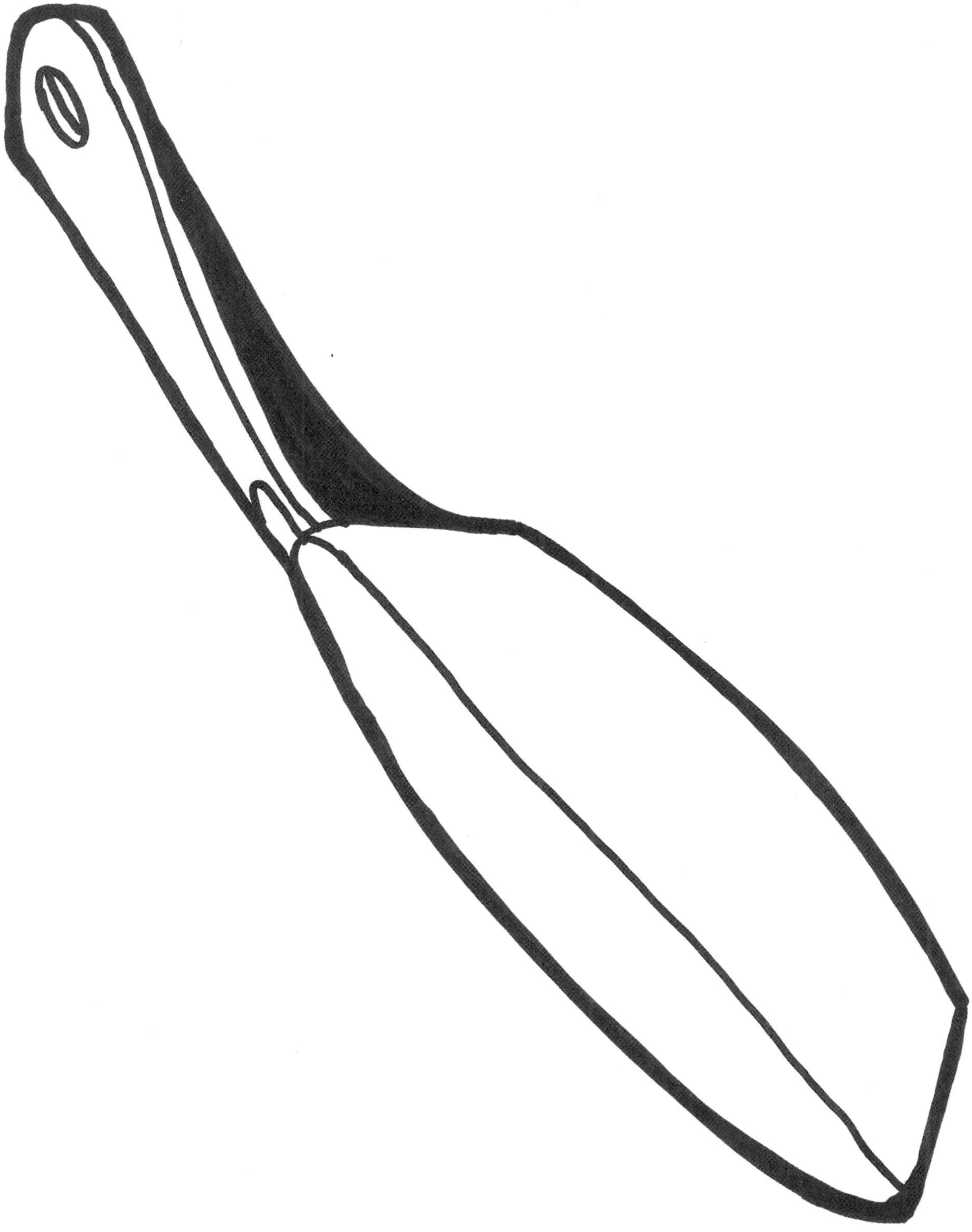

Resource B: Some Mother Goose on the Loose Felt Piece Patterns **165**

Pan

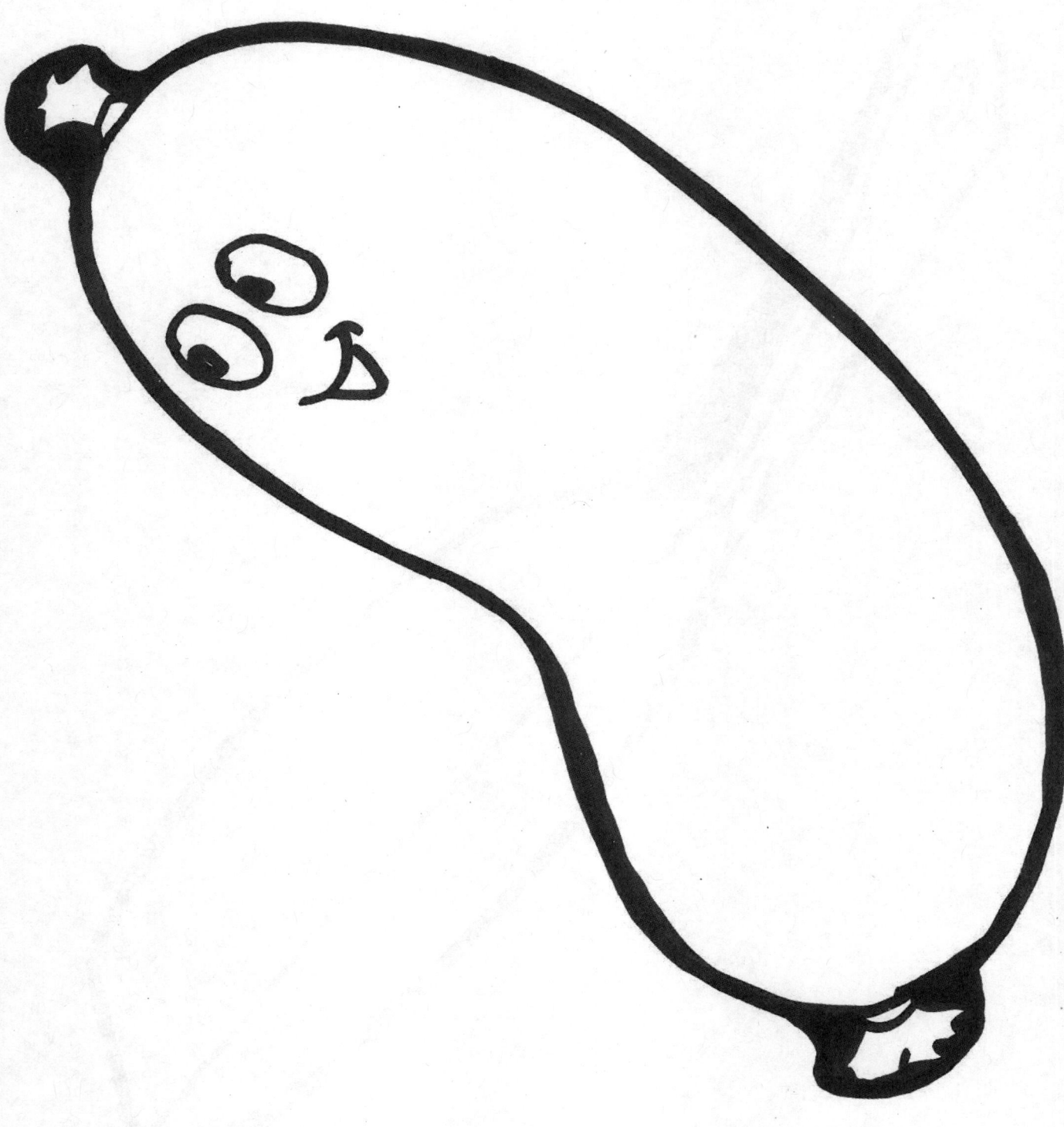

Sausage

Resource B: Some Mother Goose on the Loose Felt Piece Patterns   167

Goose on Stairs

Duke of York

Men of York

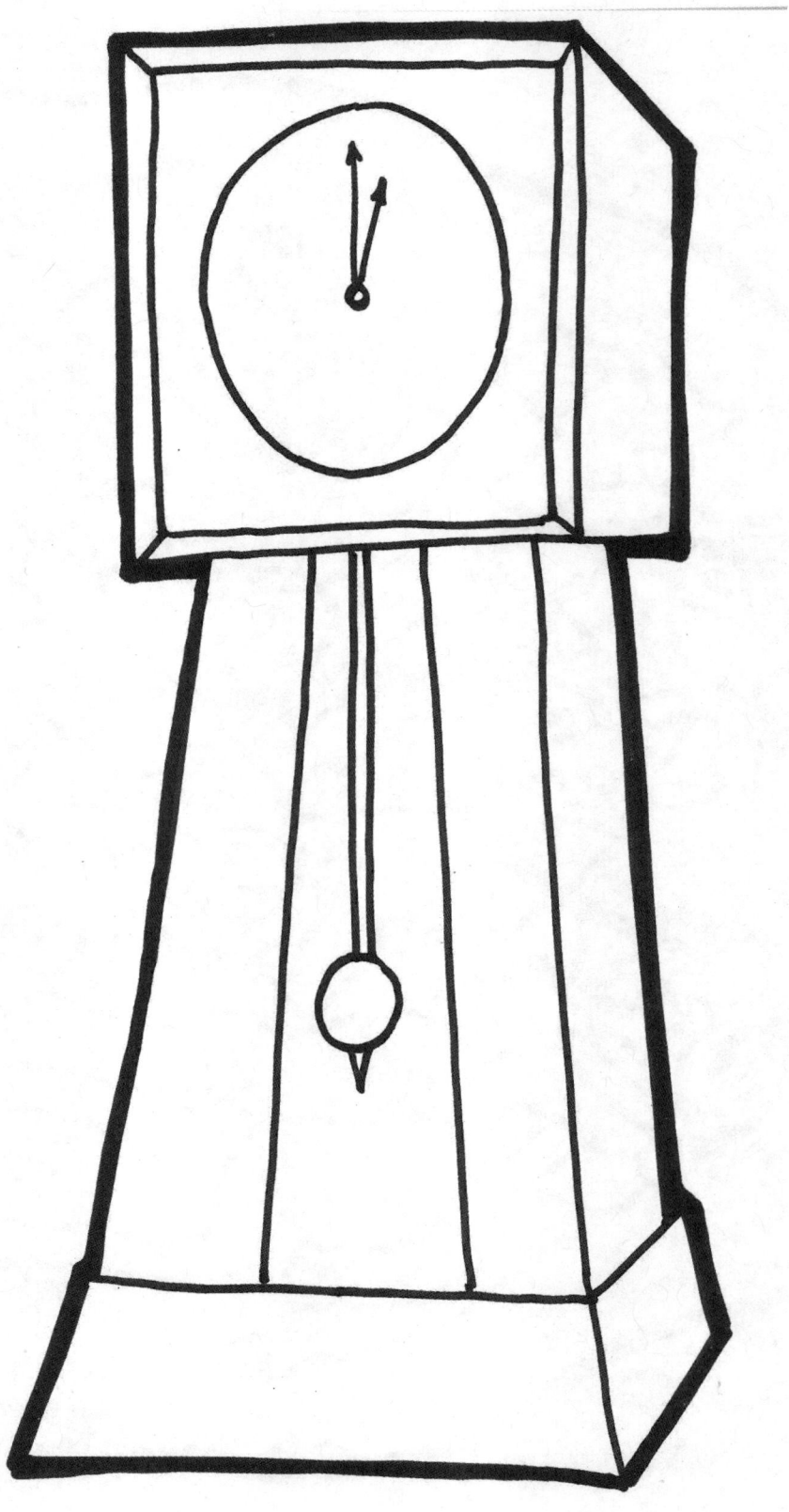

Grandfather's Clock

Resource B: Some Mother Goose on the Loose Felt Piece Patterns **171**

Mother's Kitchen Clock

172 *Part IV: Mother Goose on the Loose Resources*

Brother's Watch

Pig

Mouse

Resource B: Some Mother Goose on the Loose Felt Piece Patterns 175

Three Children Dancing

176   *Part IV: Mother Goose on the Loose Resources*

Humpty Dumpty

Wall

Jill Jumping

Resource B: Some Mother Goose on the Loose Felt Piece Patterns 179

Door

180 Part IV: Mother Goose on the Loose Resources

Train

Resource B: Some Mother Goose on the Loose Felt Piece Patterns 181

Mother Goose

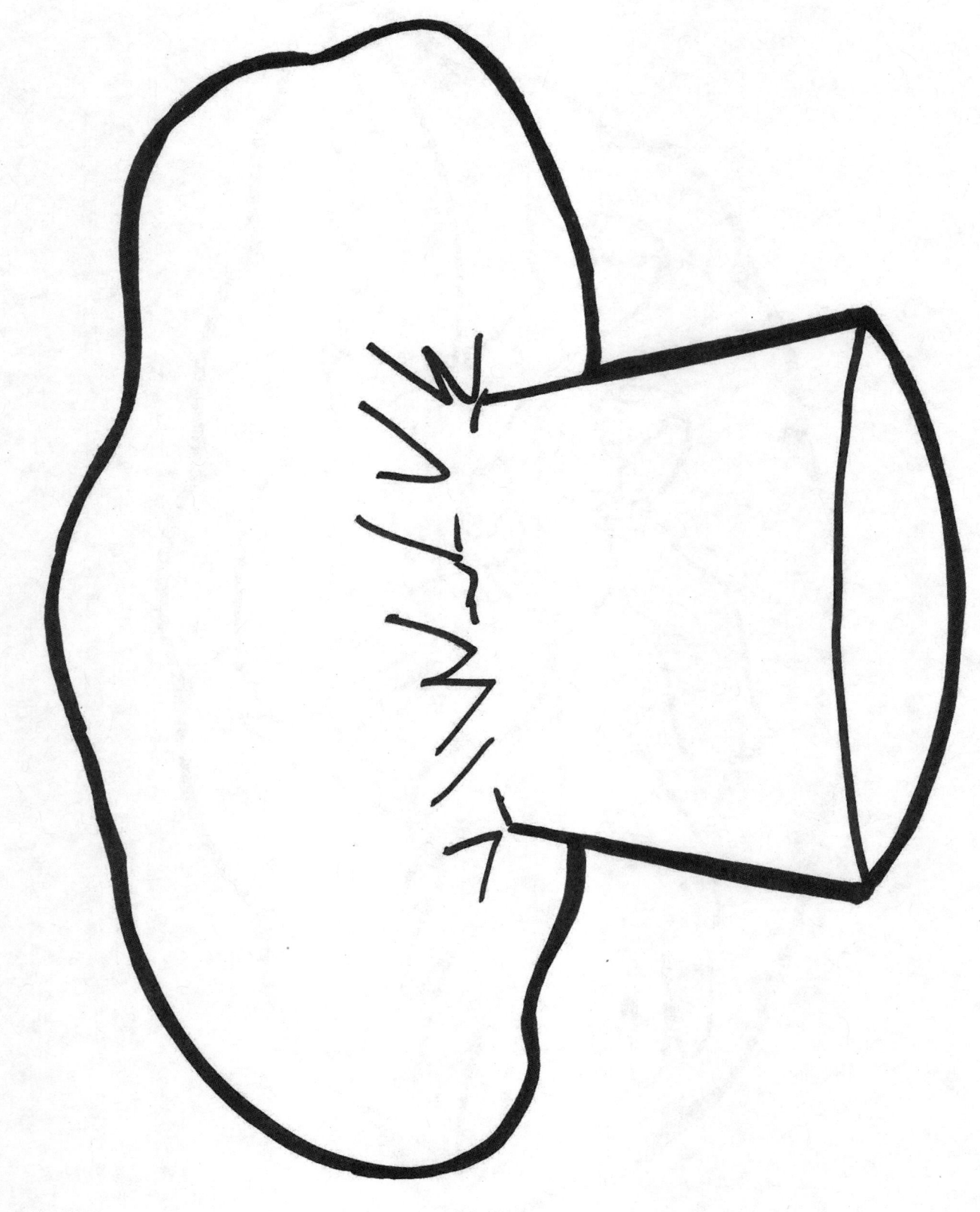

Chef's Hat

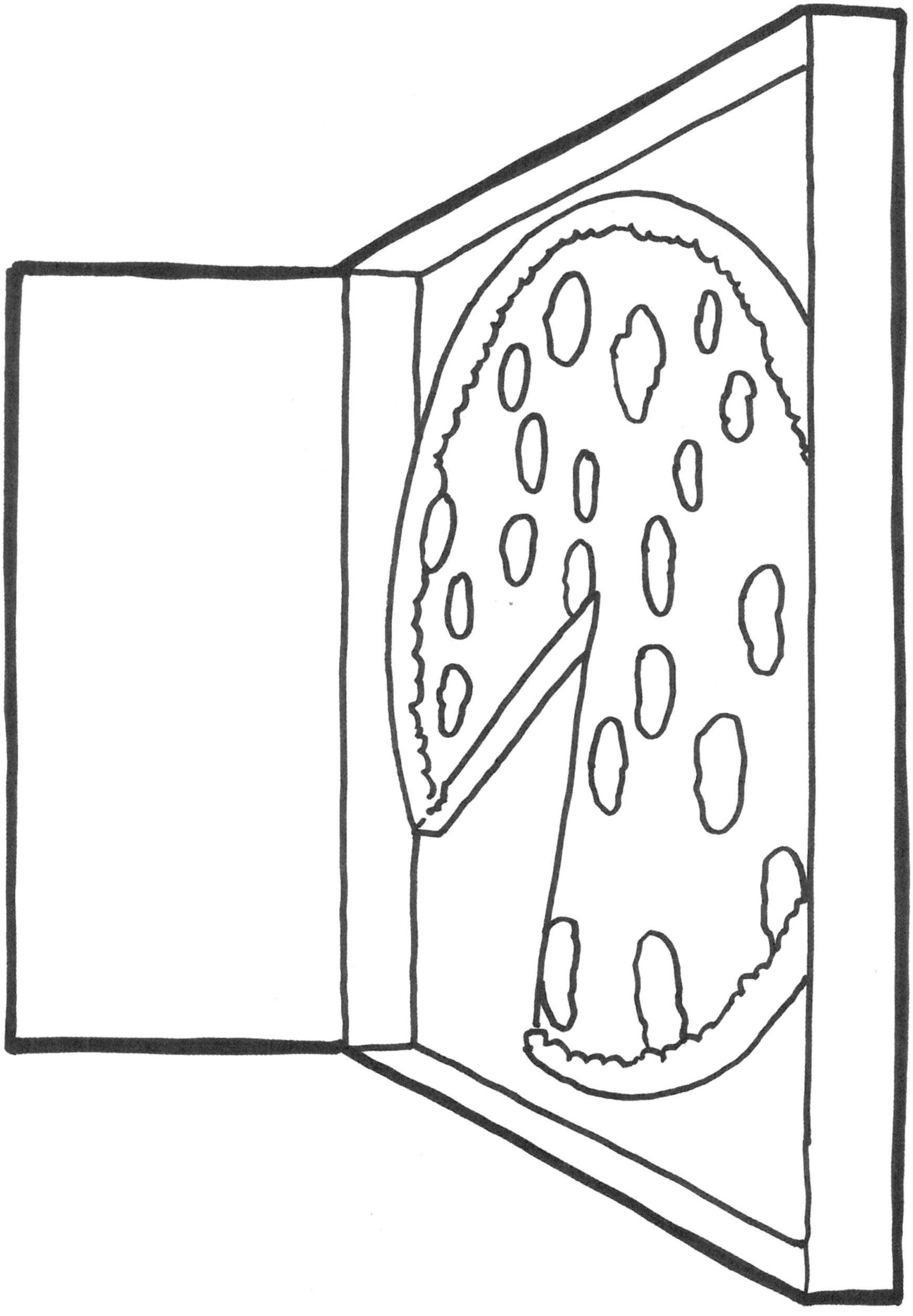

Pizza

184　*Part IV: Mother Goose on the Loose Resources*

Teddy Bear

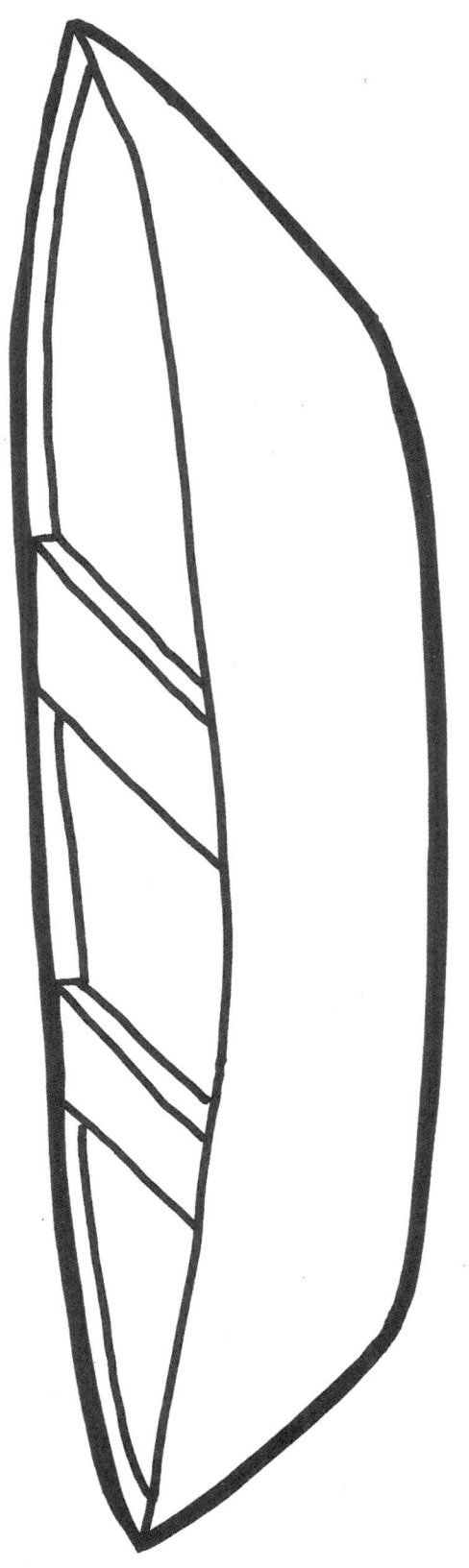

Rowboat

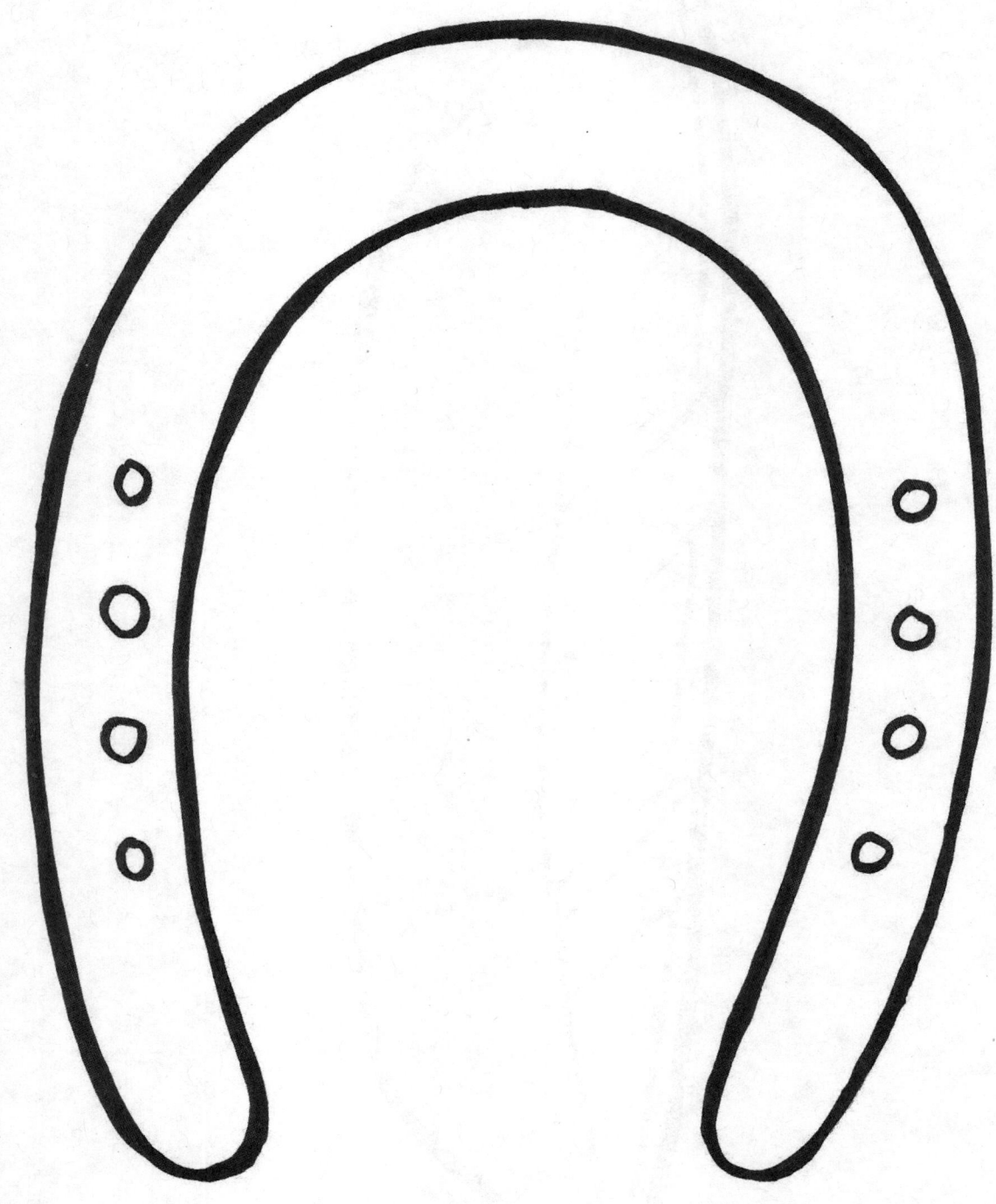

Horseshoe

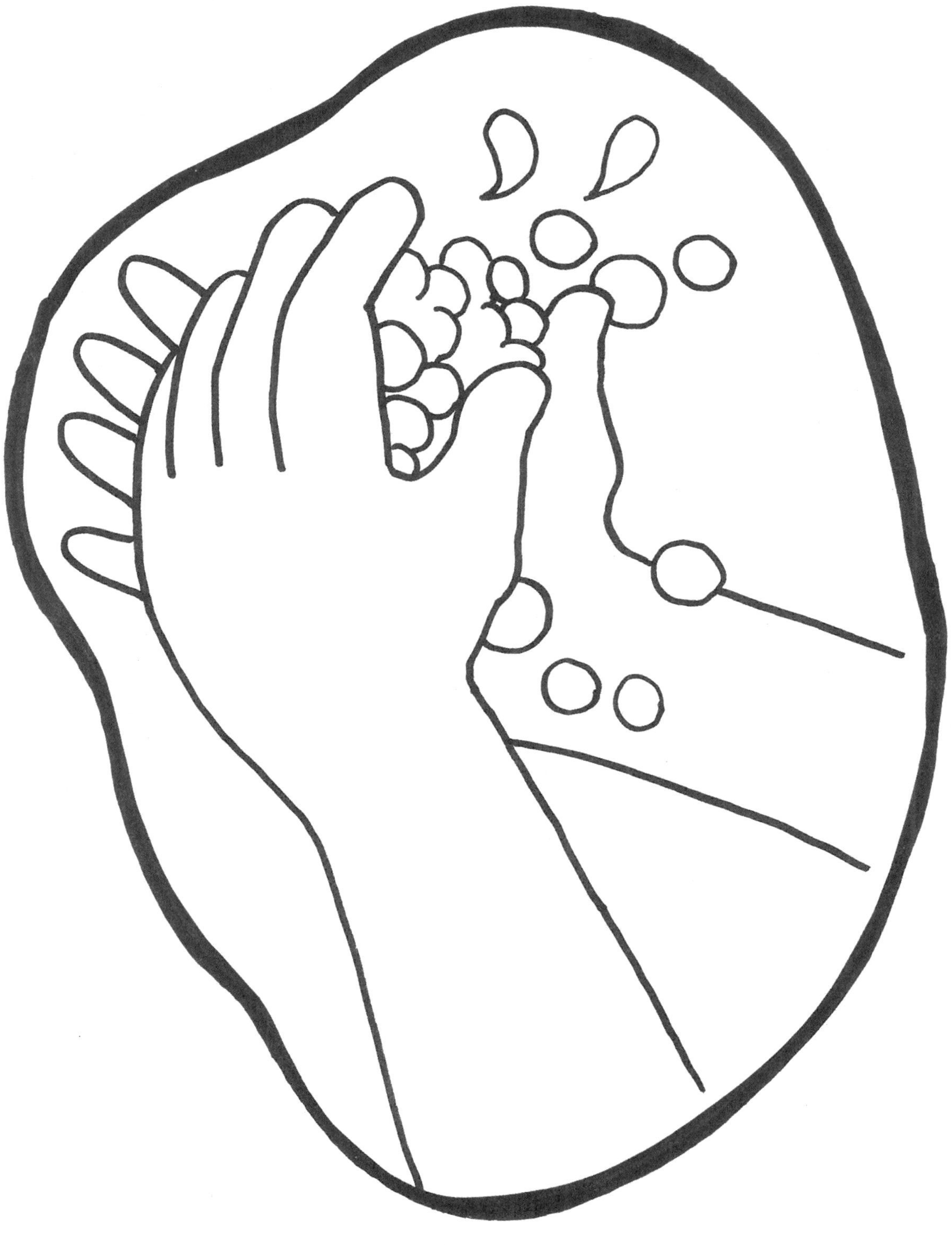

Hands Washing

188 *Part IV: Mother Goose on the Loose Resources*

Star

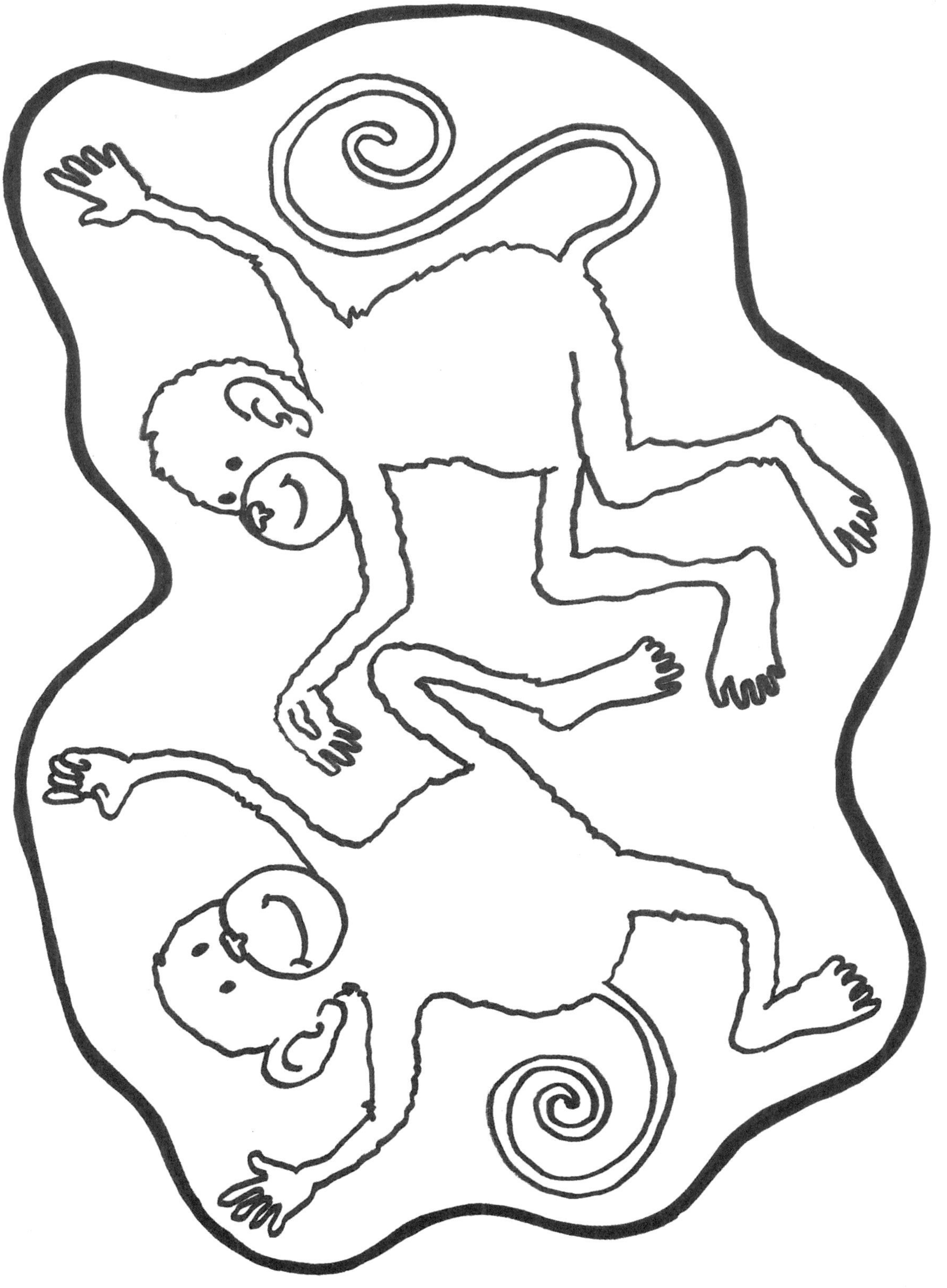

Monkeys Jumping on a Bed

190 *Part IV: Mother Goose on the Loose Resources*

Two Birds Sitting on a Cloud

Resource B: Some Mother Goose on the Loose Felt Piece Patterns 191

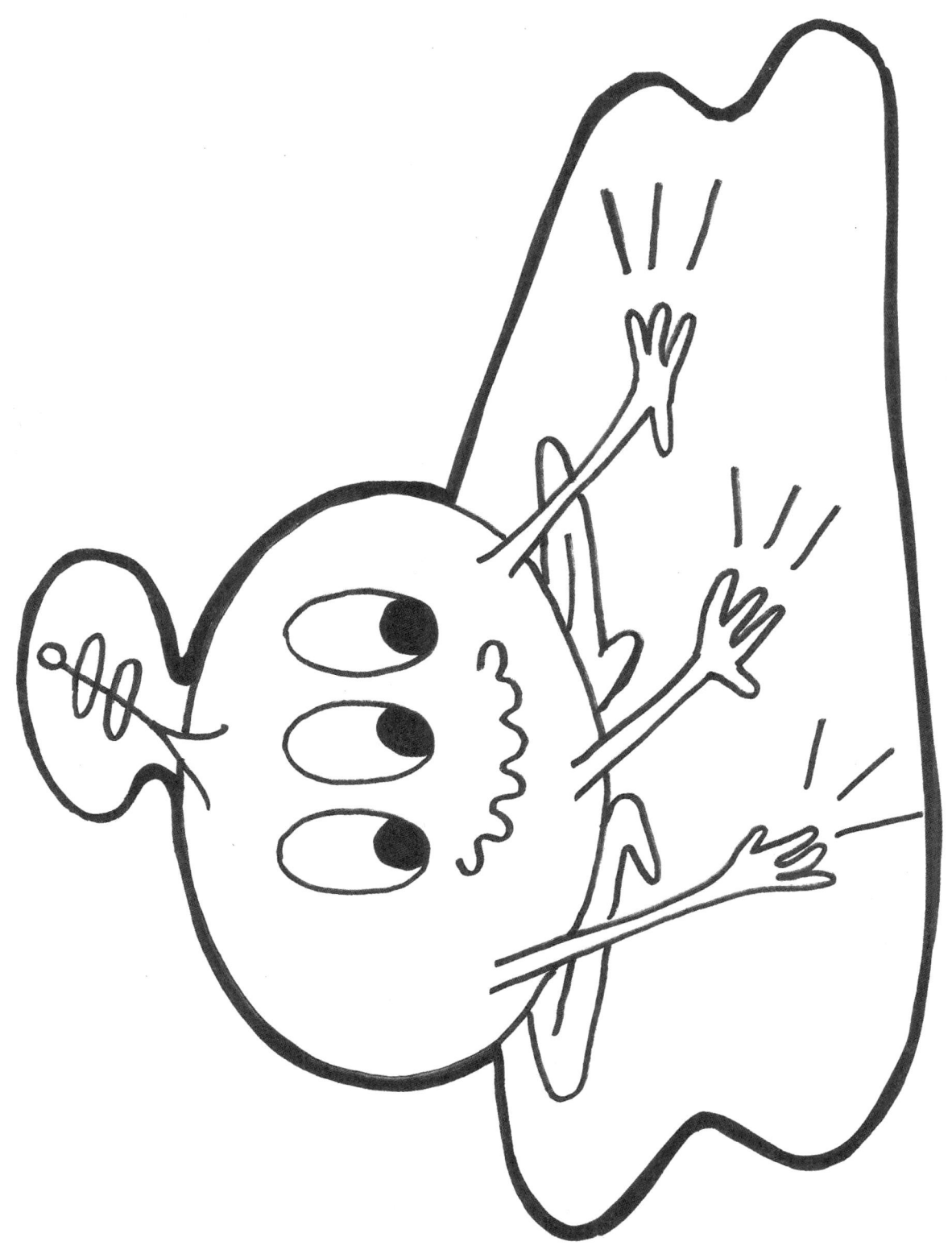

Alien Hitting the Floor with Three Hands

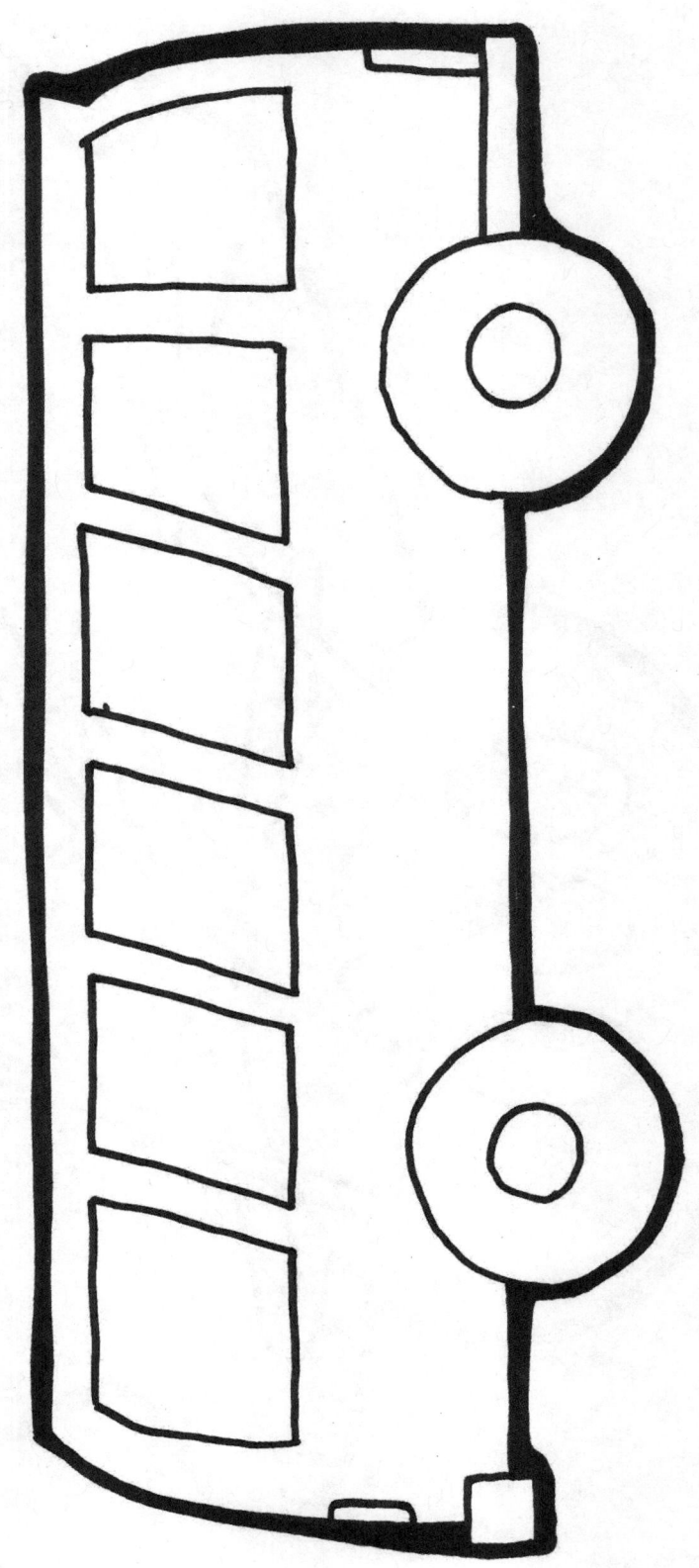

Bus

Sun

194　*Part IV: Mother Goose on the Loose Resources*

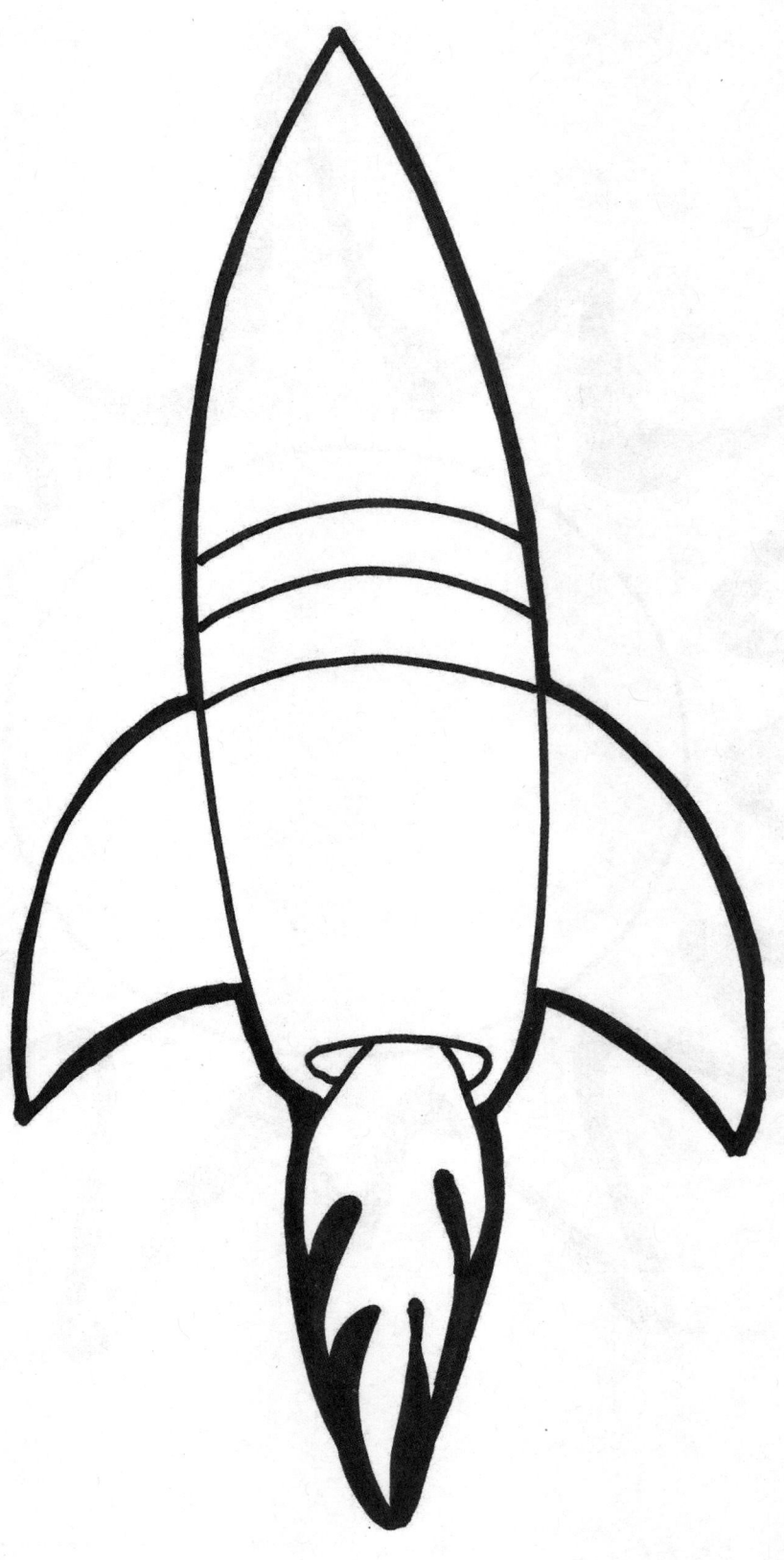

Rocket Ship

Suggested Supplies and Ordering Information

BELOW IS A LIST OF BASIC ITEMS NEEDED TO RUN A MGOL program along with suggested suppliers. Recommended vendors and websites were based on prices and availability at the time this book was written; feel free to search on the Internet to find better prices! A few brand names for sturdy and safe children's musical percussion instruments are LP RhythMix, Remo, and Hohner.

Flannelboard Easel

You'll need an easel with a flannelboard on one side, a chalkboard or a magnetic whiteboard on the other side, and a shelf in the middle. The shelf is an essential piece of equipment for keeping flannel characters, some props, and books out of sight and reach of the toddlers at your session. This flannelboard is sold by many companies; search online for "Best-Rite Magnetic Flannel Easel" to find the best price.

Materials for Making Flannelboard Pieces

Felt and Tacky Glue are needed for making flannelboard pieces. Stay away from stiff acrylic felt; it often does not stick well to the flannelboard. Buy in bulk at craft stores or online.

Recommended Sources

Lakeshore Educational, www.lakeshorelearning.com (felt packages)
NASCO, www.eNASCO.com (felt and Tacky Glue)
Aleene's, http://aleenes.com (Aleene's Tacky Glue)

Plastic Storage Tub with a Tight-Fitting Cover

Your storage tub should be large but able to fit inside the easel underneath the inner shelf. It should not be translucent.

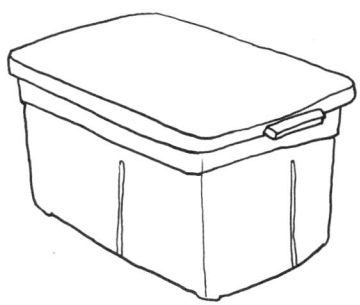

Recommended Sources
>Target, Kmart, or the Rubbermaid website (www.rubbermaid.com)

Colored Scarves

Look for brightly colored scarves. Large scarves without hems can be cut in half or even in quarters.

Recommended Sources
>Musician's Friend, www.musiciansfriend.com (Rhythm Band 12 Colored Scarves)
>Music Rhapsody, https://musicrhapsody.com (Item #3009)
>Lakeshore, www.lakeshorelearning.com (Activity Scarves)

Puppets

Puppets or stuffed animals are necessary for each program. When shopping for puppets, be sure your animals look friendly!

You may want to purchase the following:

- at least five farm animals such as dog, sheep, pig, horse, kitten, duck, or cow for singing about the sounds animals make
- two identical monkey puppets for "Two Little Monkeys"
- a colorful bird puppet for "Mrs. Perky Bird"
- a spider puppet for "The Eency Weency Spider"

Note: Many companies only have scary-looking spiders. Demco no longer sells their friendly spider puppet, pictured below. Cute spider puppets are sometimes available on Amazon, eBay, or Etsy.

Recommended Source
>Folkmanis Puppets, www.folkmanis.com

Note: Folkmanis puppets are realistic enough to help children identify the animals but are not scary or unwieldy. Talk directly with the company before placing your order; public libraries can often receive a discount.

A Tambourine or Drum

The drum sequence requires a tambourine with a drumhead or an easy-to-carry drum; you do not need drums for each participant. If using a tambourine, be sure it is sturdy and does not have metal pins holding the mini-cymbals in place. These become serious choking hazards if broken.

Recommended Sources
>Kaplan Early Learning Company, www.kaplanco.com ("Hand Drum," use without the mallet)
>Lakeshore, www.lakeshorelearning.com ("Heavy-Duty Drums—Set of 4")
>Music Rhapsody, https://musicrhapsody.com ("Remo Tambourine" or "Sound Shapes")
>Hohner Kids, honhnerkids.com ("6 Multi-Colored Tambourine")

Bells

Sturdy, colorful, easy-to-grasp animal bells from Lakeshore Educational called "Easy-Grip Jingle Bells" are fabulous.

"Cluster bells" are easy for even the youngest children to hold.

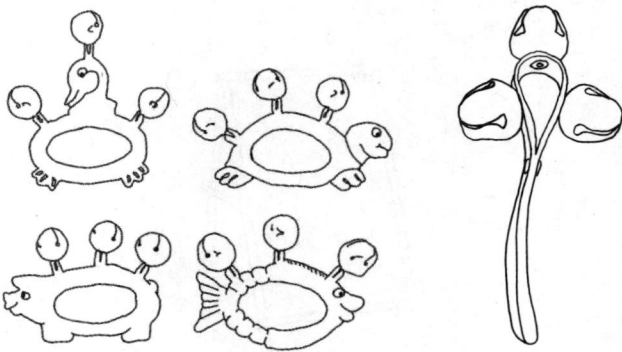

Recommended Sources
Lakeshore Educational, www.lakeshorelearning.com ("Easy-Grip Jingle Bells")
Kaplan Early Learning Company: www.kaplanco.com ("Cluster Bells")

Shakers and Chick-itas

You will need enough shakers to give one to each child and adult at your program. Maracas are often too big and too loud for children under age three. Purchase Chick-itas or "maracitos" instead. Egg shakers can be fun also.

Recommended Sources
Kaplan Early Learning Company, www.kaplanco.com ("Maracito" and "Egg Shakers")
Musician's Friend, www.musiciansfriend.com ("Niño 4-Piece Egg Shaker Assortment")
Hohner Kids, http://hohnerkids.com ("Maracitos")

Note: Look for LP RhythMix Chick-itas. They are durable and come in pairs or in bulk.

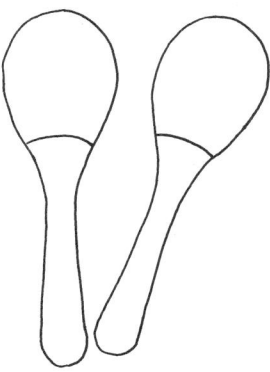

Tote Bags

Two-handled wide (but not too deep) tote bags are great for storing, distributing, and collecting musical instruments and scarves. Vendors often give away free bags at library conferences. Demco has some tote bags for under $10 with designs from children's books on them. MGOL tote bags can be purchased via ALA Editions (or the MGOL online store).

Recommended Source
Demco, www.demco.com ("Tote-Bags")

Books

Although it is best to alternate your read-aloud book from week to week, children enjoy recognizing familiar animal illustrations for "I Went to Visit the Farm One Day." *The Very Busy Spider* by Eric Carle is a book with big, cheerful pictures of farm animals that can be used weekly for this activity.

Assorted Mother Goose anthologies with large, colorful pictures that depict nursery rhyme characters are helpful for using as visual representations to go along with your rhymes. Books can be purchased through your library supplier or via Amazon.com.

After-Program Play Items

Sometimes a sturdy piece of furniture can serve as a play piece for a few children. Choose furniture that is safe and easy to move.

Recommended Source
Community Playthings, www.communityplaythings.com

Of course, it is fine (and even preferable) to use more props, such as musical instruments and a candlestick for jumping over, but these are not necessary for running the basic program.

About Barbara Cass-Beggs

by Michael Cass-Beggs

ALTHOUGH I ONLY STUDIED FOR A SHORT TIME WITH Barbara Cass-Beggs, I believe that her "Listen, Like, Learn" approach and her worldview in general have had a profound influence on the creation of MGOL. Because of this, I asked her son, Michael, to write about her for this book.

About Barbara Cass-Beggs

Passionate parents, avid teachers, discerning librarians, and doctors—and even thoughtful politicians—have come to understand the real meaning and challenge of the term *formative years*. Rather than starting with kindergarten, we have learned that the "years" begin at birth and in many ways quite a few months prior.

A key inspiration for Betsy Diamant-Cohen developing the MGOL program was my late mother, Barbara Cass-Beggs, and her work with small children. She taught Betsy the philosophy and practice of her own fabled teaching experience, as first captured in her 1974 book *To Listen, To Like, To Learn* and later developed in "Your Baby Needs Music" and, almost inevitably, "Your Child Needs Music." We all need music, and as my mother's son, I'm now happy to give both permission and this requested introduction to Barbara Cass-Beggs: she believed in "passing the word," and for me, it's only hard to be brief.

My mother began teaching while a voice student at the Royal College of Music in London. She worked to develop a new "group" approach to classes with local children ages three to seven. Not incidentally, she found that some earlier work as an assistant in a nursery school was "quite as useful" as her musical training! But what started her lifelong involvement with ever younger children was matched by her interest in folk music, and especially folk songs, which she said "represent the childhood of music."

Deceptively direct and "simple," these songs rarely exceed the range of a child's voice, yet their musicality and beauty can be profound, and my mother included "folk songs" in all her song recitals. Like ancient "sayings," these were literally "memorable"; they had to be because until the time of astute collectors and recordings, a "folk song" only survived if passed down to a new generation. I know the habit, since I too learned much of my British Isles repertoire at, or actually on, my mother's knee. Betsy carries on this tradition of passing down folk songs to a new generation with her MGOL.

In coming to Canada, my mother became a pioneer collector of folk songs in the province of Saskatchewan, and her tape recordings became a disk by Folkways Records of New York. She was also the vibrant founder and director of the Saskatchewan Junior Concert Society, which thrived on her dictum "Good music, well presented, will be accessible to young children"; it must be let to be.

Barbara Cass-Beggs always gave encouragement in a uniquely holistic way. She taught the importance of context, of conscience, and of "feeling," which can inspire actions quite different from mere thinking—when left unguided, we too easily forget our humanity. She knew that a hungry child cannot concentrate and that every child needs to be wanted. There must be food, family planning, and hope-engaging adult education.

Why did my mother emphasize music? She would quote the old Chinese proverb: "If you have two loaves, sell one and buy a lily." Everyone needs the first loaf, but you must understand that "the lily" is more essential to real living than any second loaf.

"Not by bread alone"—my mother realized that music was valuable to the unborn, and she developed classes for young mums, born of the need to promote positive care. If you sing a "favorite" lullaby to the distending tummy (partly for the mum's comfort and partly to calm a kicking foot), after the birth, you may discover proof of prebirth hearing. Sing the "favorite" lullaby, and the newborn baby knows precisely what to do: go to sleep! Because they've heard it before, they know what to do about it.

MGOL relies heavily on Barbara Cass-Beggs—and for more than her music. I will be glad, and so would she be, if all new readers can find the way to listen to themselves and for what really matters, to like what they find they can do (share and build), and therefore to learn and grow to feel, trust, and love as well as express reality, hope, and the importance of our cultural humanity. This will be the inheritance from Barbara Cass-Beggs.

Living music has always been at the center of society; it is never too soon to seek, and then to teach, a close acquaintance. I wish you joy.

Michael Cass-Beggs,
Quebec, Canada

Subject Index

A

AAP (American Academy of Pediatrics), 43
ABC felt piece pattern, 160
activities, 47, 50
after-program play items, 197
ALA Editions, 43
Alexandre Vattemare Award for Creativity in Libraries, x
Alien Hitting the Floor with Three Hands felt piece pattern, 191
American Academy of Pediatrics (AAP), 43
"And Baby Makes Three" program, ix
animal activities
    farm animal app, 43
    in five consecutive programs, 59
    "Listen, Like, Learn" approach and, 10
    in MGOL program, 25–27
    Mother Goose on the Loose Session Planning Sheet, 49, 52
    overview of, 25–27
    in Program Five, 139, 143–144
    in Program Four, 129, 133–134
    in Program One, 93, 102–103
    in Program Three, 119, 124–125
    in Program Two, 109, 114–115
apps, 42
Association for Library Service to Children (ALSC), 4, 43
Association of Specialized and Cooperative Library Agencies, x
attendees
    adapting MGOL for different-sized groups, 38–39
    Mother Goose on the Loose Participant Survey, 81–82
    of outreach MGOL programs, 73
    registration for MGOL program, 71–72
    tickets for MGOL program, 72
attitude, positive, 5, 7

B

babies, adapting MGOL for, 37–38
baby brain, 71
baby talk, 7
background knowledge, 4
barber, 73
Baruzzi, Agnese, 130
The Beatles, 66
Bed felt piece pattern, 161
Beethoven, Ludwig van, 66
bells
    "Listen, Like, Learn" approach and, 10
    musical instruments and scarves, 115
    sources for purchasing, 196–197
Bezos Family Foundation, 35
bird puppet
    in Program Five, 140
    in Program Three, 120
    in Program Two, 110
    purchasing, resources for, 196
bloggers, parent, 74
body rhymes
    "Listen, Like, Learn" approach and, 10
    in MGOL program, 22–24
    Mother Goose on the Loose Session Planning Sheet, 48, 51
    overview of, 22–24
    in Program Five, 141–142
    in Program Four, 131–132
    in Program One, 92, 97–99
    in Program Three, 118, 121–123
    in Program Two, 108, 111–113
bonding, 11
book-reading behavior
    modeling of, 22
    parents observe, 11
    as part of language development, 9
books
    book sharing, 76
    book-handling behaviors, 3
    gathering for MGOL program, 57, 77
    planning for MGOL program, 53
    sources for purchasing, 197
Bowie, C. W., 111
Boy Wiggling Fingers felt piece pattern, 164
brain, 15–18
Brooklyn Public Library, 35
Brother's Watch felt piece pattern, 172
Bus felt piece pattern, 192

C

call-and-response rhymes, 10
caregivers
    See parents
Carle, Eric
    Draw Me a Star, 105
    recognition of artwork by, 11
    The Very Busy Spider, 25, 37, 102, 114, 133, 143, 197
Cass-Beggs, Barbara
    about, 199–200
    on body rhymes, 23
    closing ritual, 30
    "Listen, Like, Learn" approach of, xiii
    materials in MGOL program, x
    memorial to, xiv
    on music, 17
    songs by, 27, 28, 149, 155–156
    "Two Little Dickey Birds," 22
    "We're Marching to the Drum," 25
    "Your Baby Needs Music" program, ix
Cass-Beggs, Michael, 199–200
challenges, taking on, 8
Chef's Hat felt piece pattern, 182
Chick-itas, 197
child development facts, 20
childbirth preparation classes, 73
childcare situation, adapting MGOL for, 40

children
- digital media in MGOL and, 42–43
- early literacy, 3–4
- early literacy program components, 15–18
- evaluation of MGOL program and, 87
- Every Child Ready To Read @ Your Library program, 4
- general knowledge, 10–11
- health/physical well-being, 7
- language development, 7, 9
- MGOL activities, benefits of, ix, x
- rewards of MGOL, xiv
- school readiness of, 5
- social/emotional well-being, 5–6
- visual literacy, 11

Children's Trust Fund, 35
Chopin, Frederick, 66
circulation, 76
closing ritual
- in five consecutive programs, 60
- instructions for, 30
- Mother Goose on the Loose Session Planning Sheet, 49, 52
- in Program Five, 139, 146
- in Program Four, 129, 136
- in Program One, 93, 106–107
- in Program Three, 119, 127
- in Program Two, 109, 117

Coles, Robert, 11
Colorado Libraries for Early Literacy site, 35
¡Colorín Colorado! 35
comfort, 32
commonsensemedia.org, 42
communication, 8
community development, 11–12
Community Playthings, 197
connections, 8
critical thinking, 8
Crosby, Stills, Nash, and Young, 66
culture, 40–41

D

Debussy, Claude, 66
Denver, John, 66
developmental tips
- on animal activities, 124
- on "Can You Kick with Two Feet?," 136
- developmental tip cards, 54
- on Humpty Dumpty rhyme, 117
- on "Mother and Father and Uncle John," 132
- Mother Goose on the Loose Session Planning Sheet, 52
- on recognition of children, 144
- resources for, 35
- on session planning sheet, 47, 49
- stop, playing games to teach, 123
- texting tips, 34–35
- types of, 31–34
- on variation in tone of voice, 144
- from websites, 35

Diamant-Cohen, Betsy
- Barbara Cass-Beggs and, 199
- on creation of MGOL, ix–x
- "Early Literacy Handbook and Tip Cards," 35
- And We Walk by, 149

digital media, 42–43
digital-storytime.com, 42
directions, 6, 20
diversity, adapting MGOL for, 37–44
Door felt piece pattern, 179
drum, sources for purchasing, 196
drum sequence
- in five consecutive programs, 59
- in MGOL program, 24
- Mother Goose on the Loose Session Planning Sheet, 48, 51
- in Program Five, 138, 142
- in Program Four, 128, 132
- in Program One, 92, 100
- in Program Three, 118, 123
- in Program Two, 108, 113

Duke of York felt piece pattern, 168

E

Earlier is Easier (website), 35
early literacy
- description of, 3
- Every Child Ready To Read @ Your Library program, 4
- FAQs, 8
- MGOL support of, 4–5
- program, components of, 15–18
- progression toward, 3–4

"Early Literacy Handbook and Tip Cards" (Diamant-Cohen & Ghoting), 35
"Early Literacy Messages in Action" (Krabbenhoft), 35
e-book, 42
Elgar, Sir Edward, 66
emotional intelligence (EQ), 6
emotions
- emotional development, 33
- positive learning attitude, 7
- social/emotional well-being, 5–6

environment
- adapting MGOL for different spaces, 39–40
- affect on brain, 16
- room setup for MGOL program, 75–77

EQ (emotional intelligence), 6
equipment, 53
evaluation, of MGOL program
- celebration of program success, 88
- evaluation tools, 87
- follow-up survey, 83
- formal evaluation, 80
- information evaluation, 79
- Mother Goose on the Loose Participant Survey, 81–82
- need for, 79
- observation and reflection survey, 83–86
- personal interviews, 79–80
- pre-MGOL survey, 80
- Self-Assessment Survey, 89–90
- self-evaluation, 87–88
- stakeholders and, 87

Every Child Ready to Read (ECRR), 4, 87
executive function skills, 5–6

F

familiarity, 32
Families and Work Institute, x
FAQs
- on animal activities, 26–27
- on body rhymes, 23–24
- on closing ritual, 30
- on drum sequence, 24
- on interactive rhymes, 30
- on lullabies, 29
- on musical instruments and scarves, 28
- on rhymes/reads, 22
- on stand-up/sit-down activities, 25
- on welcoming comments, 20

farm animal puppets, 114, 124, 133, 196
feedback, 79–80
See also evaluation, of MGOL program
feelings
See emotions
feet/toes, 59
felt piece patterns
- ABC, 160
- Alien Hitting the Floor with Three Hands, 191
- Bed, 161
- Boy Wiggling Fingers, 164
- Brother's Watch, 172
- Bus, 192
- Chef's Hat, 182
- Door, 179
- Duke of York, 168
- Goose on Stairs, 167
- Grandfather's Clock, 170
- Hands Washing, 187
- Horseshoe, 186
- Humpty Dumpty, 176
- instructions for, 159
- Jill Jumping, 178
- Men of York, 169
- Monkeys Jumping on a Bed, 189
- Mother Goose, 181
- Mother's Kitchen Clock, 171
- Mouse, 174
- Pan, 165
- Pig, 173
- Pizza, 183
- Rain Cloud, 163
- Rocket Ship, 194
- Rowboat, 185
- Sausage, 166
- Spider, 162
- Star, 188
- Sun, 193
- Teddy Bear, 184
- Three Children Dancing, 175
- Train, 180
- Two Birds Sitting on a Cloud, 190
- Wall, 177

Subject Index

felt pieces
- making for MGOL program, 57
- materials for making, 195
- planning for MGOL program, 53
- in Program One, 94–106
- in Program Two, 110

"Felt-Board Mother Goose on the Loose" app, 43

finger rhymes, 23, 58, 111–112, 141

First Book, 35

flannelboard
- for interactive rhymes section, 29
- ordering/making, resources for, 195
- setting up, 75
- *See also* felt pieces

fliers, 73

focus, 8

Folkmanis Puppets, 196

folks songs, 199

Folkways Records, 199

follow-up survey, 83

foot-patting rhymes, 23–24, 142

formative years, 199

freeze games
- developmental tip on, 31
- learning "stop" with, 10, 123, 143
- teaching with, 6

G

Galinsky, Ellen, 8

Gardner, Howard, 17–18

Garraton, Dora, 39–40

gender, 41

Ghoting, Saroj Nadkarni, 35

Godfrey Award for Excellence in Public Library Services for Families and Children, x

Golinkoff, Roberta Michnick, 9, 78

Goose on Stairs felt piece pattern, 167

Gopnik, Alison, 16, 78

Grandfather's Clock felt piece pattern, 170

groups, adapting MGOL for, 38–39

guidelines, 20

H

hairdresser, 73

hand rhymes
- choices for, 23
- in five consecutive programs, 58
- in Program Five, 141
- in Program Four, 131
- in Program Three, 122
- in Program Two, 112

Handel, George Frederick, 66

Hands Washing felt piece pattern, 187

Haydn, Franz Josef, 66

head rhymes
- example of, 23
- in five consecutive programs, 58
- in Program Five, 141
- in Program Four, 131
- in Program Two, 111

health/physical well-being, 5, 7

Hirsh-Pasek, Kathy, 9, 78

Hohner Kids, 196, 197

Horseshoe felt piece pattern, 186

Humpty Dumpty felt piece pattern, 176

I

imitation, 3

inclusivity, 11–12

Institute of Museum and Library Services (IMLS), x

instruments
- *See* musical instruments

intelligence, 17–18

interactive rhymes
- in five consecutive programs, 60
- in MGOL program, 29–30
- Mother Goose on the Loose Session Planning Sheet, 49, 52
- overview of, 29–30
- in Program Five, 139, 146
- in Program Four, 129, 136
- in Program One, 93, 105–106
- in Program Three, 119, 126–127
- in Program Two, 109, 116–117

interviews, 79–80

invitations, 20

J

Jill Jumping felt piece pattern, 178

K

Kaplan Early Learning Company, 196, 197

Katz, Karen, 140

Kingsley, Gershon, 66

knee bounces
- in childcare situations, 40
- in five consecutive programs, 59
- instructions for, 23
- "Listen, Like, Learn" approach and, 11
- in Program Five, 142
- in Program Four, 132
- in Program One, 99
- in Program Three, 122
- in Program Two, 112–113

knowledge, general
- description of, 10
- developmental tips on, 34
- as domain of school readiness, 5
- music/singing to stimulate learning, 10–11

Krabbenhoft, Libby, 35

L

Lakeshore Educational, 195, 196, 197

language development
- description of, 7
- as domain of school readiness, 5
- MGOL support of, 9

languages, 40–41

learning
- environment for, 16
- language development, 7, 9
- play and, 16
- positive learning attitude, 7

self-directed/engaged, 8

letter knowledge, 4, 5

Libana, 66

librarian, 11–12, 43

library
- developmental tips on library program, 31
- evaluation of MGOL program and, 87
- staff, evaluation of MGOL program by, 87
- website, MGOL page on, 72

"Listen, Like, Learn" approach
- in action, 10–11
- MGOL based on, xiii, 19, 199
- MGOL's use of, ix
- songs/music that use, 17

listening, 6

literacy
- assessment tool, 79
- early literacy, 3–4, 8
- early literacy program components, 15–18
- emotional, 6
- Every Child Ready To Read @ Your Library program, 4
- general knowledge, 10–11
- MGOL support of, 4–5
- visual literacy, 11

local resources, 72

lullabies
- in five consecutive programs, 60
- "Listen, Like, Learn" approach and, 11
- in MGOL program, 28–29
- Mother Goose on the Loose Session Planning Sheet, 49, 52
- overview of, 28–29
- in Program Five, 139, 146
- in Program Four, 129, 135
- in Program One, 93, 105
- in Program Three, 119, 126
- in Program Two, 109, 116
- for relaxation, 17
- to unborn child, 200

M

Mallett, Dave, 66

maracas
- *See* shakers

materials
- *See* supplies

media coverage, 73–74

meetup app, 74

Men of York felt piece pattern, 169

MGOL
- *See* Mother Goose on the Loose

Miller, Margaret, 97

Mind in the Making, 35

Miranda, Anne, 112

monkey puppets, 196

Monkeys Jumping on a Bed felt piece pattern, 189

Mother Goose felt piece pattern, 181

Mother Goose on the Loose (MGOL)
- adapting for different ages/abilities, 37–38
- adapting for different cultures/languages, 40–41

Mother Goose on the Loose (MGOL) (cont'd)
  adapting for different spaces, 39–40
  adapting for different-sized groups, 38–39
  adapting to address social justice concerns, 41–42
  adapting to include digital media, 42–43
  animal activities, 25–27
  Barbara Cass-Beggs and, 199–200
  based on research, 3
  benefits for children, ix
  body rhymes, 22–24
  closing ritual, 30
  community development/inclusivity, 11–12
  developmental tips, 31–35
  drum sequence, 24
  early literacy FAQs, 8
  early literacy program components, 15–18
  early literacy, support of, 4–5
  evaluation of program, 79–88
  for every situation, 43–44
  finishing up session, 78
  interactive rhymes, 29–30
  introduction to, xiii–xiv
  language development, support of, 9
  launch of, x
  lullabies, 28–29
  musical instruments and scarves, 27–28
  music/singing stimulate learning, 10–11
  parent education, 77–78
  positive learning attitude, support of, 7
  preparation to present, 75
  promotion of program, 72–74
  registration for, 71–72
  rewards of, xiv
  rhymes/reads, 21–22
  rhymes/songs, list of, 149–158
  room setup for, 75–77
  scheduling, 71
  school readiness, support of, 5
  social/emotional well-being, support of, 6
  stand-up/sit-down activities, 24–25
  tickets for, 72
  time after session, use of, 77
  transition into program, 77
  welcoming comments, 19–21
Mother Goose on the Loose (MGOL) program, planning
  activities, 47
  encouragement about, 61
  five consecutive programs, 58–60
  gathering/making supplies, 57
  Mother Goose on the Loose Session Planning Sheet, 48–49, 51–52
  organization of materials, 57
  planning second, third, fourth sessions, 57–58
  preparing for program, 49, 57
  repetition/new material, 47
  sorting, listing, gathering, 53–56
Mother Goose on the Loose (MGOL) scripts
  Program Five, 138–146
  Program Four, 128–136
  Program One, 92–107
  Program Three, 118–127
  Program Two, 108–117
Mother Goose on the Loose Participant Survey, 81–82
Mother's Kitchen Clock felt piece pattern, 171
motor skills, 17, 32
Mouse felt piece pattern, 174
movement, 16–17
Mozart, Wolfgang Amadeus, 66
multiple intelligences, 17–18
music
  Barbara Cass-Beggs and, 199–200
  developmental tip on, 32
  as early literacy program component, 17
  planning for MGOL program, 53
  preparation for, 75–76
  for stimulating learning, 10–11
Music Rhapsody, 196
musical instruments
  "Listen, Like, Learn" approach and, 10–11
  planning for MGOL program, 53
  setting up for program, 77
  sources for, 196–197
musical instruments and scarves
  in five consecutive programs, 60
  in MGOL program, 27–28
  Mother Goose on the Loose Session Planning Sheet, 49, 52
  overview of, 27–28
  in Program Five, 144–145
  in Program Four, 129, 134–135
  in Program One, 93, 103–105
  in Program Three, 119, 125–126
  in Program Two, 109, 115–116
Musician's Friend.com, 196, 197

N

name tags, 76–77
narrative skills, 4, 5
NASCO, 195
National Education Goals Panel, 5
nursery rhymes
  See rhymes

O

observation and reflection survey
  instructions for, 83
  Survey: Reflections on Today's Session, 84–86
observations, 79–80
Opie, Iona, 99
oral language, 4
ordering information, 195–197
outline
  for Program Five, 138–139
  for Program Four, 128–129
  for Program One, 92–94
  for Program Three, 118–119
  for Program Two, 108–109
outreach program, 39–40, 73

P

Pachelbel, Johann, 66
Pan felt piece pattern, 165
parents
  adapting MGOL for babies, 37–38
  developmental tips for, 31–35
  digital media in MGOL and, 42–43
  education after MGOL session, 77–78
  evaluation of MGOL program and, 87
  follow-up survey for, 83
  health/physical well-being of children and, 7
  lullabies section and, 28–29
  MGOL for community development/inclusivity, 11–12
  MGOL program evaluation, observations for, 79–80
  MGOL program promotion by, 74
  pre-MGOL survey, 80
  reading to children, 16
  registration for MGOL program, 71–72
  scheduling MGOL and, 71
  time after session, use of, 77
  use of term, 4
  vocabulary of children and, 9
  welcoming comments for, 19–20
participants
  See attendees
personal interviews, 79–80
perspective taking, 8
Peter, Paul, and Mary, 66
phonological awareness
  drum sequence section for, 24
  as early literacy skill, 3
  in ECRR program, 4
  MGOL support of, 5
photographs, 74
physical activity, 16–17
Piaget, Jean, 16
picture book, 11, 22
Pig felt piece pattern, 173
Pizza felt piece pattern, 183
planning, xiv
  See also Mother Goose on the Loose (MGOL) program, planning
play
  after-program play items, 197
  as early literacy program component, 16
  modeling after session, 77
positive learning attitude, 7
positive reinforcement, 6
preliteracy skills, 33–34
pre-MGOL survey, 80–82
presentation space, 75–77
press release, 73–74
print awareness, 4
print motivation, 3, 4
Program Five
  animal activities, 143–144
  body rhymes, 141–142
  closing ritual, 146
  drum sequence, 142
  interactive rhymes, 146
  lullabies, 146
  musical instruments and scarves, 144–145

outline for, 138–139
rhymes and reads, 140–141
stand-up/sit-down activities, 143
welcoming comments, 140
Program Four
animal activities, 133–134
body rhymes, 131–132
closing ritual, 136
drum sequence, 132
interactive rhymes, 136
lullabies, 135
musical instruments and scarves, 134–135
outline for, 128–129
rhymes and reads, 130–131
stand-up/sit-down activities, 132–133
welcoming comments, 130
Program One
animal activities, 102–103
body rhymes, 97–99
closing ritual, 106–107
drum sequence, 100
felt figures, books, props for, 53
interactive rhymes, 105–106
lullabies, 105
musical instruments and scarves, 103–105
outline for, 92–94
rhymes and reads, 94–97
stand-up/sit-down activities, 100–102
welcoming comments, 94
Program Three
animal activities, 124–125
body rhymes, 121–123
closing ritual, 127
drum sequence, 123
interactive rhymes, 126–127
lullabies, 126
musical instruments and scarves, 125–126
outline for, 118–119
rhymes and reads, 120–121
stand-up/sit-down activities, 123–124
welcoming comments, 119–120
Program Two
animal activities, 114–115
body rhymes, 111–113
closing ritual, 117
drum sequence, 113
interactive rhymes, 116–117
lullabies, 116
musical instruments and scarves, 115–116
outline for, 108–109
rhymes and reads, 110–111
stand-up/sit-down activities, 113–114
welcoming comments, 110
Project Outcome website, 87
promotion
childbirth preparation classes, 73
fliers, 73
local resources, 72
media coverage, 73–74
MGOL page on library website, 72
outreach visits, 73
by parents, 74
sample programs, 72–73

via hairdresser/barber, 73
word of mouth, 74
props
gathering/making, 57
planning for, 50, 53
setting up, 77
supplies/ordering information, 195–197
written reminders, 54–56
Public Library Association, 4, 87
puppets/stuffed animals
gathering for MGOL program, 57
planning for MGOL program, 53
in Program Five, 140
in Program Four, 133–134
in Program Three, 120, 121, 124–125
in Program Two, 110, 114–115
purchasing, resources for, 196

Q

questions
See FAQs

R

Rain Cloud felt piece pattern, 163
reading
being read to, 16
for early literacy skills, 3–4
e-books, 42
language development and, 9
MGOL support of early literacy, 4–5
positive learning attitude, MGOL support of, 7
rhymes/reads section of MGOL program, 21–22
Reading Rockets, 35
READY4K! 34
registration, 71–72
rehearsal, 57
relaxation, 17, 28–29
release form, 80
Remind app, 73
reminder cards, 57
reminders, written, 54–56
repetition, 15, 47
resources
for developmental tips, 35
felt piece patterns, 159–194
local resources, informing about program, 72
Mother Goose on the Loose Participant Survey, 81–82
Mother Goose on the Loose Session Planning Sheet, 48–49, 51–52
overview of, xiv
rhymes/songs, list of, 149–158
Self-Assessment Survey, 89–90
suggested supplies/ordering information, 195–197
Survey: Reflections on Today's Session, 84–86
rhymes
adapting MGOL for social justice, 41–42
benefits of, 6

body rhymes section of MGOL program, 22–24
developmental tip on, 31
for general knowledge, 10–11
interactive rhymes, 29–30
for language development, 9
list of, 149–158
for MGOL program, choosing, 50
MGOL support of early literacy, 4, 5
Mother Goose on the Loose Session Planning Sheet, 48–49, 51–52
in rhymes/reads section of MGOL program, 21–22
to target learning, 9–10
See also interactive rhymes
rhymes and reads
in five consecutive programs, 58
in MGOL program, 21–22
Mother Goose on the Loose Session Planning Sheet, 51
in Program Five, 138, 140–141
in Program Four, 128, 130–131
in Program One, 92, 94–97
in Program Three, 118, 120–121
in Program Two, 108, 110–111
ritual, 15–16, 30
See also closing ritual
Rocket Ship felt piece pattern, 194
Rogers, Fred, 16
room setup, 75–77
Rowboat felt piece pattern, 185
Royal College of Music (London), 199
Rubbermaid, 196

S

sample programs, 72–73
Saskatchewan Junior Concert Society, 199
Sausage felt piece pattern, 166
scarves
in five consecutive programs, 60
musical instruments and scarves, 27–28
planning for MGOL program, 53
recommended sources for, 196
sources for purchasing, 196
See also musical instruments and scarves
scheduling, 71
Schickedanz, Judith, 3–4
school readiness
definition of, 5
developmental tips on, 34
in observation and reflection survey, 83
social/emotional well-being, 5–6
School Readiness Consulting, x
scripts
See Mother Goose on the Loose (MGOL) scripts
secret formula, 47
Self-Assessment Survey, 89–90
self-control, 8
self-esteem, 6
self-evaluation, 87–90
self-regulation, 5

shakers
- "Listen, Like, Learn" approach and, 10–11
- in Program Four, 134–135
- sources for purchasing, 197

singing, 10–11
social justice, 41–42
social media, 74
social skills, 33
social/emotional well-being, 5
socialization time, 77–78
songs
- list of, 149–158
- MGOL support of early literacy, 4–5
- singing to stimulate learning, 10–11

space, 39–40
Spanish language, 40–41
special needs, 38
Spider felt piece pattern, 162
spider puppet, 121, 134, 196
Spurr, Elizabeth, 141
Staines, Bill, 66
stakeholders, 87
stand-up/sit-down activities
- in five consecutive programs, 59
- in MGOL program, 24–25
- Mother Goose on the Loose Session Planning Sheet, 49, 52
- in Program Five, 138–139, 143
- in Program Four, 129, 132–133
- in Program One, 93, 100–102
- in Program Three, 119, 123–124
- in Program Two, 109, 113–114

Stanford University, 34
Star felt piece pattern, 188
Stewart, Georgiana, 66
sticky notes, 56, 57
Stockdale, Susan, 120
Stoop, Naoko, 141
storage tub
- for MGOL program materials, 53, 57, 70
- suggestions for/ordering information, 195–196

story-reading behavior, 4
Strauss, Johann, 66
stuffed animals
- *See* puppets/stuffed animals

Sun felt piece pattern, 193

supplies
- for after MGOL program ends, 76
- gathering, making, 57
- organization of, 57
- preparation for presentation, 75
- setting up for program, 77
- sorting, listing, gathering, 53–56
- suggested supplies/ordering information, 195–197

surprise, 15
survey
- follow-up survey, 83
- Mother Goose on the Loose Participant Survey, 81–82
- observation and reflection survey, 83
- pre-MGOL survey, 80
- Project Outcome website for, 87
- Self-Assessment Survey, 89–90
- Survey: Reflections on Today's Session, 84–86

Survey Monkey, 83

T

Talking Hands, Talking Feet, 66
tambourine, 196
Tandem Partners in Early Learning, 35
Taylor, James, 66
Teddy Bear felt piece pattern, 184
Text4baby, 34–35
texting, 34–35
Three Children Dancing felt piece pattern, 175
tickets, 72
tickle rhymes
- in five consecutive programs, 59
- instructions for, 23
- in Program Four, 131
- in Program One, 97–99
- in Program Three, 122
- purpose of, 6

Too Small to Fail, 35
tote bags, 53, 197
Train felt piece pattern, 180
21st century skills, 8
Two Birds Sitting on a Cloud felt piece pattern, 190

V

VIEWS2 (Valuable Initiative in Early Learning), 8
VIEWS2 Planning Tool (VPT), 8
visual literacy, 11
visual skills, 34
Vivaldi, Antonio, 66
vocabulary
- of children, impact of, 4
- as early literacy skill, 3
- in ECRR program, 4
- MGOL support of, 4
- music and, 17
- as part of language development, 7, 9

W

Wall felt piece pattern, 177
website, library, 72
websites, developmental tips from, 35
welcome card, 54
welcoming comments
- in MGOL program, 19–21
- Mother Goose on the Loose Session Planning Sheet, 48
- for non-English speakers, 40
- in Program Five, 138, 140
- in Program Four, 128, 130
- in Program One, 94
- in Program Three, 118, 119–120
- in Program Two, 108, 110
- sample, 21

welcoming space, 76
Wells, Rosemary, 99
what's next cards, 55
"whole child" approach, x, xiii
word of mouth, 74
worksheets
- *See* resources

writing, 3
written reminders, 54–56, 57

Y

"Your Baby Needs Music" program, ix

Z

Zero to Three, 34–35

Title Index

A
ABC Song, 126, 135, 149
All My Loving, 66
And We Walk, 114, 123, 149
Are You Sleeping Brother John/Frère Jacques, 149

B
Baa Baa Black Sheep, 41
Bells Away, 28, 145, 149
The Blue Danube, 66
Busy Fingers (Bowie), 111

C
Can You Kick with Two Feet? 30, 106–107, 117, 127, 136, 146, 149
Clair de Lune, 66
Country Road, 66

D
Draw Me a Star (Carle), 105

E
"Early Literacy Handbook and Tip Cards" (Diamant-Cohen & Ghoting), 35
"Early Literacy Messages in Action" (Krabbenhoft), 35
Early Literacy Programming en Español (Diamant-Cohen), 40
The Eency Weency Spider, 11, 26, 121, 133–134, 150
Eine Kleine Nachtmusik, 66
"Escucha y Disfruta con Mama Gansa" CD, 40–41
Eye Winker, 111, 121, 150

F
The Farmer in the Dell, 41, 100–101
Fingers Like to Wiggle Waggle, 23, 97–98, 111, 121, 150
Five Fat Sausages, 10, 42, 130–131, 140, 150
The Four Seasons, 66
Freight Train (Crews), 96

G
The Garden Snail, 131, 150
The Garden Song, 66
Gavotte, 66
Georgie Porgy, 41
Good Morning, Mrs. Perky Bird, 110, 140, 150–151
Goosey, Goosey Gander, 22, 41, 94–95, 110, 151
The Grand Old Duke of York, 9, 23, 113, 122–123, 132, 142, 151
Grandfather's Clock Goes Tick Tock, 28, 125, 134–135, 151

H
Handy Spandy, 25, 102, 114, 124, 133, 143, 151
Hickory Dickory Dare, 10, 26, 103, 114–115, 144, 151
Hickory Dickory Dock, 134, 144, 151
The Hokey Pokey, 25, 123–124, 132–133, 151–152
Humpty Dumpty, 29–30, 105–106, 116–117, 126–127, 142, 146, 152

I
I Had a Little Rooster by the Old Barn Gate, 26
I Had a Little Turtle, 26
I Hear Thunder, 111, 130, 141, 152
If I Had a Hammer, 66
I Went to Visit the Farm One Day, 25, 43, 124, 133, 143, 152
If You're Happy and You Know It, 9, 23, 120, 131, 141, 152
I'm a Little Teapot, 25, 133, 143, 152
I'm Driving in My Car, 134, 152
In the Rain (Spurr), 141
It's Time to Say Good-Bye, 30, 127

J
Jack Be Nimble, 29, 136, 152–153
Jack-in-the-Box, 25, 124, 143, 145, 153
Jingle Bells, 27–28, 103–104

K
Knock on the Door, 111, 131, 153

L
Let's Go Fly a Kite, 66
Library Journal, x
Little Bo Peep, 29
The Little Train, 122, 153
London Bridge, 25, 101, 153

M
Mind in the Making (Galinsky), 8
Minute Waltz, 66
Mother and Father and Uncle John, 9, 23, 99, 112, 122, 132, 153
Mother Goose on the Loose: Here, There, and Everywhere (Diamant-Cohen), 44
Mother Goose on the Loose: Updated (Diamant-Cohen), xiii–xiv
Much More Than the ABCs (Schickedanz), 3–4
My Face Is Round, 121, 131, 141, 153
My Very First Mother Goose (Opie & Wells), 99

O
Oh Where, Oh Where Has My Little Head Gone? 116, 126, 135, 153–154
Oi Dai, 66
Old MacDonald, 26
Old Mother Goose, 22, 94, 110, 120, 130, 140, 154
Old Woman Who Lived in a Shoe, 41
Open Them, Shut Them, 23, 112, 122, 131, 154
Opposite Surprise (Baruzzi), 130
Our House, 66

P

Pachelbel's Canon, 66
Pat-a-Cake, 10, 154
Peek-a-Boo, 116, 125–126, 145, 154
Peter, Peter Pumpkin Eater, 41
Peter Piper Picked a Peck of Pickled Peppers, 9
Pizza, Pizza, Hot, 111, 154
A Place in the Choir, 66
Polly Put the Kettle On, 9
Pomp and Circumstance, 66
Pop Corn, 66
"Positive Parenting Tips" (Children's Trust Fund), 35

Q

Quintet in E Flat Major, 66

R

"Ready, Set, Kindergarten" (Brooklyn Public Library), 35
Ring Them Up High, 27, 144, 154
Ring Your Bells, 28, 115, 154
'Round and 'Round the Garden, 112, 154–155
Row, Row, Row Your Boat, 9, 142, 155
Rum Pum Pum, 10, 100, 113, 123, 132, 142, 155

S

Scarves Away, 105, 126, 145, 155
Scrunch Your Scarf into a Ball, 126, 145, 155
See the Ponies Galloping, 122, 132, 155
Seesaw, Scaradown, 23, 112, 122, 155
Shake Your Rattles like the Leaves, 125, 155–156
Shakers Away, 125, 135, 156
Shoe the Little Horse, 23, 142, 156
Shoo Fly, Don't Bother Me, 28
Sing with Me (Stoop), 141
Stretch Up High, 156
Stripes of All Types (Stockdale), 120
Supercharged Storytimes (Campana, Mills, & Ghoting), 87
Surprise, 66

T

This Is the Way the Ladies Ride, 41
This Is the Way We Wash Our Belly, 126
This Is the Way We Wash Our Face, 10, 28, 116
This Is the Way We Wash Our Legs, 156
This Little Piggy, 141, 156
Three Gray Mice, 41
To Listen, To Like, To Learn (Cass-Beggs), 199
To Market, To Market, 112, 156
To Market, To Market (Miranda), 112
Toys Away, 9–10
Twinkle, Twinkle, 29, 105, 116, 156
Two Little Dickey Birds, 9, 22, 95, 110, 120, 130, 156–157
Two Little Monkeys, 41–42, 95–96, 140, 157

V

The Very Busy Spider (Carle), 25, 37, 102, 114, 133, 143, 197
"Vroom" (Bezos Family Foundation), 35

W

Water, Water, 66
The Water Music, 66
We Hit the Floor Together, 23, 27, 96–97, 110, 141, 157
We Ring Our Bells Together, 27, 115, 144, 157
We Shake Our Shakers Together, 125, 134, 158
We're Marching to the Drum, 25, 113, 143, 157
We're on the Way to Grandpa's Farm, 26
We're So Happy, 30, 117, 136, 146, 157
The Wheels on the Bus, 23, 145, 158
When the [Cow] Gets Up in the Morning, 26, 114, 124–125, 144, 158
Where Is Thumbkin? 10
Wind, Oh Wind, 115, 116, 125, 126, 135, 145, 158

Y

You Are My Sunshine, 146, 158
Your Baby Needs Music (Cass-Beggs), 17, 199
Your Child Needs Music (Cass-Beggs), 199
You've Got a Friend, 66

Z

Zoom, Zoom, Baby (Katz), 140
Zoom, Zoom, Zoom, 130, 158